keepin' it real

keepin' it real

A TURBULENT SEASON AT THE CROSSROADS WITH THE NBA

LARRY PLATT

SPIKE

AN AVON BOOK

Grateful acknowledgment is given for permission to reprint lyrics from "Dear Mama," words and music by Joe Sample, Tupac Shakur, Tony Pizarro, Joseph Jefferson, Charles Simmons, and Bruce Hawkes, copyright © 1995, 1996 by FOUR KNIGHTS MUSIC, JOSHUA'S DREAM MUSIC, WB MUSIC CORP., THE UNDERGROUND CONNECTION, and IRVING MUSIC, INC. All rights for FOUR KNIGHTS MUSIC and JOSHUA'S DREAM MUSIC administered by MUSIC CORPORATION OF AMERICA, INC., a division of UNIVERSAL STUDIOS, INC., WARNER BROS. MUSIC CORP. and WARNER-TAMERLANE PUBLISHING CORP. All rights for THE UNDERGROUND CONNECTION administered by WB Music Corp. (Contains elements from "Sadie" by Joseph Jefferson, Bruce Hawes, Charles Simmons—Warner-Tamerlane Publishing Corp.) International copyright secured. All Rights Reserved.

avon books, inc.
1350 Avenue of the Americas
New York, New York 10019

Copyright © 1999 by Larry Platt
Interior design by Kellan Peck
ISBN: 0-380-97714-1

Library of Congress Cataloging in Publication Data:

Platt, Larry.
    Keepin' it real : a turbulent season at the crossroads with the NBA / Larry Platt.—1st ed.
        p.   cm.
    Includes index.
    1. National Basketball Association.   2. Basketball players—Professional ethics—United States.   3. Basketball—Moral and ethical aspects—United States.   I. Title.
GV885.515.N37P53 1999   99-12059
796.323'64'0973—dc21   CIP

First Spike Printing: April 1999

SPIKE TRADEMARK REG. U.S. PAT. OFF. AND IN OTHER COUNTRIES, MARCA REGISTRADA, HECHO EN U.S.A.

Printed in the U.S.A.

FIRST EDITION

QPM 10 9 8 7 6 5 4 3 2 1

www.spikebooks.com

To Mom and Dad for doing the nasty thirty-five years ago, not to mention their subsequent support; to Scott Mac, whose thinking about the NBA's cultural place litters these pages; and to Bet, whose eloquent example of everyday kindnesses informs the type of person I'm striving to become.

Character, that's what God and the angels know about you. Reputation, that's what men think of you. I'll live with what God knows.

—Randall "Tex" Cobb, former heavyweight contender and movie actor

The body is the one thing you can't fake; it's just got to be there.

—Lewis in *Deliverance* by James Dickey

contents

keepin' it real

introduction

it's the eve of the 1997–98 season and the suits at Olympic Tower, also known as NBA headquarters, are nervous. Sure, the league continued its unprecedented popularity last season, its fiftieth year. Michael Jordan led his Bulls to yet another league title, the TV ratings were stellar, and the talent pool of young hoopsters seeking to impact the league is deeper than ever.

But these are perilous times for the NBA and Commissioner David Stern knows it. Make no mistake: The suits are worried.

Indeed, its fifty-first season promises to be the NBA's most critical since 1978, Stern's first year as general counsel to a moribund league riddled with drug scandals and off-putting on-court personalities. By the time he rose to commissioner in 1984, the league had begun its transformation into the sport of the '90s. It was done through a fortuitous amalgam of luck and marketing savvy. For the league was blessed with a charismatic crop of newcomers—Larry Bird, Magic Johnson, Michael Jordan, and Charles Barkley among them—whom Stern cleverly recognized and hyped as the league's assets.

But now 1997–98 looms as another turning point. It may very well see Michael and Charles's last hurrahs, and the hand-wringing is all too audible: To whom could they possibly pass the torch?

With the ascendancy of the Generation X hoopsters, a crescendo of league officials, pundits, and even coaches can be heard bemoaning the future of their game. Three years ago, *Sports Illustrated* ran a cover story on the league's "prima donnas" and, two years ago, it opined: "The NBA should write B. B. King a nice royalty check, because one of his hits is the theme song for this season: 'The Thrill Is Gone, baby . . .' " Recently, it's only gotten worse. Grumblings about the young players' frequent run-ins with the law have dominated this off-season.

Undoubtedly, there is a clash of cultures at work in the NBA. On one side is Stern and veterans like Jordan and even Barkley, who long ago signed on to the advice given to them by erstwhile star Julius Erving, who served as a different sort of generational signpost; Dr. J reigned, after all, in the '70s, and he came to represent the possibilities of integration. It made sense, then, that he would tell a youthful Barkley, "This is a billion-dollar business and we're the assets. It's our job to grow the business."

But coming of age in the wake of Erving, Jordan, and even Barkley has been a host of young millionaire basketball players, raised not on the crossover-inspired ethic of Motown but on the in-your-face aggressiveness of rap music. They're a presence throughout the league, mega-talented players who value their street credibility as much as their endorsement deals, who are anything but conciliatory to what they perceive as mainstream taste.

Into this old school versus new school chasm step five players, all facing unique challenges at the dawn of the 1997–98 season. There's Jerry Stackhouse, who, at twenty-one, consciously adopted the Erving and Jordan crossover mantle and, in the process, may have increased the pressures on himself to perform like a superstar right away. There's Barkley, the former bad boy turned philosopher prince, whose take-no-prisoners aggressiveness in the late '80s and early '90s ironically spawned the generation of hip-hoppers he now disdains and who, with diminishing skills, hopes to take one final run at the title that would cement his name in the game's pantheon. Matt Maloney is the throwback, a white player whose physical skills are judged as even more limited by the reverse (and growing) stereotype that white guys simply can't ball up as well. Vernon Maxwell, on the other hand, is the original gangsta hoopster. He has gotten by on a mix of athletic ability and boyish charm, but his career has been continually threatened by his own impulses to court danger. Finally, there's Chris Webber, the raw but immensely talented superstar-to-be. He spent the last four years combating his reputation as a prima donna, and like the hip-hopper he is, obsesses on being "respected" above all else.

As they negotiate the mine-laden terrain that is the modern-day NBA, each of their stories illustrates what's gone wrong with the league, what needs to be changed if the league is to continue to flourish—and what is still very right about the game itself.

Daunting issues may be on the horizon, but these five players share an abiding faith in the game that, like the prodigies they are, has been their vehicle of self-expression since early childhood. In the late nineteenth century, after all, basketball's founder Dr. James Naismith observed: "I had in mind the tall, agile, graceful, and expert athlete, one who could reach, jump, and act quickly and easily."

Whether it's a new generation demanding a handoff

from an older one or the modern manifestation of Naismith's dream, these players, if given the chance, would tell
the suits to quit their nail-biting: The more things change,
the more they stay the same.

FIRST QUARTER

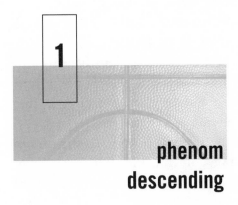

1

phenom
descending

opening night just ended badly, and Stack is facing the music. The Philadelphia 76ers, winners of only 40 games the past two seasons, came out sporting new uniforms and a new coach, but delivered the same old result: a loss, this time at the hands of the Milwaukee Bucks.

Now the media throng is crowded around Jerry Stackhouse's locker, microcassette recorders bobbing in front of his mouth, camera lights blinding his eyes. It's a jostling, sweating mass of mostly middle-aged, paunchy white guys who want to know *what happened*.

By now, at all of twenty-three years old, Stack is a grizzled veteran of this routine. In his velvety smooth baritone, he recites all the right phrases. How, with a lot of new faces, you can't expect a team to gel right away. How, without Allen Iverson (suspended for this game because of an off-season arrest for possession of marijuana), tonight wasn't a good barometer of this team. How he never really felt in rhythm tonight. How you'd have to ask the coach why he wasn't put back into the game in the fourth quarter.

Just moments before, the media horde had heard Larry Brown, the new coach of the 76ers and Stackhouse's third in a three-year career, talk about "one or two guys in that locker room who aren't buying into what we're trying to do. . . . They say the right things, but if you're not going to guard somebody, you're not going to play for me." There was little doubt he was referring to Stackhouse, who got lit up in the first half by Milwaukee shooting guard Ray Allen.

The stat sheet told all: twenty minutes played, one for five from the floor, 5 points. This after leading the 76ers in scoring during the preseason, at 17 points per game, not to mention leading all rookie scorers in 1995–96 (19.2) and all second-year players last season (20.7). This year, though, there are a lot of doubts about Stackhouse's game—but one thing he could always do is score. Not tonight.

Now, sound bites exhausted, he straightens his tie, takes one last look at the hang of his olive green Donna Karan suit, slings a pair of his signature Fila sneakers over his shoulder, and steps into the hallway that leads to the players' lounge, where his girlfriend, Shondra, awaits. "Man, coach keeps saying not to think about scoring," he says softly, looking down. "That's hard to do when you're a scorer. That's my game."

I volunteer that this was a one-game aberration: In the preseason, after all, he shot over 50 percent and dropped in 17 a game. "Yeah, but that's misleading," he says softly, clearly concerned. "Look at the Boston game."

In the 76ers' final preseason game, Stackhouse led all scorers. "Sure, I got thirty-three points, but even that was only on eight shots," he says, noting that his points came from the foul line, where he hit seventeen of nineteen.

He sighs, before spying Shondra and their six-month-old baby, Jay Alexander. "Basketball sucks, but life is great," he says, making eye contact with his baby and breaking out into the wide grin that marketing mavens once thought would change the NBA. That was two years ago. A lifetime.

When Jerry Stackhouse opted to enter the 1995 NBA draft after his sophomore year at the University of North Carolina, it was big news. He was *Sports Illustrated*'s College Player of the Year and the comparisons to another athletically gifted UNC graduate started almost immediately. In fact, in a summer pickup game on campus, the legend went, he had even dunked on His Airness. Right in his face.

Yes, Stackhouse would be the latest "next one," following in the footsteps of Grant Hill and Penny Hardaway. The cliché-tossing commenced; hardly a column about the NBA was written that didn't attach the prefix "Air Apparent" to Stackhouse's name.

Of course, the twenty-year-old prodigy was into the hype. He had seen how first Jordan and then Hill had parlayed their on-court skills into the beginnings of empire; that's what he wanted, too. He had watched as they—both, not coincidentally, products of the ACC—adopted the legacy of Dr. J. He saw them do as Erving had done in the late '70s: By cleverly combining an infectious smile with positive (if a bit boring) sound bites and a gracious demeanor, they had "crossed over." They had achieved the pinnacle of media integration: Whites who knew no blacks in real life felt they knew the Doc, Michael, and Grant. And they bought their sneakers.

So even before he had played a minute of pro basketball, Stackhouse made his own crossover moves. He signed for $7 million over three years with the 76ers after getting picked third in the 1995 draft, but before his rookie season began he had almost equalled that figure in endorsement income. Along with "Team Stackhouse"—a bevy of business advisers—he interviewed the sneaker companies who wanted his name on their shoes. Nike couldn't offer top billing; they already had Jordan and another of his heir apparents, Orlando's Hardaway. He chose Fila—not coincidentally, the company Hill had gone with right out of college—after the upstart company pledged to feature him in a series of national commercials. Other deals followed with Mountain Dew, Schick, and Fleer trading cards.

But the rush to join Jordan and Hill in the endorsement sweepstakes had its downside, too. If you're accepting—indeed, cultivating—superstar hype, you'd better play like one. Last season, Stackhouse's second in the league, things went sour. Sure, he averaged 20.7 points, but there was widespread dissatisfaction with his game. Along press row, the mavens who had anointed him the next Jordan were now mumbling that he might turn out to be a bust. He was a gifted athlete, but he hadn't improved in three key areas: outside shooting, ballhandling, and defense.

The reconsideration of Stackhouse reached its peak in midseason of his sophomore year, when the dismal chemistry between him and backcourt mate Allen Iverson showed no signs of improving. He and Iverson, a breathtakingly athletic but often out-of-control rookie point guard, don't play together so much as compete for the spotlight. "I'm the shooting guard. I think I should be leading this team in shots," bemoaned Stackhouse after Iverson's own shooter's mentality became obvious.

The adjustment to Iverson wasn't made easier by the media's intense scrutiny. USA Today's Peter Vecsey reported that both players' respective "posses" brawled outside a 76ers' practice; vehement denials followed and Vecsey later apologized to the team.

The posse fight may never have occurred, but there's no question that both young guards were having trouble accommodating each others' games on court. At one point, good-natured trash-talking between the two at practice morphed into ill will when Stackhouse made a crack about Iverson's failure to give up the ball; punches were thrown.

Much is made in the NBA about "chemistry," a loosely used term. Too often, it is confused with camaraderie. When Dennis Rodman joined the Chicago Bulls, he and Scottie Pippen didn't hold a personal conversation for an entire year. Yet, on court, they blended together seamlessly. Partially, their success was due to their respective maturity levels and to the wisdom of their coach, Phil Jackson, who preached tirelessly about "putting 'we' before 'me.' "

Personally, Stackhouse and Iverson do get along. When the team played at Charlotte, Minnie Stackhouse cooked up some artery-hardening Southern delicacies for her son's backcourt mate. No, their problems go deeper than the personal. Persuading young players like Stackhouse and Iverson to embody the selflessness exemplified by Rodman and Pippen has become a trying task, because, more and more, tomorrow's superstars have been treated as such since early adolescence.

Add to the mix the vagaries of youth, not to mention their different backgrounds, and it's no wonder the Stackhouse–Iverson combo hasn't clicked. Both left college early to enter the NBA. Consequently, denied full apprenticeships, both have had to learn as they go. Moreover, but for their precociousness, they are mirror images of each other, each one representative of the divergent paths open to modern-day hoopsters. In his rookie season, Iverson became emblematic of the gangsta player, with his corn-rowed hair, in-your-face rhetoric ("I don't have to respect nobody," he said in reference to—gasp—Jordan), and trouble with the law. Stackhouse, on the other hand, is a conscious crossover-era throwback.

Now, as Stackhouse's pivotal third year begins—the final season of a three-year deal—there are few signs the 76ers' backcourt will gel. Few fans realize just how competitive the NBA is, even among teammates. There are, after all, only 348 jobs—and everybody wants one. As a result, all players share the same mantra: Minutes and shots (even the so-called role players). The truth is, while coaches might tell a player his role is to rebound and play defense, the first thing general managers focus on come contract time is scoring—or the lack thereof, a contradiction not lost on a generation of players who count among their favorite songs Puff Daddy's "It's All About the Benjamins, Baby." And this is a show-me-the-money moment for Jerry Stackhouse.

For the first time in his life, he hears doubts about the one thing no one has ever questioned before: his game. And they are everywhere he turns. They're coming from the stands, where a smattering of boos is discernible during pre-game introductions. They are implied in the thinly veiled public criticisms uttered by his new coach, Brown, who stripped Stackhouse of his team captaincy during training camp in favor of newcomer Jim Jackson, who plays a similar go-to-the-hole (though less spectacular) style. They are in the paper, where one local writer suggests the 76ers hire a shooting coach to work with him. They are on talk radio, where the phone lines light up around the time his latest Fila commercial airs and his shooting percentage hovers below 40 percent; irate fans complain that a top draft pick making millions in endorsements *should at least know how to shoot the ball.*

How fickle conventional wisdom is. The same media that overhyped him has now reached a damning conclusion: Stackhouse is a perfect example of the type of player who should have stayed in college. By chasing the big bucks, the argument goes, he sacrificed the development of a well-rounded game. That may turn out to be true, but the thinking derives from an overwhelmingly middle-class myopia.

For many NBA fans, choosing a college was about finding a major that meshed with our career goals, but, like so many of the kids today forgoing a B.A. for the NBA, Stackhouse faced different dilemmas. He was the last of eleven children born to Minnie, a cook and preacher at the local church, and the only child of George Stackhouse, a sanitation truck driver whom Minnie married twenty-eight years ago. Minnie was forty-six when she had Jerry and, by the time he'd completed his sophomore season at UNC, she was in failing health. She had diabetes, breast cancer, and had just undergone gallbladder surgery when Stackhouse—agonizing all the while—opted for the NBA money. It was not an easy decision. But he had already lost a sister to diabetes and it dawned on him: You don't often hear about the siblings of millionaires dying from diabetes. After he signed, he bought Minnie a Lexus, George a new pickup, and gave them a checkbook so they could pay off all their bills.

Now those who once proclaimed him ready to come out have thought better of it. But what really gnaws at him are the league-wide rumors about his future. It is a given that any day now, he might be traded. The rumors have swirled for close to a year, ever since it became apparent that he and Iverson didn't mesh and that he'd be looking for something in the neighborhood of $10 million a year to re-sign with Philadelphia. "It's like any job—how would you like to keep hearing that you may be going someplace else and you have no idea where?" he says. "It could be anywhere in the United States, in a city where you don't know anyone. They expect you not to think about that?"

More and more lately, he has. Two years ago, a smiling, wide-eyed rookie, Stackhouse was the only Sixer to leave the hotel on road trips and explore new cities, happy to be recognized, to sign autographs. Now he's brooding, more private. On off-nights, he tends to hang around the house he's renting on Philadelphia's opulent Main Line, where he lives with Shondra; Jay Alexander; his rottweilers, Rendo and Heidi; and a rotating assortment of friends and relatives from back home: guys named Allen, Fen, Drake, and Chuck, who grew up with him in Kinston, North Carolina. They were in his corner before the big money; they were his boys before all the hangers-on started pulling at him. And they are expert, if biased, at analyzing their friend's situation.

Playing without a true point guard, they'll offer, is wreaking havoc with his shooting. Every shot Stack takes, he has to create for himself. "Allen is really a shooting guard," Stack agrees. "He's not interested in being a distributor."

It is as close as Stack will come to criticism of his back-court mate. Ever-mindful of the crossover ethic to "say the right thing," he refrains from making it personal. When it's pointed out that it was he who showed up to unveil the team's new uniforms at a local mall, while Iverson was no-where to be found, he simply shrugs. He's a good citizen who doesn't want a medal for it. He just wants the ball. Minutes and shots, minutes and shots.

Tucked away just miles from the 76ers' practice facility is the home Stackhouse escapes to, set deeply in a heavily wooded, all-white enclave where his neighbors share his tax bracket but have little sense of the pressure he works under. Who among them, after all, has literally millions of people watching them, analyzing them, and making moral judg-ments about their work every day? They are far more con-cerned that their kids are accepted at the right private schools so they can get into the right Ivy-clad universities. To them, having their offspring attend UNC would qualify as a family disaster.

The pressure on Stack exerts itself in ways fans haven't begun to contemplate. In his first two seasons, for instance, Fila sold over 1 million Stackhouse sneakers; this year, though, hardly any are on the market. "Until they know where I'm going to be, they're not sending them out," Stack-house says. Other signs abound of his strangely precipitous fall from can't-miss phenom to disappointment, like the fact that he no longer needs to register in hotels under an alias. The clamoring fans of his rookie year have found new fla-vors of the day.

So it is here, in this house, after games, that Jerry Stack-house, a self-described "homebody," gets all the encouragement he needs from those who, he keeps reminding himself, are the only ones who truly matter. "It don't matter where they trade me. It's all the same," he says, entering his kitchen and greasing up a tin pan. It's a chocolate chip cookie and milk night. "I'm always going to have my family with me. Can't break us up."

Once the cookies are in the oven, he picks up the phone for his daily phone call back to Kinston, where his mother awaits news of tonight's game with an assortment of home-spun aphorisms and biblical verses. One by one, Stack's friends and family disappear to different wings of the house, until it's just him, a twenty-two-year-old millionaire man-child, checking periodically on his cookies—"I like 'em real soft"—while taking comfort in the voice of his mom at his ear.

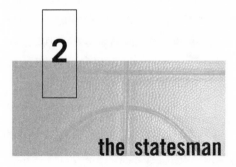

2

the statesman

governor Barkley is practicing damage control. Last season, his first with the Houston Rockets, this veteran team got off to a 15–1 start in November. Not so this year. Tonight Stackhouse and Iverson and the rest of the Sixers come in, looking for their first win after an 0–5 start, against a struggling 3–2 Rockets team.

Suddenly the Rockets—with aging superstars Barkley, Clyde Drexler, and Hakeem Olajuwon—look old; center Olajuwon, in particular, looks mortal. More important, there are indications of internal dissent. After last week's last-second loss at Portland (Barkley missed two layups with the game on the line), Olajuwon complained about not getting the ball down the stretch. Barkley told Eddie Sefko, a beat writer for the *Houston Chronicle*, that Hakeem is "a big baby." Drexler chimed in, taking Olajuwon's side, unable to resist the opportunity to needle Barkley publicly.

Now Barkley is flanked by Olajuwon and Drexler as he addresses the media on the corner of the court where tonight his team will take on the organization he anchored for years. He's about to display a talent perfected through thirteen years in the national spotlight, a talent for spin control he hopes to take with him into his next career: politics. That's right, the most impolitic of sports stars plans on running for governor of his native Alabama in 2002 and, like countless savvy pols before him, he's about to use humor to quell a brewing controversy.

"There is no dissension on this team," Barkley announces. "Ya'll have been printing misleading things to divide us and it's going to stop now. It is not true that Dream and I don't get along. I respect Dream. It's not true that I ever told Dream to shut up. He never speaks—how can you tell him to shut up?"

The press giggles. Olajuwon clears his throat and inches forward into the microphones, about to speak. Before he can, though, Barkley, grinning wildly, jumps in: "Man, shut up, Dream!"

There is thunderous laughter. Olajuwon and Drexler issue some pro-forma quotes and, just like that, all is well in Rocket Land. For now.

Charles Barkley, statesman. It is just the latest incarnation of one of the most singular athletes of our time; for the last thirteen years, the evolution of Charles Barkley has been a riveting work in progress. Like his hero, Muhammad Ali, he is always in a state of becoming, a consummate showman who, despite appearances, is never in the final act.

He is expert at makeover. When he broke into the league in 1985, Barkley was an anomaly, a fat jumping jack in a world of sinewy athletic hardbodies. He was also a shy "country bumpkin" in the words of one who knew him well then, a backwater Alabama kid who rarely ventured out of his Philadelphia apartment, so intimidated was he by the big city.

Within a few years, though, he would grow into the first hip-hop hoopster, serving as a symbolic rejection of cross-over, that prevailing ethic for black basketball stars. He had, after all, inherited leadership of a team from Erving, who, toward the end of his illustrious career, was championed by the press and league alike as the game's "great ambassa-dor," a hardcourt Cosby.

"I grew up listening to Motown—Marvin Gaye, the Temptations, the Supremes," recalls Erving today, now a vice president with the Orlando Magic after an inauspicious stint as a hoops commentator on NBC. " 'Crossover' was an important word to me. It became important to be able to be accepted in all different kinds of neighborhoods. These kids today don't feel the same."

In fact, Erving, bespectacled and graying now, is critical even of Jordan. "Closing your eyes when you shoot a free throw?" he says. "That's all about 'Look at me, look at me.' "

And Jordan is the *closest* approximation in demeanor to Erving among today's black stars. Barkley, during his time in Philly, was the antithesis. Where Erving was dutifully apolitical, Barkley was brash and outspoken. In the late '80s, he began talking to Jesse Jackson and calling himself a " '90s nigga." Visits to the 76ers' locker room were the stuff of great theater, as Barkley would regularly castigate the over-whelmingly all-white press and a city still divided by race. "Just because you give Charles Barkley a lot of money, it doesn't mean I'm going to forget about the people in the ghettos and slums," he lectured. "Ya'll don't want me talk-ing about this stuff, but I'm going to voice my opinions, because this stuff's important. Me getting twenty rebounds ain't important. We've got people homeless on our streets, and the media is crowding around my locker. It's ludicrous."

He called Philly a "racist city" and the town's sports punditocracy shot back in kind, beating him up for taking on issues beyond rebounds and free throws. "I don't have to be what you want me to be," he told them in 1990, echoing an Ali line from the '60s, after he read Thomas Hauser's oral history of the boxing great. "I'm a strong black man."

Once he pointed across the locker room at genteel teammate Hersey Hawkins. "I ain't no pussy black man like Hersey," he said. Hawkins shook his head—Charles was just being Charles, after all—and the press nervously giggled. When I told him I was writing a magazine profile of Erving, he dismissed the legend: "Man, I ain't got no time to talk about no Uncle Tom," he said.

His was a voice that resonated at street level at the precise cultural moment when rap music was breaking through to the mainstream. The innovative rap group Public Enemy even paid homage in its hit "Bring the Noise by celebrating Barkley's ferocious dunking style."

Yet, even then, he exhibited a greater potential for growth than any other athlete on the public scene. He was constantly answering questions—with that stunning forthrightness—and questioning answers. "I'm somebody who has always thought for myself," he says. "Most people don't question what they're told."

That was clear in 1988, when he told his mother he was considering voting for George Bush. "But, Charles, Bush is only for the rich," she said. "Mom, I *am* the rich," he replied.

Similarly, his iconoclasm was on display in 1991, when Magic Johnson tested HIV positive and other players like Kevin Johnson were calling for uniform testing in the NBA. Barkley simply stated: "I'm disappointed in myself that I haven't felt the same compassion for other people stricken with AIDS that I now feel for Magic."

In 1992 Barkley was traded to Phoenix, where he'd star for the Suns and where he would enter his Republican makeover phase. His world view began to mature; he became more focused on class, less virulent on race. He also grew close to Rush Limbaugh and Dan Quayle, dined with Clarence Thomas, and endorsed Steve Forbes in the presidential primary. Exit polls showed that his imprimatur sealed Forbes's win.

And now here he is, in Houston, playing for one last chance at a championship while gearing up for his post-hoops political career. As his politics have developed, so has his place in the game. Somehow Charles Barkley has become one of the league's premier elder statesmen, a soundbite machine capable of putting into immediate perspective the problem with these kids today, as he did last season when he publicly lambasted Iverson about his posse: "Your teammates should be your posse," he said. (Iverson, in true hip-hop fashion—you dis me, I dis in return—fired right back: "What has Charles Barkley ever won? How many rings does he have?")

This isn't to suggest, however, that anything in Barkley's world is cut-and-dried. To the contrary, there is an ongoing internal conflict between his hip-hop roots and mainstream aspirations; the schism is manifested in his emotional—rather than cerebral—outbursts, as when he launched an obnoxious heckler through a plate-glass window in an Orlando bar prior to the season. But that's what is so intriguing about his foray into politics: He may be the only figure, in sports or politics, who carries cache with the brothers in the 'hood *and* with Stackhouse's blue-blooded neighbors.

"I don't think I run my mouth. That's just what redneck sportswriters say when you voice an opinion they disagree with," he says. "And I don't think I'm someone who gets in trouble. If someone throws a drink in my face, I'm gonna defend my damn self."

Indeed, it was the hip-hop Barkley talking when, after meeting with NBA honchos following the Orlando incident, he announced: "Let there be no conflict in America. If you bother me, I whup yo ass."

*   *   *

On this day, Barkley would have been better served to save the in-your-face rhetoric for his former team. The Sixers, though winless, have shown signs of coming together in practice.

Iverson and Stackhouse were impressively in synch during the shootaround, seeming to know where the other would be at all times during a run-through of countless offensive sets. But when the two took a breather, sitting together on the sideline, Iverson rose to make his way to the Gatorade and Stackhouse called out, "Get me one, too."

"Do I look like Mr. Fuckin' Belvedere?" responded Iverson, walking away with his cup. Stackhouse just shook his head.

At game time, the Sixers come out energized. Stackhouse scores 17 points on eight of thirteen shooting, but Iverson is the story of the night: 26 points, 15 assists, and, astonishingly, no turnovers. The Rockets look their age, scoring just 4 points in the fourth quarter; Barkley goes for 19 points and nine rebounds, but he appears sluggish and plodding. The Sixers get their first win of the season.

After the game, though, Barkley is his usual gregarious self. After thirteen seasons in the league, he knows how to handle defeat. In fact, league-wide, it is the coaches whose faces drain of color for days after tough losses; veteran players know that the key to winning is dealing with the losing, which is why NBA locker rooms can seem oddly jovial after crushing losses. It's not that the players don't care; they simply digest the blow and move on. There is always a next game. So it is tonight, when 76ers' announcer Steve Mix enters the locker room to say goodbye to Barkley.

"Hey, Mix, tell your wife to stop calling me so late when you're away on road trips," Barkley roars. "If she wants to call me, tell her to—"

"Call earlier?" Mix deadpans.

"That's right. Call earlier," Barkley says, breaking into a

wide grin. "I'm getting tired of it." Then he pours himself a Lite beer, grabs his stuff, and mumbles something about tomorrow being another day at the office.

In general, the great ones don't lose it all at once. No, the first thing to go tends to be consistency. It's why, in his final season, Larry Bird was able to score 49 points one night, but just 7 the next: The reserve of energy that has overcome countless back-to-backs in the past simply isn't there.

Barkley may have been running on close to empty against the Sixers, but he's refueled two nights later when the Lakers come to town. He grabs 22 rebounds and hits a baseline jumper at the end of regulation to send the game into overtime. But the Rockets can't overcome the play of Laker point guard Nick Van Exel, one of the hip-hop hoop-sters often vilified in the press. (Two seasons ago, Van Exel shoved a referee and then apologized not to the ref, the fans, or his teammates, but to his sneaker company.) He drains three after three en route to 35 points, silencing the Houston crowd. Then, late in the game, just for good measure, Van Exel cups his hand to his ear and stares wide-eyed at the stands, a quintessential playground moment.

Tonight it is Olajuwon who looks his age. He makes just two of eleven shots and is dominated by Shaquille O'Neal.

The next day, before the Rockets leave for a game at Phoenix, the locker room talk is about the weirdness of the season so far. The Rockets, after all, are now 3–4 after a 57-win regular season last year, not to mention a trip to the Western Conference Finals. More shocking is that, with last night's home loss to Washington, the mighty Bulls, playing without the injured Scottie Pippen, are now 4–4; there is general accord, however, that Washington star Chris Webber spoke too soon when, after last night's game, he said, "They're still a good team, but I don't think people are going to come in being afraid of them right now."

The strangeness of this fledgling season can be seen off the court as well. There is a new preoccupation among the league's powers with its image. New emphasis is being put on curbing everything from the wearing of baggy shorts to the use of trash-talking and foul language to smoking pot. (A *New York Times* piece on the eve of the season estimated that over 70 percent of all players smoke; management decried the paper's methodology, but most players privately concede that the figure sounds too low.)

The latest memo from the league, warning players to refrain from profanity on the court, prompts some Rocket veterans to reminisce about their ex-teammate Vernon Maxwell, one of the more linguistically inventive players in the league. Seems San Antonio's pious Avery Johnson begins every game by shaking his opponents' hands and saying, "May the Lord bless you tonight." Maxwell's response was pure Mad Max: "This a muthafuckin' basketball game, muthafucka, so God ain't got fuck-all to do with it."

Despite the jocularity, the league's increasing enthusiasm for issuing edicts speaks to a real tension between the players and the NBA. The hip-hoppers are taking over and David Stern doesn't like it, as evidenced by his declaration four years ago, when Dream Team II, led by Derrick Coleman, Larry Johnson, and Alonzo Mourning, preened and strutted and trash-talked its way through the World Championship Games. "We are going to take back our game," Stern said then.

But the street-wise sensibility of hip-hop among players hasn't decreased. Already this season, when a fan charged toward Gary Payton on the floor during the waning moments of a game between the Philadelphia 76ers and the Seattle SuperSonics, Payton responded by keeping it real: The two jawed at one another, faces pressed together, while security rushed to the court. When asked later why he didn't just walk away, Payton responded, "Hey, I'm from the 'hood in Oakland. If he pulled a gun, I'd knock him out."

Payton is just one of a generation of ballplayers who, in keeping with their roots, see Stern as "the Man" and his dictums as indicative of a hostility to black culture. Ironically, it was Barkley's defiance through the years that, above all else, shaped their view. He may scoff at the new generation's tendency to see every mandate from the league or their teams as either an assault on their manhood or a stifling of their creativity, but it was only two years ago that he reacted similarly when the Suns shopped him around the league: "The days of cotton-picking are over," he said. "They disrespected me by shopping me around like a piece of meat."

Now, though, the wannabe politician will have none of it. He is hanging around the Rockets' state-of-the-art practice facility at the Westside Tennis Center, getting ready for tonight's trip to Phoenix. "I don't care what the younger guys think. They're wrong," he says. "The shorts now are getting to the point where they don't even look like shorts. I think the NBA has to be concerned with a lot of black guys getting arrested, doing drugs, wearing shorts down to their ankles. That's not hostility to black culture. That's just reality. The NBA can't go back to the way it was once thought of. It's an image thing."

I tell him that, ten years ago, he would have agreed with the younger guys and his response is classic Barkley: a traditionally conservative message delivered with an in-your-face 'tude that has street credibility. "That's not true," he snaps. "Don't tell me what I thought ten years ago, muthafucka. I'll tell you what I thought ten years ago."

And I am on the receiving end of similar forthrightness when I make the mistake of calling his gubernatorial ruminations a "fantasy." "What you mean, man?" he barks, eyebrows arching. "I'm doing this. Ain't no ifs. I think about it every day. I wake up thinking about it."

That's when it becomes clear: For Barkley, basketball is his job. Finding something to stand for is his passion.

* * *

Two yeas ago, Charles Barkley sat in a darkened movie
theater, transfixed. He was watching *When We Were Kings,*
the Academy Award–winning account of Ali's epic "Rumble
in the Jungle" against a younger, seemingly invincible
George Foreman. Of course, the film is much more than a
chronicle of a prizefight. It paints a glowing portrait of Ali,
whom Barkley has long admired.

"Man, I sat in that theater and that was a humbling
experience," Barkley says now, riding a stationary bike in
the bowels of the Rockets' arena. Two days ago, his team
dropped its third straight in Phoenix, but, more importantly,
Barkley left the game with a sports hernia, an injury that
will keep him out for a couple of weeks. Tonight's game,
against the Knicks, will be the first of three games he'll miss.
For now, he's grimacing through his workout, beads of
sweat dripping off his forehead. This is work and he doesn't
enjoy it. "That was a different kind of human being right
there, Muhammad Ali. I don't think there's ever been a
greater black man, besides Malcolm X. I just sat there and
kept thinking about how that man stood for something.
Stood for principle."

As he pedals, he welcomes the opportunity to talk issues—anything to serve as a diversion to the workout. It's
a generation later, but Ali's symbolic influence is never far
from Barkley, who is, after over a decade of celebrityhood,
similarly looking for something to stand for that is bigger
than himself.

"What Ali said in that film about rich and poor is true,"
he says now. "I don't want to run for office necessarily to
win. I just want to wake people up. See, nobody cares about
poor black kids or poor white kids. The have-nots in
America are left on their own, because it ain't to nobody's
advantage to help them. I think it's up to the haves."

At home, Barkley is a classic couch potato, expert with
the remote control. But he watches political talk shows as

much as sporting events—CNN's "Crossfire" is a particular favorite. And he reads, currently wading through Jonathan Kozol's *Savage Inequalities,* a scathing indictment of the public school system, after finishing Colin Powell's autobiography and Mumia Abu-Jamal's *Live from Death Row.* It is when he's watching "Crossfire" that he gets most agitated, turned off by the partisan bickering, often yelling back at the screen and calling the talking heads "knuckleheads."

"Somewhere along the line, something's gotten lost," he says. "Politicians are supposed to take care of all the people, not just the special interests. That really bothers me. I like Clinton. I think he's improved as a president and I think he truly cares. But he gets bogged down in that system, too. I'm going into it with this mindset: I don't need the job and I'm just here to help the people."

In that sense, Barkley might be the perfect candidate for the post-ideological age: a pragmatic populist. Neither left nor right, he is in favor of what works. He regularly lambastes liberalism, to the proud applause of his friends Limbaugh and Quayle, as "not having done anything for black America in the last twenty years. All my old friends are still back in the 'hood, on welfare. Welfare gave the black man an inferiority complex. They gave us some fish—instead of teaching us how to fish."

In the next breath, though, he will similarly skewer the Republican revolution of 1994 as "mean-spirited" and denounce conservatives like Pat Buchanan, whom he calls a "neo-Nazi." The Barkley panacea? Education for all. He is intrigued by, but still noncommittal on, conservatives' calls for school choice, whereby local municipalities provide parents with a voucher for a set sum and the parents send their kids to any school—public or private—they choose. He is convinced, however, that the way we fund public schools— through local property taxes—is fatally flawed, designed to produce good schools in good neighborhoods and run-down schools in run-down areas.

Education is at the heart of his criticism of Fob James, the current occupant of Alabama's statehouse (the name of which Barkley pledges to change upon his election to "the Crib"). James opposed Goals 2000, Clinton's education reform package, and opposes new taxes dedicated to education spending in a state that has the nation's fifth-lowest percentage of college-educated citizens. Instead, James has made national news by leading a Bible-thumping crusade, going so far as to threaten to call in the National Guard in support of Judge Roy Moore's refusal to obey a court order to remove the Ten Commandments and to cease holding prayer services in his courtroom. To Barkley, it stinks of political pandering.

"I just think people spend so much time worrying about little things, they don't look at the big things, and politicians know this and take advantage of it," he says. "The first thing we've got to do is correct the way we fund public schools. I mean, my daughter goes to a private school because I can afford it. But shouldn't everyone have great education available to them? Where do you think crime comes from? A lot of it happens because these kids don't have self-esteem or pride through education. And what little education they get ain't gonna give them any opportunity out there."

Where does this social conscience come from? Self-esteem is not some New Age feel-good buzzword to Barkley; it's been the story of his life. Unlike so many sports superstars, he wasn't a prodigy, coddled from a young age and trained to focus on a game at the expense of all things human. No, Barkley grew up, by all accounts, shy, sweet, fat, and unathletic. Were it not for a sudden growth spurt his senior year of high school, he reminds himself daily, he'd have been just another minimum wage worker in Leeds, Alabama. He was raised by his mother, Charcy Glenn, and his grandmother, Johnnie Mae Mickens, to be empathetic, but with a stern dose of tough love, a recipe he borrows now as a father: Nine-year-old Christiana is forbidden from playing sports until she gets straight A's.

And once he made it big, he watched his younger brother, Darryl, grappling with his sibling's fame and fortune, suffer a stroke due to cocaine abuse. Of course, Barkley resents delving into these issues as a pretext for understanding his political motives. "Why does it have to be about stuff that's happened to me?" he asks. "I believe it's up to the haves to help the have-nots because that's the right thing. Period."

He does this a lot nowadays: steer the conversation back to tried-and-true sound bites, another sign of the emerging politico. In one week's time, he uses the "They gave us some fish instead of teaching us how to fish" line at least three times.

It's not as far-fetched as it may sound: Governor Barkley. Not when, until his untimely death, Sonny Bono was a respected member of Congress, as was Fred Grandy, a.k.a. Gopher on "The Love Boat." Not at a time when Alec Baldwin plots a senate or gubernatorial run in New York. And don't forget the veritable all-star team of ex-jocks who have joined the political fray: from presidents-in-waiting Bill Bradley and Jack Kemp to Congress's Steve Largent, Jim Bunning, Tom McMillan, and J. C. Watts. The lines between celebrity and public officeholder have blurred, thanks to the modern-day prerequisites of the job: More than ever, candidates need to have instant name recognition, personal charisma, access to money, and media skills. Who better to fit the bill than professional athletes, who have grown up on the public stage, before our very eyes? We complain about them, but we love them. We even call them by their first names—Michael really needs Scottie in the lineup—as if they were our personal friends.

But there's still something about "Governor" Barkley that strains credulity. We're talking Barkley here, the pre-Rodman bad boy, a self-professed anti–role model who has been involved in more than his share of high-profile bar fights over the years. This is chief executive material?

Yes, actually. We live, after all, at a time when our sports stars come to us prepackaged, complete with a bevy of handlers, not unlike our political candidates. Both come into our living rooms and sell, sell, sell—hawking products ranging from sneakers to flat taxes. It is said that political consultant Frank Luntz devised the Contract for America from polling data; well, so too did the marketing gurus at Nike create Michael Jordan.

Barkley has been the one rare exception. His is a totally self-generated phenomenon, and the political zeitgeist calls out—finally—for someone genuine. And who is more authentic than the impetuous Barkley, sports' most engaging personality since *his* role model, Ali? America has seen Barkley defiant, repentant, joyous, and, yes, unthinking. It still likes what it sees.

The numbers bear out that if he wants it, his most stunning public act may lie ahead. In a statewide poll conducted in 1993, when he first publicly ruminated on running, Barkley would have had 19 percent of the vote, without spending a nickel on image enhancement. Indeed, Republican Party leaders in Alabama, who tried to get him to run for Congress in 1996 and 1998, believe he has as much name recognition as the sitting governor right now. And don't forget his status as hometown hero. When Barkley is in Alabama, he busies himself with charitable acts throughout the state— though you won't hear him talk about them. Throughout the years, the one condition to Barkley's charity has been that there be no media coverage. Barkley underwrites academic scholarships at Auburn University, which he attended for two years before turning pro. And, an obsessive neat freak, he's paid the teens of Leeds to clean up his hometown in the summers.

"I don't do it for recognition," he says. When pushed, he gets testy. "Ain't it enough to say I send underprivileged kids to school? I'm not trying to impress America. Fuck America. America don't give a shit about me. America only cares about me as long as I'm making baskets. Hell, Moses Malone can't get a job in the NBA, but if you're Larry Bird, Danny Ainge, and Kevin McHale, you step right in. They don't give no brothers jobs like that. I'm very realistic. I'm under no illusions."

The outburst comes out of nowhere and the fury recedes just as quickly. But far from alienating or frightening the white middle class (as Ali did for a time), Barkley has a message that leaves them salivating at the thought of his candidacy. It happened on "Crossfire" in March 1997, when he held forth on the state of race relations. "The family structure in the black community has been destroyed." he said. "You have to realize that black people have become our own worst enemies through gang violence, black-on-black crime, teenage pregnancies, and, in the black community, if you're articulate, educated, and do well, they call you a sellout and things like that."

The show closed with another endorsement for Barkley for governor, this one from right-wing cohost Lynne Cheney: "This message about self-help, about self-reliance, may be the most important message around today, and I sure do hope Charles Barkley carries it into politics, and I'll be there to campaign for him."

"Hey, franchise."

Charles Barkley enters the trainer's room and greets Olajuwon, who is icing his thirty-five-year-old knees. They share a laugh over a note in this morning's paper about how Barkley will be donating his full salary for each game that he misses to a food bank in Houston and one in Phoenix. "Hey, how much money is that?" he calls out. Someone does the math and tells him it's over $30,000 a game. "That much? Damn. I'm lucky I'm not making as much as you, Dream. I'd be giving all of it away."

As staffers and teammates and visitors come and go, there is one constant: Barkley dominates the room. The league has just signed a whopping four-year, $2.64 billion contract with NBC and Turner Sports at a time when Commissioner Stern is threatening to reopen the collective bargaining agreement because the players are getting 57 percent of league revenues. This sudden windfall, Barkley says, is proof that the "people running this league are bad people. . . . They have the audacity to complain that they're not making any money and then they do this? Those are some corrupt guys right there. We have to start preparing for a lockout."

Last time, Barkley didn't join the hard-liners, who were led by Jordan and Patrick Ewing. Now he pledges it's going to be different. There will be unity in the upcoming labor war.

And it's clear that this wannabe politician will be a leading voice. As he's sitting on the trainer's table, filibustering, it's hard to remember that he was once a fat, shy kid in Leeds who spent a lot of lonely hours on the basketball court and had a lot of doubters. Folks who thought he couldn't make his high school team, let alone get a scholarship to college, let alone make the pros, let alone become one of the greatest to ever play the game.

That Charles Barkley didn't know things would turn out as they have. All he knew was that if he worked as hard as his mom, who cleaned white people's houses, and his grandmom, who worked in a meat factory, and if, like them, he considered no task too menial (rebounding, diving for loose balls), good things had to happen.

Now it's some twenty-five years later and Charles Barkley is receiving ultrasound treatment on a trainer's table, alongside teammate Eddie Johnson. This Charles Barkley knows a lot more than the shy, fat kid; this Charles Barkley glows with self-confidence. He's become the self-esteem kid.

So when he talks about running for governor, dare you dismiss it?

Across the room, a TV catches Barkley's eye. It is tuned to "Entertainment Tonight"; the actor Leonardo DiCaprio appears on the screen.

Barkley lets out a low whistle while gazing at the screen, mesmerized. "If I could be a star, I'd be Leonardo DiCaprio, man," he says softly. "This guy's got it going on."

Johnson looks over. "You think you can act?" he asks, skeptical.

While never taking his eyes from the TV, Barkley tells his teammate how he's looked at plenty of movie scripts—including the abysmal *Celtic Pride*—but hasn't found the right one yet. He says he'll probably star in his first film (save *Space Jam*) this summer.

He says all this in the most matter-of-fact of ways. And then this most improbable of Republicans says very softly, almost to himself, the truest thing he's said all day: "I believe I can do anything if I put my mind to it."

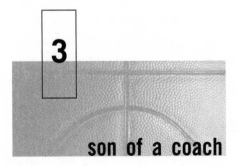

3

son of a coach

he's cornered. "Let's go. Now. All those people want to do is just jabber at me. And they get right in your face and they smell like alcohol."

Matt Maloney is stage-whispering, pleading with his older brother, Paul, who is trying to get him to make a postgame appearance in the Compaq Center bar. Maloney has just had his best game of this young season, scoring 23 points in his team's 95–84 win over the Knicks in the Rockets' first of three without Barkley, and now Paul, his business manager, roommate, and best friend, wants him to schmooze. Matt won't budge, so Paul brings the bar to him. Maloney backs up against the wall next to the exit, rolling his eyes as Paul parades a host of fans past him. One middle-aged man introduces his young son, and Maloney signs for him while engaging in awkward chitchat:

"You like basketball?"

The kid nods.

"Well, come back, you know, any time. And do good in school." He clumsily—and very momentarily—puts his arm around the kid's shoulder, the kid as impassive as Maloney is on court. Maloney inches toward the door again. Paul is slapping backs, shaking hands, and bellowing loudly, while Matt looks down, aware of all the eyes in the hallway and from the bar resting on him. The only time the second-year starting point guard for the Houston Rockets with the movie star good looks doesn't feel self-conscious, it seems, is on the court.

Last year, Matt Maloney was the surprise story of the NBA. He came out of nowhere, signing with the Rockets for the league minimum of $247,000 after apprenticing for a year in the minor league CBA; in college, he'd starred at the University of Pennsylvania in the Ivy League, not exactly a hoops hotbed. Yet he started every game for the 1996–97 Rockets and made the league's All-Rookie Second Team. In the playoffs, he picked it up a notch, scoring 26 points in a game against the heralded point guard Stephon Marbury and matching that career high against Seattle's Gary Payton—one of the NBA's best point guards ever—in a seven-game series win that included an unlikely sight: Matt Maloney crossing over Gary Payton, "breaking his ankles," as they say, on a drive to the basket.

Arguably, Houston would not have advanced past the Sonics to the Western Conference Finals had it not been for Maloney. At twenty-four, Matt Maloney had become the sudden embodiment of the ultimate suburban adolescent dream—as those of us who spent our youth in the driveway with a ball and a hoop can attest. For Maloney, it was a dream nurtured and cajoled by his demanding father, Jim Maloney, the longtime assistant to John Chaney, head coach at Philadelphia's Temple University, who died of a heart attack on the eve of his son's big break—a tryout with the

Rockets just prior to what would become his storybook rookie year.

But the storybook had a downer of an ending. Following the Sonics came the Utah Jazz and veteran point guard John Stockton, flawlessly running the pick and roll; after the Jazz's six-game win, Maloney's playoff run—not to mention his regular season consistency (9.4 points on 44 percent shooting and 3.7 assists per game)—was forgotten. The Houston call-in shows focused on the point guard position as the team's weak link.

So far this season, the widespread displeasure with the play of Maloney, Brent Price, and Emanual Davis—Houston's point guards—has continued, even escalated. For Maloney in particular, it's been a frustrating start to his sophomore season: His minutes are down, the criticism up.

Tonight he played a season-high thirty-four minutes en route to his 23 points, but that's attributable to his hot start, when he buried four of five three-pointers and totaled 14 points in the first quarter alone. On nights when his first few shots don't fall, Maloney sees more bench time than last year. Two weeks ago, it was a mere fourteen minutes against Seattle; against the Lakers four nights ago, he sat the whole fourth quarter.

Now as he enters the Green Room, a dimly lit, fashionably furnished Houston cigar bar full of blondes in dresses with plunging necklines, he orders a Greyhound, which he'll nurse throughout the night, and declines a cigar. "I don't smoke during the season," he says. A big screen shows highlights of tonight's NBA action, and he is featured; the room erupts in applause. He doesn't smile, because he's still apprehensive about the way his season is starting.

"I just figure, you know, we won fifty-seven games last season and went to the conference finals," he says as, nearby, a woman is asking Paul if it would be all right to sit on Matt's lap for a photo. "Maybe it was coincidence, but we were winning last season when you knew you'd be getting thirty to thirty-six minutes a game."

Maloney's teammate Matt Bullard enters the room, puffing a stogie and wearing a loud multicolored leather jacket with a bull—his nickname—on the back. Paul and Bull hug and compare notes on endorsement deals. We are here as guests of a couple of local businessmen who, in exchange for an occasional commercial spot and live appearances, give cars to players, replacing old with new when the odometer hits 5,000. Today, however, there was a miscommunication and one of the businessmen took away Matt's Navigator at the shootaround, failing to replace it. Brent Price had to give him a lift home.

Paul is livid. This is what he came to Houston for—to watch out for Matt. He holds an animated conversation with the businessmen at the bar; suddenly Paul's blaring guffaw cuts through the room. He's just found out that after they took the car they were in a traffic accident. "See that! See that!" he's bellowing. "You were saying, 'Aw, fuck Matt Maloney' and then—BOOM!"

He is laughing uproariously and all eyes in the intimate bar are on him, which is precisely as Matt would have it. Last season, Matt's life off the court wasn't nearly as uplifting as one might think. Particularly nightmarish was the trek from the locker room to the court at the Compaq Center on game nights; he would be accosted by a never-ending stream of marketing mavens, all hawking one deal or another. Ever the accommodating suburban kid, Maloney said yes to virtually anyone who asked him to make an appearance. In the off-season, back in Haddonfield, New Jersey, his mom, Barbara Maloney, convened a family meeting, where it was decided that thirty-seven-year-old Paul, an analyst in the pharmaceutical field, would split time between his home in the Bay Area and Houston, where he would look out for Matt's interests.

"Last season, it got so I dreaded walking from the locker

room to the court," Matt says now as he looks over and sees Paul handling things. "Now I can just hand people Paul's card and tell them to talk to my brother."

They are a study in contrasts: Matt shy and obsessively single-minded, Paul gregarious, curious, and outspoken. "Basically, I'm here to put his life together, so all he has to think about is his game," Paul explains once his business at the bar is smoothed over. "Guys were making money off his signature and likeness and he didn't see anything from it. And Matt is so focused on the game, it's not in him to pay attention. He's the kind of kid who won't pay his bills, not because he's derelict, but because he's so *responsible* about what he has to do in terms of basketball. I'm here so that focus won't hurt him."

So Paul sets up his appearances, like the upcoming one in the lobby of a local office building, where a makeshift hoop will be erected and Matt will put on a shooting exhibition. As Paul describes the gig, Matt doesn't look thrilled. "Paul will be there to talk to people, so that's good," he says in his clipped monotone. "But you feel like an animal in the zoo. All these eyes on you."

But Matt is relieved to finally have someone doing his speaking for him. Paul, for instance, does the talking to Fila now, with whom Matt has a $25,000 contract—a paltry sum compared to Stackhouse's $3 million per year deal—in exchange for a set number of personal appearances.

Paul's is a twenty-four-hour job. Now, for instance, Matt's cell phone rings and Paul promptly answers it. It's someone named Michelle, wondering where Matt is. Paul tells her he doesn't know; he hopes to meet up with him later. "I'm out with a friend of Matt's from Philly—say hello to Larry," Paul says, handing me the phone as he mouths the words: "Matt's not here."

Michelle and I have a brief, stilted conversation. "I don't know how these girls get the cell phone number," Paul says; he has once again shielded his brother from distracting encroachments. With his aqua eyes and Alec Baldwin–like looks, Maloney has become a local heartthrob. Teenage girls sit in a section behind the visitors' basket at the Compaq Center, waiting for play to stop so they can shout in unison: *"We love you, Matt!"*

But Maloney hasn't started living large. Last season, for example, after a live interview, a local TV station gave him the use of the limo they sent until nine the following morning. After thinking it over, he gave the driver directions to Blockbuster Video, where he rented Eddie Murphy's *The Nutty Professor*. "I can't go out," he explained. "I have a game in twenty-four hours."

So he spends his time renting movies (He's seen *The Cable Guy* at least four times) or watching TV ("Beverly Hills 90210") or reading (Christopher Buckley is a favorite author) or playing Pictionary with teammate Brent Price and his wife. He is a white man in a black man's game, a relative choirboy in an after-hours league, a gym rat nonplussed by the game's trappings. Everything he does, it seems, is atypical—even the way he decided to stay in Houston after his rookie year.

League salary cap rules prohibited Maloney from re-signing with Houston for more than a 20 percent increase—$326,000. He could, however, sign with any other team for whatever the market would bear. And they came calling. Pat Riley of the Miami Heat envisioned Maloney as a three-point specialist and steady backup to Tim Hardaway. The most serious interest came from the Lakers' Jerry West, who, rumor had it, was looking to jettison point guard Nick Van Exel. There was talk of signing Maloney as their $1 million exemption to the cap—whether they retained Van Exel or not.

It was tempting, but the Maloney camp didn't encourage the Lakers. The Rockets were making it clear that if Maloney came back for the $326,000, they'd reward him after the season with a two-year, $2.3 million deal. But more than that, Maloney felt indebted.

"The Rockets discovered me last year, gave me a shot," he says now, checking his watch. It's time to leave, but he can't drag Paul away from his glad-handing. "I just thought I owed them, you know? I mean if, after this season, I get a two-year deal with them and then can parlay that into another five-year contract, I'll have had a nine-year career in the NBA. That's pretty good."

Ironically, compared to most of those he now plays against, players who come from less and who have adopted an "It's about getting paid" attitude, the Ivy Leaguer may have made a naive business decision. Aware of his loyalty, is it reasonable to assume the Rockets will reciprocate?

For Maloney, though, it was more than a bottom-line, dollars-and-cents decision. Loyalty, after all, was among the lessons he learned from his father, who spent twenty-three years by John Chaney's side, turning down chance after chance to become a head coach himself. A devout Catholic, the senior Maloney, through the silent eloquence of his own example, taught his son that loyalty is not about getting something in return. It's an end in itself.

When Matt Maloney was four years old, he practiced dribbling with his head up so he could survey the terrain in front of him. When he was five, he concentrated on developing picture-perfect shooting form: elbow in, follow-through extended. As he entered his teens, he would mutter play-by-play to himself like all driveway Dr. J's, fantasizing that he was in a Sixers uniform, taking it to the hole in the NBA.

But that "goofing around," as he calls it, was an occasional luxury he allowed himself during those daily three-to-four-hour hoop sessions. Afternoons on the court were like days at the office; Barbara Maloney would look out the window and see her youngest son working on drills to improve his quickness or his ability to shoot off the dribble. It was there that the poker face and utter confidence at which his teammates marvel took hold, thanks to the never-ending counsel of his father, who preached the importance of "believing in yourself" and "focusing on the task at hand."

It is a dedication Maloney still displays. After one recent practice, for instance, most of his teammates hurry to their cars. But not Maloney, and not Barkley. Maloney continues to work, alone, shooting three-pointers after running fifteen minutes of suicide sprints. Off to the side, Barkley is, as usual, holding court, keeping a mixture of hangers-on and media enthralled. He's talking about how much he hates Houston—too much traffic and too many Uncle Toms, he says—when a three-year-old girl is encouraged by her mother to waddle up to him. "You are *sooo* beautiful," he says, scooping her into his big hands just before she bursts into tears and starts straining for Mommy. "Girl, don't you know I'm a world-famous sex symbol? You gonna regret this one day," he says, putting her down, the crowd laughing.

Maloney, oblivious, keeps on draining threes. Barkley watches his young teammate's smooth stroke. "See, Matt's a quiet kid, but he plays with a cocky confidence," says Barkley, who convinced Coach Rudy Tomjanovich to give Maloney the starting point guard job last year after Brent Price got hurt. "He's not afraid to put the ball between his legs or behind his back. He plays with a pep in his step. I love that attitude."

"When I see Charles putting his arm around Matt, I'm so proud," says John Chaney from his office at Temple University. Chaney's eyes still well up at the mention of Jim Maloney, his best friend. A proud surrogate dad, Chaney tapes Rockets games off his satellite dish and shows them to his players. "Charles knows Matt doesn't play flashy like so many kids today, pulling shots out their asses and talking junk out their mouths. He's like the pound cake I eat: plain.

That's what happens when a youngster follows his father's lead."

It's as if his success is a surprise to everybody but Matt Maloney. And that serene confidence is the main difference between him and the countless other gym rats still languishing in obscurity: He possesses not a scintilla of self-doubt, despite consistent critics and dissenters through the years.

"I'm not sure I wasn't one of those skeptics," recalls Coach Fran Dunphy of Penn, for whom Maloney played from 1993 to 1995, leading the Quakers in scoring at 14.6 points per game his senior year, when he was the Ivy League Player of the Year. "I tried to introduce some caution to his dream. I loved how hard he worked, but I didn't want to see him end up crushed. So I'd say, 'You know, Matt, it's not going to be easy.' It turns out it didn't matter what my opinion was, anyway. In his mind, he was going to play in the NBA." When he transferred to Penn from Vanderbilt, Coach Eddie Fogler (now coaching at South Carolina University) told him in no uncertain terms: "You're not going to the NBA."

Maloney heard the doubts, but never listened. In college, the backcourt tandem of Maloney and Jerome Allen (who plays in France) was much lauded, yet it was Allen who pundits claimed had the quickness for the NBA. Maloney and Allen both saw such analysis as typical racial stereotyping; Maloney was labeled the slow, heady (white) point guard and Allen the natural playground (black) athlete. But Matt was used to hearing from nonbelievers.

"Now here I am, starting for the Rockets," Maloney says today without the rancor that informs most I-told-you-so's. That he is where he is can be traced to the senior Maloney. By all accounts, they were close, with Jim filling multiple roles: father, coach, friend, disciplinarian. In tenth grade, Matt gave up soccer and baseball to focus on basketball—a commitment to the sport none of his older siblings (brothers

Pete, Paul, and Chris and sister Sarah) had made. Soon Matt
was rising at five o'clock every morning to attend John Chaney's legendary 6 A.M. Temple practices, and not just to
watch; he'd suit up, often guarding All-American guard
Mark Macon for a couple of grueling hours before Jim
would get him back in time for homeroom at Haddonfield
High. At night, there'd be ferocious two-on-twos: Matt and
Chris or Paul versus Jim and Coach Chaney. "We'd cheat
'em and beat 'em," Chaney recalls.

During Matt's games, Jim could be seen frantically scrib-
bling notes—scraps of paper he and Matt would huddle
over for hours. When Matt was starring at Penn, Jim would
rush over for his practices and work with his son at one
end of the floor after Dunphy had dismissed the rest of the
team. In the basement of the Haddonfield home, there was
a never-ending series of videotapes to watch and dissect.

"I'm sure that sometimes Matt resented Jim," Barbara
recalls. "It was like, 'Oh no, I've got to look at tape again.'
And I'd say, 'Jim, why don't you let him be?' He'd just tell
me to stay out of it. They were relentless, but they were
relentless together. Really, it was like in any family: Jim was
telling Matt to do his homework."

Maloney says, "It wasn't like my dad would say, 'You
missed two shots, so now you've got to run ten laps.' The
physical part was up to me. He and I would work on the
mental part. And he was such a great teacher, I was always
soaking up his knowledge. Now I feel like I know everything he knew about the game. On the court, I can actually
hear him correcting little things I do wrong, like if I allow
my man to get into the passing lane and intercept a pass.
Little things like that—but there are a million of them during
each game."

There are these moments when you're with Matt Maloney when he's not there. And you notice his lips moving
ever so slightly or the barely perceptible motion of his up-

turned wrist: He is repeating old mantras of his father's and correcting the subtlest of hitches in his shot. It happens tonight, at the Green Room, amid all the frivolity. He's bemoaning two of the threes that swirled around the rim and bounced out, trying to analyze what went wrong.

He is only in his second year, but has had a lifetime of experience in shaking off the doubts that others have raised. Despite tonight's performance, he is in store for more, especially if the Rockets' big three—Olajuwon, Clyde Drexler, and Barkley—continue to show their age. When all three are healthy and on their game, Maloney flourishes: They draw the double team, he hits the three-pointer. But when opposing defenses can afford not to forget about him, his game suffers and the critics will come out again.

I ask how he's going to handle the naysaying. Maloney smiles. "By listening to my dad," he says, shrugging. "People speak from places of ignorance all the time. I mean, I knew what I did against Mark Macon in high school and what I did against guys from the 76ers in the summers. I was taking guys, breaking their ankles. Some of the stuff I did would have made people's jaws drop. But no one noticed. I'd complain to my dad and he'd point out that I have no control over how others see me. All I can do is focus on what I have to do. He always told me, 'You can never replay the last play.' "

4

one last chance?

midway through the third quarter, Vernon Maxwell's cell phone rings. It is late November 1997, the NBA season is close to a month old, and here he is, on the sidelines of a junior high school football game in Alpharetta, a suburb of Atlanta, holding the down marker.

On the field, Little V—Maxwell's twelve-year-old son, Vernon Jr.—is evading tacklers left and right, while his dad, so preoccupied with barking out encouragement, time and again forgets to flip the down marker.

"It's *third* down!" the ref yells over as Maxwell fishes his cell phone from his pocket.

Maybe this is Dwight, Maxwell thinks, frantically juggling the marker—which still reads 2—with the cell phone. Dwight Manley is his new agent, the man who, Maxwell hopes, can resurrect his once-promising NBA career. He came recommended by Maxwell's bud Dennis Rodman, whose image the thirty-one-year-old Manley, a coin collector by trade who met Rodman at a Vegas craps table, transformed into a stardom that transcended basketball. Over the summer, the three shared a beach house in Orange County, California, where Maxwell worked out with a personal trainer for the first time in his life, arguing constantly with Rodman about the music played on the house's state-of-the-art sound system: Max wanted Tupac, while Rodman wanted Pearl Jam.

Instead of Dwight, though, it's an old friend, wondering whassup: How come Maxwell's name is nowhere to be found in the box scores?

"I retired, man," he says, keeping his eyes on Little V, who appears winded.

"Suck it up, V!" Maxwell yells. "Suck it up, man!" He puts the phone back to his mouth. "Sorry. Yeah, man, that's it. I'm out. Sick of this bullshit. This muthafuckin' league. Wes Unseld talking 'bout signing me to the minimum. Fuck that."

The call over, he checks the phone, making sure it's on. Despite the hard-bitten posturing, Vernon Maxwell wants desperately to hear from Dwight. At thirty-two, he's got a lot of ball left. He knows it and he knows general managers throughout the league know it. He proved that last season in San Antonio, where he averaged 14 points a game but still had to split time at shooting guard with popular Vinny Del Negro, despite Del Negro's inability to even get his shot off against him in practice. When a teammate told him that Coach Greg Popovich, an Air Force veteran, referred to him as a "rebellious nigger"—shortly after Maxwell gave the finger to a heckling fan in Indiana and was perplexed by his subsequent suspension: "It ain't like I flipped off one of *our* fans," he said—he knew he was history there.

But the phone didn't ring all summer as Maxwell watched lesser players sign for big bucks elsewhere. In fact, the phone has been deafeningly silent ever since that horri-

ble night last May, a night of off-the-court troubles unprecedented even for Mad Max, a night that, ironically, has
helped calm him down.

Long before Allen Iverson broke a single NBA ankle,
before Chris Webber trash-talked his way into America's
homes, and before a corn-rowed Latrell Sprewell became a
household name, Vernon Maxwell was the NBA's original
gangsta hoopster. Throughout the early '90s, he was the
walking embodiment of Ice Cube's lyric: "Niggaz always
gotta show they teeth . . . Be true to the game." Throughout
his erratic career, one thing has been constant: Vernon Maxwell has always "kept it real," has always embodied the
type of street authenticity Ice Cube rapped about. In the
Maxwell ethic, the worst thing you can do in the NBA is
kiss ass or play by the Man's rules.

And as the starting shooting guard for a Houston Rockets team that won back-to-back titles in '94 and '95, Maxwell
offered plenty of evidence that his ethic took precedent over
mainstream mores. There was the time, for instance, he
climbed seven rows into the stands to go after a wise-ass
fan and as a result received an eleven-game suspension. Few
reported what the fan had done, however: taunted Maxwell
about his recently stillborn daughter, Amber, whose loss he
had literally burned into his skin. His left bicep bears a
young angel and the words: IN LOVING MEMORY OF AMBER.
REST IN PEACE. No way was he going to stand for such a dis.

Then there was the traffic stop in Houston in 1995, for
which he still faces jail time as his appeal winds through
the courts. The crime? Possession of less than a gram of
marijuana. Few reported the ostensible reason for the stop:
a black man driving a Mercedes. Fewer still defined in lay-
man's terms what a gram is: a half a joint.

In fact, Maxwell has been tried and convicted in the
court of public opinion for conduct unbecoming a role
model ever since, shortly after graduating from his home-

town school, the University of Florida, as the SEC's second all-time leading scorer (behind Pistol Pete Maravich), he admitted having accepted cash and gifts from a sports agent while in college and testified about his own dalliances with pot and cocaine during the trial of a Gainesville, Florida, drug dealer. What bothered the press was not so much what Maxwell did, but his lack of remorse; in other words, his 'tude, which resonated as "real" in hip-hop culture. As Larry Guest, the *Orlando Sentinel* sports editor who broke the news of Maxwell's failure to pass a drug test during the 1988 NCAA Tournament, said, "We attempted to give him a chance to show some signs of contrition. . . . Frankly, he didn't show as much contrition as we portrayed."

Throughout his time on the public stage, he's been Mad Max, a player so passionate, so peripatetic, he was often in danger of spinning out of control. But it is that passion—whether for shots of Rémy Martin, V.S.O.P., the cognac that is the NBA drink of choice, or ham hock and pea soup, which recalls his Gainesville youth—that explains his personal charisma. And it is that passion that fueled his game. Even now, now that the phone has stopped ringing after that night last May, there are no doubts about the kind of player he is.

"He's a poor man's Michael Jordan," says John Lucas, his coach in Philadelphia during the 1995–96 season, when Maxwell averaged over 16 points per game while playing a new position—point guard—and refused to sit out with sprains to both ankles that were so severe one doctor referred to them as "twin fractures." Indeed, Jordan himself has long volunteered that Maxwell plays him as tough as any opposing shooting guard in the league.

"Vernon was never a choirboy, but he was a warrior," says Houston's Tomjanovich, who points out that, bad press notwithstanding, Maxwell has always been popular with his teammates—thanks to his reputation as a money player, forged on Houston's championship teams. When a big shot needed to be made—like the three-pointer that buried the Knicks in game seven of the 1994 finals—Mad Max wanted the ball.

But in the media, his off-court controversies—rather than the heart he fiercely displayed on court—defined him. "They [the media] put us up here and then when we do something everymuthafuckin'body else do, they say now we just bad people," he says. "The people who know me know I'm a good person. They also know I've made some mistakes."

In part, Maxwell's inability to recognize himself in media portrayals—something Manley has been hired to turn around, as he did for Rodman—relates to a racial and generational divide between him and his interlocutors. This became apparent during the recent Rockets–76ers game, where, in the press room, a beat writer from Philadelphia and one from Houston joked about rumors that Vernon might be signed by the Bulls.

"God, I would have thought Vernon would be dead by now," said Michael Murphy of the *Houston Chronicle.*

"Hey, I covered Vernon for a year and he never said my name," said Phil Jasner of the *Philadelphia Daily News.* "He always called me 'baby.' "

"That's better than what he called me: 'muthafucka,' " laughed Murphy.

When I relay the story to Maxwell, he's troubled. Didn't these guys know that he meant no disrespect? "That's just the way I am. It's how I came up," he says. "Like, 'Yo, muthafucka, whassup?' You know? But you know what? Other black people can say shit like that and it's cool. Like if Grant Hill talked like that to them, it'd be cool. See, I can only be who I am. I ain't come up all phony. I ain't no phony muthafucka. What you see is what you get."

It's an attitude straight from the 'hood, which is where the shit that might have ended his career went down last May.

*   *   *

Maxwell noticed the sport utility vehicle with tinted windows following them around 3 A.M. after a stop at Whataburger, the usual destination once the clubs closed. They were in Houston's tough Fourth Ward and he was in the rear passenger seat during a night out with his boys, guys he hung with during his days as a Rocket.

They were in Peanut's Expedition, with Moses in the passenger seat and Li'l Gangsta next to Maxwell in back, on their way into the heart of the 'hood to visit one of Peanut's friends, who Peanut had just called on the cell phone. "I'm coming by with Vernon Maxwell," he said.

Meantime, Maxwell kept looking behind them. "Some muthafucka be following us," he said.

"Aw, nigga, you just drunk," replied Peanut.

When they got to the house, Maxwell was still aware of the tail. He told Peanut to pull over, let them pass. The rest is all in slow motion, and it visits him every day—how the car slowly glided by, windows lowering, and how it dawned on him and Moses at the same time: *Drive-by.* They both bolted from the passenger side, amid a cacophony of screeching tires, slamming doors, and the rubber-peeling sound of Peanut and Li'l Gangsta, still in the Expedition, taking off. "Where's that nigga Vernon! Where's that nigga Vernon!" someone screamed. And then a pistol was in Maxwell's face while Moses was thrown to the ground, gun to his head, and then Maxwell was being screamed at, told to "Get on the ground!"

There was a momentary pause. "Nigga, I ain't getting on the ground," he said slowly, peering at the barrel. "Kill me right here."

That's when the beating started, a pistol-whipping that sent Maxwell down to the fetal position, blood cascading into his eyes. "Stop fucking around and kill the muthafucka!" the one who held Moses yelled as sirens rang out.

Their attackers fired a shot in the air and fled. Maxwell started crawling, wanting to get away, obsessed by one thought: I don't have a contract. I can't get in no trouble. Moses tried to get him to his feet and a stranger offered a lift to the hospital, where, despite their best intentions— Maxwell registered as "Craig Jones"—the media was alerted. The next night news of Vernon Maxwell's pistol-whipping made it onto ESPN's "SportsCenter."

But the effects of last May run much deeper. As Maxwell suspected in those groggy post-beating moments, for general managers in the NBA, it was the last straw: Vernon Maxwell was not a good risk. Moreover, as he puts it, it fucked with him mentally. He's replayed the night again and again in his head, trying to figure out who might have had it in for him. His initial reaction was to stay in the Fourth Ward, to ask around, to find out who did him like that, and then to pay them a visit, 9-millimeter in tow.

But he left Houston instead, returning to the Atlanta burbs, to his wife, Shel, his sweetheart since the fourth grade, and their three kids. Since that night in May—his last foray to an inner-city club—this is where he's been, rediscovering family life. He hasn't spoken to Peanut since that night, convinced his former friend set him up.

But there's one thing he can't shake. Ball. It haunts him. He stays up all night, watching NBA games on DirecTV, mumbling to himself, "I can take this muthafucka," shaking his head. It gets so bad that Shel catches him watching the Spanish station when it broadcasts an international game. She teases him—"You don't even know that language"—and he laughs, but it's a worried laugh, because the NBA season has begun and for the first time in nearly a decade he isn't a part of it and it's all he knows in this world and he never thought he'd be retired at thirty-two. He keeps telling himself, Dwight'll come up with one more chance for me.

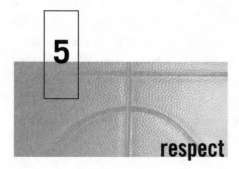

5

respect

this is the part they don't see, Chris Webber keeps telling himself, the part away from the cameras. All the doubters, the talking heads, the know-it-alls who hold forth about your character. This is the part where you take what they say, all those asinine lines about how you lack heart and maturity and the "right attitude," you take them and replay them, you repeat them to yourself, over and over, and it keeps you out here, an hour after practice, in the silence of this empty old gym, where the only sound bouncing off the rafters is the squeak of your Filas on the hardwood, the pounding of your dribble, and finally that sweet swish, the sound of your youth.

Yes, this is the part they don't *want* to see, Webber keeps telling himself, his rebounder rifling the ball back to him for more midrange jump shots. This is my answer. With each swish, a feeling washes over him, a half-formed thought: *Take that.*

His teammates are long gone on this early December day
at Bowie State University in suburban Maryland, where his
Wizards are practicing until the practice gym at their brand-
new state-of the-art arena, the MCI Center in Washington,
D.C., is open. Webber's lone presence is not an aberration.
Throughout the league, the best players, those with seemingly the least room for improvement, are the last to leave;
Jordan's work ethic, of course, is legendary. But there are
others, too. In Detroit, it's Grant Hill, struggling from the
floor this season, working on his form. In Los Angeles,
there's Kobe Bryant, who launched a succession of air balls
in last year's playoff loss to Utah, then spent the next morning in a high school gym, shooting the exact same shots,
again and again.

And here it's Webber, twenty-four-year-old reluctant
leader of the Washington Wizards, a team that once again
is hearing it from the fans and media. This was to be the
Wizards'—and Webber's—year after all. Last season, though,
swept by the Bulls in the first round of the playoffs, the
then-Bullets* performed well enough to prompt Jordan's as-
sessment that this young team with the league's sixth-highest payroll was one to watch. He was particularly impressed
by Webber: "He's got the look," Jordan said once the series
was over. "He's hungry."

Finally it seemed Webber had buried the reputation that
has haunted him since his days as the most talented member
of Michigan's famed Fab Five—that he's the poster boy for
today's Generation X hoopster, a breed long on ability but
also greed and short on time-honored attributes like teamwork and hard work. Finally, by making the playoffs and
impressing Jordan, he had put his laundry list of Gen X
transgressions behind him: the infamous last-second timeout, which cost Michigan an NCAA title; the showdown

*Owner Abe Pollin, disturbed that the team from the murder capital of
the country would have a lethal nickname, changed it.

with Coach Don Nelson of the Golden State Warriors his rookie year, which saw Webber labeled as petulant and hard to coach; and the on-court showboating, a series of histrionics that offended the NBA's old guard because he hadn't won anything yet. Finally there was optimism. For he had responded to the challenge laid down by Bullet General Manager John Nash, now with the New Jersey Nets, who, after acquiring Webber in a trade, told him: "You can be the next Charles Barkley or you can be the next Derrick Coleman. It's up to you."

The implication was clear: You can be a winner—a guy who makes teammates better, like Barkley—or you can be an immensely talented player like Coleman, who has never played for a winner and whose work ethic has been questioned around the league (by Barkley, among others). Webber nodded then, but filed the challenge away.

However, the challenge is still in his thoughts as the start of the 1997–98 season sees the Wizards once again languishing in fourth place in the NBA's Atlantic Division with a 7–11 record. Like their star, these Wizards are strangely mercurial: They've already beaten the Bulls and Utah Jazz (Webber went for 26 points and 13 rebounds while shutting down reigning MVP Karl Malone) and lost to the woeful 76ers and Orlando Magic. Last night, in the team's second game at the MCI Center, the Wizards did what they were expected to do, dispatching the Sacramento Kings, 118–96, behind Webber's 26 points and 14 rebounds. Tomorrow night they will host the Minnesota Timberwolves and young phenom Kevin Garnett, otherwise known by the price tag of his new contract as the $126 Million Man.

With Webber's post-practice practicing completed, he ambles out of the gym and into a phalanx of reporters. One, Ric Bucher of *The Washington Post*, asks, "Do you think Rod [point guard Strickland] saying he wants to lead the league in assists is a selfish goal?" Webber looks up and holds back a crooked half-smile.

"I'd love for Rod to lead the league in assists," he says. "Just like I want to lead it in rebounding. That's good for the team."

Most of the other questions aren't about the game or his team's record or even the new arena. No, they are about the heretofore obscure hoopster who has the whole country talking: Webber's best friend, Latrell Sprewell, also known as Spree, who, six days ago, went from being a great player nobody had ever heard of to Public Enemy No. 1. Sprewell's premeditated attack on his coach, P. J. Carlesimo, instantly transcended the insular world of sports. Suddenly talk show hosts who couldn't identify a zone defense had Exhibit A in the case against professional athletes: too much money, too little respect for authority.

Unlike the rest of America, Chris Webber knows Latrell Sprewell. He knows, too, that Spree's attack on his coach had its genesis in Webber's own troubles with Coach Nelson, back when he and Sprewell were Golden State teammates and inseparable. So now he has no choice: He'll support Spree, as he did last night on the phone, but he'll be diplomatic with the press.

"You know, I'm no authority when it comes to player-coach relations," he says into the camera, smiling and moving for the door to the parking lot. "But Spree is my friend and I'm there for him."

Once away from the pack, he throws his stuff inside his Mercedes 600 sedan and settles behind the wheel. Old Al Green classics blare out of his six speakers as he slowly shakes his head, pulling out of Bowie on the way to chill at his Mitchellville, Maryland, home. He's still thinking of his friend on the other coast. "Man, how can I not stand up for Spree, when he's the only one who stood up for me back in Golden State?" he says. "I'm not saying he wasn't wrong, but it's like nobody wants to be the defense attorney anymore. It's easy to see a situation and then jump on one side. I see it in the name 'Generation X.' Being one of the so-called poster boys of Generation X, I want to say, 'Hey, X means no identity.' So when you don't give a generation an identity, you basically look at people my age, twenty-seven on down, and demean us by saying, 'We don't know what's coming out of that.' Instead of trying to understand."

He pauses as the opening guitar riff of Green's "Love and Happiness" fills the air. "One thing I know to be true now," Chris Webber says, "is that, a lot of times, you're guilty until proven innocent."

He may be on the verge of entering the elite pantheon of NBA superstars, but when he was twenty years old, Chris Webber learned firsthand how your public image can get away from you and take on a life of its own, something his friend in the Bay Area is learning now.

Webber had just showboated his way through two controversial seasons at Michigan, where, with Jalen Rose, Ray Jackson, Jimmy King, and current Wizards teammate Juwan Howard, he had a greater impact on the culture at large than any collegiate hoopster in recent memory. The Fab Five, with their shaved heads, droopy shorts, black socks, and black sneakers, not to mention their high-fiving, chest-thumping, trash-talking ways, were the hardwood embodiment of rap music. Their theme song was Public Enemy's "Shut Em Down" and they even had an immediate foil: Duke University. The instant rivalry with Duke—led by white stars such as Christian Laettner and Bobby Hurley and crossover icon-in-training Grant Hill—provided the perfect, if simplistic, narrative backdrop: It was playground versus the old school.

The old school won. Webber led the Wolverines to the NCAA championship game both seasons, losing to Duke and then North Carolina in the infamous timeout game (when Webber called a timeout his team didn't have and was assessed a technical foul in the game's closing seconds), yet he heard the catcalls: The Fab Five were underachievers.

There hadn't been such a widely disliked team in recent memory; to Webber's mind, it grew out of a hostility to mainstream expressions of black culture.

But few looked past the street histrionics on the court, the finger-pointing, the trash-talking, to see what was really there. When he thinks back on those days now, after all he's been through since, Webber smiles. "Man, we were so naive, we were just so pure, as far as just having our eyes open real wide," he recalls. "As kids, I thought we were supposed to have fun. We played like we did out of pure love, love for the game and for each other. We would cry after we lost regular season games—that's love for the game. We were playing for our mothers to see us on TV. And then we had to listen to how bad that was, how bad our expressiveness was."

Webber and his teammates may have thought they were just kids having fun, like on the playground, but to viewers and the media, they represented something more sinister: a threat. It has always been such; throughout the recent history of sports, black athletes have been at the forefront of an aesthetic of celebration that stands in stark contrast to the repressed model of sportsmanship taught in the suburbs, where Matt Maloney honed his game. Think of it: In football, it was Billy "White Shoes" Johnson who invented the end zone spike and a host of other black stars who refined the act before the NFL outlawed such displays of emotion. In college basketball, it was reportedly the all-black Louisville team of 1980 that founded the high-five, now a staple of expressiveness in all sports. So the Fab Five were not prepared for the backlash against them, as when, of all people, Dick Vitale lambasted them on national TV for their "histrionics and carrying-on."

Nor was Webber prepared for the old school, drill sergeant-type coaching of Don Nelson. The Warriors signed Webber to a fifteen-year, $76 million contract, but the deal had an out clause after one year, which Webber, fed up with his coach's tongue-lashings, sought to exercise.

"I never heard anybody talk to people the way he talked to some of our players," Webber says today. At the time, Webber and his teammates said Nelson would use Webber's salary—"You know what we call that? A seventy-six-million-dollar turnover!"—and an in-his-face aggression (which, in other circumstances, would no doubt lead to a fistfight) to try and motivate his star. Webber attempted to smooth things over. "I said, 'Coach, I know you're trying to push my buttons,' " Webber says. " 'But it doesn't work on me. Here are some things I think will work.' " And he proceeded to tell Nelson, who had coached his way to over eight hundred NBA victories without Webber's advice, how Steve Fisher, his easygoing college coach, had worked with him.

Webber's stand earned him no points in the media. Nelson—who would later be run out of New York by older star players for many of the same reasons—was portrayed sympathetically. Calling Nelson "a symbol of resistance in the fight to retain discipline in the NBA," Sam Smith of the *Chicago Tribune* urged fans to root for Nelson, "not to fall to the monsters of greed, immaturity, and selfishness." When the confrontation ended with Webber's trade to Washington and Nelson's resignation, *The New York Times* opined: "Nelson is the latest coach unable to master Generation X."

All the hand-wringing, though, confused discipline with control. The battle between Webber and Nelson was actually symbolic of the passing of an outdated management style. Nelson is a throwback to a time when teamwork was thought of in terms of the military style—a place where everyone has a defined position, wears an identical uniform, where the self is suppressed. Webber—like so many new players in the league, including Sprewell—saw Nelson's tirades as an effort to control his creativity and assault his manhood. His seeming insubordination sent shock waves through the sport, despite the widespread evidence that the old school methods don't work anymore.

In Miami, rumor has it that Pat Riley's players have grown tired of his nonstop in-your-face intensity, as they did in New York and Los Angeles. Even at the collegiate level, the style is becoming antiquated. Indiana University's Bobby Knight, who brandished a whip over a black player in 1992, has seen his recruiting suffer and has made four successive early exits from the NCAA Tournament. (When asked for the main difference between playing for Bird and Larry Brown, his former coach, Indiana star Reggie Miller recently replied, "Bird isn't always screaming at me.")

Meanwhile, the most successful coaches in the new NBA, guys like Phil Jackson, Rudy Tomjanovich, Danny Ainge, and rookie Larry Bird, are those who eschew their own ego, who purposefully treat their charges like professionals, who talk about "empowering" their players, and who have borrowed progressive management techniques from examples that range from Zen philosophy to Microsoft.

Despite this trend, the fallout from the Nelson imbroglio turned Webber into nothing more than a caricature to those who knew him. The real Webber had gone to Detroit Country Day, a predominantly white upper-middle-class prep school, and had long been a student of history. Since college, he has collected signed historical documents of prominent African Americans, including items from Martin Luther King, Jr., and Frederick Douglass; the collection is currently housed at Wayne State University.

Yet, like hard rappers who hail from the middle class and adopt a street 'tude, Webber's image was all hip-hop. And gangsta at that. Those who knew him—like Grant Hill, at whose home Webber stayed when the two were thirteen and playing AAU tournaments together—saw the dichotomy. "Grant is always pointing out I'm not a hard guy, and I like that comment," Webber says. "I'm a tough athlete, not a tough guy."

But the distinction was lost on most people. Now Webber fears the same thing will happen to Spree; after all, every time he picks up the paper, he reads about a Latrell Sprewell that he doesn't recognize. "When I went through my stuff with Nelson, Spree was there for me, man," Webber recalls. "It took Spree to write my number on his shoes. The first time I went back there I hugged him at halfcourt for so long they started booing him. Spree didn't like getting booed by his fans. But when he was hugging me, he was taking all that weight off of me. People will never understand how comfortable that makes you feel, to go into an arena where you're not liked and have that former teammate, who loved you, who was your friend when other guys on the team were scared to talk because of their contracts or scared of being blackballed by the league, and have him hug you."

Now it's Sprewell needing the hugs. Webber's been speaking to him regularly since the incident, consoling him. "He regrets doing it, but only because of the judgment that was put onto him," he reports. "It was two men, and he feels like nobody can tell what two men go through. Just like nobody can tell you and your wife not to get a divorce, that you should stick together, when they don't know the situation."

When Webber had his confrontation with Nelson, it did not start a dialogue about the tactics of old school coaches. Similarly, Sprewell's attack of Carlesimo—who comes from the same in-your-face breed as Nelson—hasn't prompted any reconsideration of how coaches treat players. In fact, when Sprewell said the attack followed two months of verbal abuse by Carlesimo, no one followed by reporting precisely what Carlesimo had been saying to Sprewell over that period or how he was saying it.

Instead, the pundits got self-righteous. Vitale posited that Sprewell should be banned for life. Tim Keown, *San Francisco Chronicle* columnist, wrote "[Sprewell's] appearance has gone full gangster this year, with his braids and wispy sideburns. He's a hard shadowy figure." "If this were the real world, Latrell Sprewell would be in jail or awaiting trial," piped in Mike Lupica.

Commissioner Stern adopted Lupica's rationale in announcing Sprewell's suspension for one calendar year without pay the day after the Warriors terminated his four-year, $32 million contract for violation of a standard morals clause. "A sports league does not have to accept or condone behavior that would not be tolerated in any other segment of society," Stern said.

On talk shows throughout the country, irate callers agreed, arguing that if they strangled their bosses, they'd be tossed, too. (Of course, this view ignores the economic reality in the NBA, an industry where the boss is regularly paid considerably less than his employees.) To players like Webber and Sprewell, Stern's dictum was hypocritical. The type of abuse practiced by coaches like Carlesimo—in-your-face snarls, laced with emasculating epithets like "pussy"— would likewise not be tolerated in the private sector. Why the silence on *that* conduct?

In fact, Carlesimo's coaching methods should have been taken into account when trying to gauge the severity of Sprewell's punishment; none other than the Supreme Court has found that there is something called "fighting words"— epithets so aggressive and offensive that their use could incite a reasonable person to violence. Could that be the case here? No one has even asked the question.

Moreover, there's selective prosecution. It was no big deal when Detroit Piston Alvin Robertson attacked General Manager Billy McKinney four years ago or when Tom Chambers punched out the Suns' strength and conditioning coach earlier this season. Why the uproar over Sprewell, with its way-too-literal reading of events? Much has been made of Sprewell's "threat" to "kill" Carlesimo; on urban playgrounds and street corners, that's no threat—it's lan-

guage you hear on the court, in pool halls, and when throwing down. It means: "I'mo kick yo ass."

Without excusing his behavior, many players see this
sudden fixation on the Sprewell incident as inextricably
linked with the upcoming labor strife. Barkley, a close friend
of Carlesimo's, said as much during the past week, pledging
that "We [the NBA Players' Association] ain't gonna let
them take his money" and raising the specter of an All-
Star Game boycott if the league pursued such a hard-line
punishment. (Within days, Barkley will back off the boycott
call, but he will reiterate his concern that allowing a team
to cancel a contract for violation of a vague "morals clause"
sets a dangerous precedent.)

Barkley understands that in the short run, it is to management's advantage to turn public opinion against the players at a time when an ugly argument looms this off-season
between the two sides over just how to split the $2.64 billion
windfall recently collected from the networks. But it's a risky
long-term strategy: By degrading their asset—the players—
the NBA's powers-that-be might be borrowing a page from
the baseball owners script circa 1994 and devaluing their
own product.

So management and veteran players like Barkley approach the Sprewell case with a host of strategic concerns
while younger players like Webber see it essentially in moral
terms. To them, there's a principle at stake: respect.

In urban street culture, respect—demanding it and will-
ingly bearing severe consequences in order to get it—has
become the dominating ethic, a sentiment forged in gang
life and reflected in rap music as well as basketball. "Where
I lived, stepping on someone's shoe was a capital offense
punishable by death . . . a recognized given for the crime
of disrespect," writes Sanyika Shakur, a.k.a. Monster Kody
Scott, in his compelling *Monster: The Autobiography of an L.A.
Gang Member.* "Regardless of the condition of the shoes, the
underlying factor that usually got you killed was the princi-

ple. The principle is respect, a linchpin critical to relations between all people, but magnified by thirty in the ghettos and slums across America."

Like other style crazes that have come to define American youth—the $150 sneakers, the baggy jeans—the premium placed on respect has gangland roots. It is an ethic, thanks in large part to the widespread appeal of rap, that has spread throughout youth culture—which helps explain Webber, who didn't come up as a gangsta, or Sprewell, who is a multimillionaire, reacting as they did to being dissed.

"I've thought about this a lot, about the respect factor, about how you treat people," Webber says. "It all starts with not being a coach, a player, a lawyer, or a teacher. It starts with being a person. If you're a person who respects others, who encourages people before criticizing, that habit transcends into your job. I was brought up to believe you shouldn't degrade people."

Chris was the firstborn child of Doris and Mayce Webber in a lower-middle-class Detroit neighborhood. Doris was a special education teacher who, early in Chris's formative years, began running a daycare center out of the house. Mayce was a blue-collar guy through and through who worked at the local GM plant. Soon there would be three more sons and a daughter; at a time when the intact nuclear family was becoming an inner-city anomaly, the tight-knit Webbers stood out. Chris's friends teased him, calling his family "the Waltons" or "the Brady Bunch," getting on him about the family's weekly church sojourns and their daily "quiet time" sessions—an hour a day set aside for everyone to sit and either read or think.

When Webber stood up to the taunts of Nelson, he found himself thinking of his father. "He never made more than twenty thousand dollars a year, with five kids," he recalls. "He wasn't going to beg anybody to help him care for his family—he made five kids and that was his responsibility. But he also demanded you treat him like a man who has five kids. It would have been funny to see somebody disrespect my father like Coach Nelson did to me."

Webber smiles. "I can tell you this," he says, "the dissing would be short-lived."

It's two hours to game time and Webber is in the trainer's room, hiding from the media horde. They want to talk more Spree. This morning's *Washington Post* contains a story quoting Pollin as the first NBA owner to say he would consider signing Sprewell: "I would never close the door on someone forever," said the league's senior owner. "If he would open his heart and ask for forgiveness, I would consider it."

The addition of Sprewell would make the Wizards a premier team. So far this season, Strickland has been the best point guard in the league and Webber one of its most dominant power forwards. (Strickland is leading the NBA in assists, at over 11 per game, and Webber is posting his usual 20 points and 10 rebounds.) Howard has been solid, if unspectacular; the center position has been a bust, due largely to the absence of seven-foot-four Gheorghe Muresan, who injured himself in the off-season filming of *My Giant* with Billy Crystal. There is no date set for his return, and his shot-blocking is key to the team's fortunes.

The other hole appears to be at shooting guard, where Calbert Cheaney starts. Tonight, against Minnesota, the crowd—perhaps fantasizing about Sprewell in his place—boos him and Cheaney, a sensitive kid, struggles, hitting only four of thirteen shots. But Webber is huge; he scores 33 points, grabs 12 boards, dishes 4 assists, and, as is his style, wears his emotions all over his uniform. He talks, he smiles, he high-fives, he dunks, and he glares at the courtside cameras. He outplays Garnett and the Wizards win their third straight out of three in their new downtown home, which has a giant mural of Webber facing it on the side of a building across the street.

After the game, however, there is a sign of trouble on the horizon. Webber sits at his locker, clad only in a towel around his waist, huddled next to Cheaney, who sits slumped over, looking down, despondent. It was a tough day for Cheaney, beginning with the newspaper account detailing how much better his team would be with Sprewell in his position and culminating in a poor shooting game while the fans booed. Webber leans in, lecturing his teammate, who is two years his senior, trying to lift his spirits. The two stay that way for nearly fifteen minutes, with the young superstar reassuring the shooting guard that he's an integral part of the team, that he has confidence in him.

It is the predominant question about this young team: veteran leadership. Ten players on the roster are in their twenties; of those in the regular rotation, only Strickland, who is thirty-one, has vast NBA experience. Consequently, Webber has had to speak up in the locker room more than he's accustomed to. Even at Michigan, where he was the resident superstar, he'd defer to Jalen behind the scenes. Here there is no one to defer to.

When the powwow with Cheaney is over, Webber is frowning. "I definitely don't like being a vocal leader," he says on his way to the showers. "I want to be the quiet guy who shows you by action. Instead of saying, 'Let's go, fellas,' I'd rather be the first guy to sprint, you know?"

It is an issue, this reluctance to lead, this inability to stamp the Wizards as *his* team, that will haunt him throughout this season that began with so much promise.

SECOND QUARTER

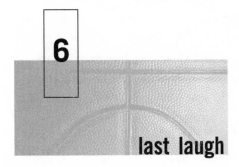

6

last laugh

it's almost nine o'clock on a chilly early winter night and in dorm rooms throughout Philadelphia—at Villanova, Temple, or the nearby University of Pennsylvania—kids in their early twenties sit cross-legged around tables, open bottles of liquor before them, playing cards or quarters or any one of a handful of other drinking games, and, as the night wears on, they giggle and drink and giggle some more. It is a middle-class American rite of passage, these gatherings.

On this night, this group of twentysomethings sits before a half-filled bottle of Rémy Martin, V.S.O.P., the expensive stuff, playing blackjack. The loser of each hand has to down a shot while the others look on, razzing. There is an open bag of sweet-smelling pot on the table and a towel shoved under the door. Just like in the dorms.

Only these kids aren't away at school and one of them is already a professional. A millionaire, in fact. Jerry Stack-

house is, in his words, "just muthafuckin' chillin" at the
two-bedroom penthouse apartment he's renting in the city,
where he stays some off-nights. Tomorrow is a home game,
which requires a 10 A.M. appearance at the arena for the
shootaround and a 6 P.M. return for the game; crashing at
the house all the way out in the burbs is too troublesome,
so here he is, joined by his brother, Tony Dawson, his homey
Allen, and a couple of girls he doesn't seem to know that
well, flicking channels on the big-screen TV, playing blackjack, and drinking.

Stackhouse is sprawled out on the floor, wearing a DKNY
sweatshirt and jeans, looking at his hand, when a thought
occurs to him. "You still freelancing, man?" he asks me as
I wince and down a couple of shots, trying to catch up,
while the others try to hide that they are laughing at me.
"You got to get me in GQ, man. I got more shit going on
than them muthafuckas they got in there."

The room erupts in earnest agreement. In a crowd like
this, Stackhouse often punctuates his speech with more col-
orful language than, say, when he's home baking cookies.
Later, for instance, we leave a message on Maxwell's cell
phone and Stack—usually so careful about his choice of
words, in keeping with the crossover tradition—is all hip-
hop: "Yo, nigga, give a nigga a call and quit acting like a
bitch," he barks into Maxwell's voicemail. (The two became
the best of friends during Stackhouse's rookie year, Maxwell's one season in Philly, a relationship that Coach John
Lucas was particularly proud of. "Vernon's like Jerry's big
brother and Jerry looks up to him so much, Vernon's self-
esteem has skyrocketed," Lucas explained at the time.)

As the night wears on, Allen and the girls continue to
play cards and laugh and drink. But the remote control has
found a college basketball game featuring the University of
Arizona, the reigning NCAA champion. Stackhouse—who
moments ago was indistinguishable from the other kids in
the room—zones in on the game, to the exclusion of all

around him. He is now on the sofa next to Tony, who, at thirty, is visiting for a couple of weeks before returning to Greece, where he plays ball professionally and averages over 28 points per game. A six-foot-seven shooter, Tony has had a couple of ten-day contracts with the Celtics.

The two fixate on the game. When Arizona's shooting guard Miles Simon, who has been held scoreless, finally hits a shot, announcer Bill Raftery exclaims: "Now he's getting untracked!" Tony smiles knowingly.

" 'Untracked?' Muthafucka hit one shot, talking 'bout him getting untracked," he grumbles. "Man, basketball is the weirdest fucking game. You ain't never thought you'd be dealing with these muthafuckas talking this shit about you, you know what I'm saying? All your life, you never thought you'd have anything to do with this muthafucka talking 'bout you, talking 'bout your game."

Stack keeps his eyes on the screen, but smiles slightly and drapes an arm around his brother's shoulder. Lately, every muthafucka in Philly has been talking about Tony's sibling. The trade rumors are reaching a crescendo and many are being reported as fact. One has him going to the Lakers along with teammate Derrick Coleman for Eddie Jones and Elden Campbell, a deal the Sixers would make in a heartbeat. Another has him Toronto-bound, where no one wants to go: Not only is it too far away, the tax rates are too high. Still another would take him to tomorrow's opponent, Denver, for LaPhonso Ellis.

The Sixers are desperate to get something for him, because they know they'll lose him once the season—and his contract—ends. Stackhouse's agent, Lee Fentress, has made it clear: Given Garnett's six-year, $126 million deal and Rasheed Wallace's six-year, $80 million contract in Portland, Stackhouse, also of the 1995 rookie class, will be looking for something along the lines of seven years and $70 million. The team and the player simply disagree as to his worth.

To Stackhouse's dismay, the improvements he's made

this season have been overshadowed by the money talk and trade speculation. His points per game are down to 15.5, but he's shooting 46.4 percent from the floor, up from last season's 40.4, and his turnovers have dropped. None other than his hard-to-please coach, Larry Brown, has praised him: "Stackhouse has really worked on his medium-range jumper. . . . Except for Michael Jordan, the midrange game is a lost art. I'm just happy Stack is working on that," he told the *Philadelphia Inquirer* a couple of weeks ago, though many read the comments as an attempt by Brown to raise Stackhouse's trade value.

But numbers aside, Stackhouse has once again been a model of inconsistency. A week ago, he played an animated, high-flying game against the Knicks, scoring 20 points on seven of fifteen shooting and dishing out 6 assists; but he followed that with a one for eight shooting performance against Orlando, scoring just 8 points while seeming dispirited.

"I wish I could explain it," Stackhouse shrugs when asked about the inconsistency. Of course, it may just be that he is a streak player and his career will forever be dotted with highs that raise fans' hopes followed by lows that crush them. Or it could be that the pressure to be the Man at such a young age has gotten to him, though he is loath to acknowledge it.

In fact, Stackhouse got a lesson in the job insecurity of the NBA even before he played his first game. Just after the Sixers drafted him in 1995, prior to training camp, Coach Lucas invited a lanky sixteen-year-old to the gym where the Sixers were scrimmaging. There the sixteen-year-old and Stackhouse—the College Player of the Year, the third pick of the draft, the savior of the 76ers—played one-on-one. And the sixteen-year-old spanked him. It wasn't even close.

The sixteen-year-old's name was Kobe Bryant, then about to start his junior year at Lower Merion High, a suburban school also attended by Lucas's daughter that was not known for its basketball prowess. Some months later, when I asked him about being whipped by Bryant, Stackhouse reacted defensively: "Is he saying that? You tell Kobe I got a deal for him. We'll play one-on-one, and if he wins, he comes to the pros. If I win, he goes to college. How much you want to bet his ass be in school next year?"

Even now Stackhouse denies he lost to Bryant, who, in his second pro season at the tender age of nineteen, has become the talk of the league and is being hyped as the newest heir to Jordan's throne. But the message of that nearly three-year-old confrontation resonates: You never know where your next challenge is coming from or who your next challenger might be.

So tonight, while the others play cards and drink and giggle, Stack watches Miles Simon intently. He's learned to always be on the lookout for the next phenom, particularly among shooting guards; you want to know, after all, who is after your job. Finally, late in the game, Stackhouse speaks.

"He's a good college player, but he shoots from here," he says, imitating a shooting motion from just beside his ear, rather than the usual straight-armed extension. "That shit'll get blocked up here."

He's scouted the opposition and can now relax. Almost instantly, he falls asleep, his head back, mouth open. It's after eleven o'clock and his guests file out, leaving the NBA player there, zonked on the sofa, big-screen TV still on.

Stack is going off. In the first quarter against Denver, he hits a bundle of midrange jumpers and gets out on the break, where he excels. He scores 17 points in the game's first quarter and finishes with a season-high 32 on twelve of twenty shooting and the Sixers win, 106–91.

Afterward, though, he is conspicuously joyless. The media crowds around his locker, but he responds in a bored monotone. One writer notes the improvement of his shooting and asks what else he'd like to improve on. "My individual defense," he says.

Another scribe asks about the trade rumors. "I just live it day by day," he says.

"Is that a terrible way to live?" someone calls out.

"It's been going on for a year and a half," he says. "All I want is to play ball and make a living for my family."

"That's a mature attitude," Phil Jasner of the *Philadelphia Daily News* observes, confusing Stackhouse's joylessness with maturity. "How do you come by it?"

"I have a good support group," he says to the writers who, at other times, have lambasted him for having a "posse." "As long as I can go home and have this baby to play with and my mom, she's always there. I talk to her every day."

Some twenty-four hours later, Stackhouse appears wise not to have gotten too excited by his offensive outburst versus Denver. At the Garden in New York, he plays thirty-four minutes against the Knicks and hits just one of nine shots and scores all of 5 points.

Less than a week later, it finally happens. The Sixers, now 6–16, lose at home to Minnesota in a revealing show-down of point guards. Minnesota's Stephon Marbury concentrates on distributing the ball to his teammates, accumulating 9 assists before scoring a single point, finishing with 14 points and 14 assists and no turnovers in forty-one minutes. Iverson, despite being the flashier player, once again takes more shots than anyone on his team, including an ill-advised jumper with ten seconds on the shot clock and the game on the line that leaves Brown livid.

But he won't have Stack to kick around anymore. The game ends with Stackhouse launching an air ball from behind the three-point line. It would be his last shot as a 76er.

The next day it's official: Jerry Stackhouse and underachieving center Eric Montross to the Detroit Pistons for

shooting guard Aaron McKie and power forward Theo Ratliff. By the day's end, Stack will be on the Pistons' team
plane, headed for a showdown with Indiana the next night.
He asks for and receives the same uniform number: 42. His
debut is storybook: With no time to learn his new team's
offensive sets, he enters the game near the end of the first
quarter and decides to take the ball to the hole. He ends up
scorching the Pacers' Reggie Miller, going for a team-high
33 points. Back in Detroit, the *Detroit News* publishes an
instant poll: 93 percent of the team's fans like the trade.

But what goes unreported is that one crucial person dis-
approves: Grant Hill. Stackhouse doesn't know it, but the
organizational instability that dominated his tenure in Philly
isn't behind him. The Pistons, after 54 and 46 wins the last
two seasons, are struggling at 11–15 after the Pacers game.
And there is deep discord.

Coach Doug Collins is neither old or new school in terms
of coaching style; he's simply anal. Veterans like Hill and
aging shooting guard Joe Dumars can often be seen rolling
their eyes during timeouts as the ever-intense Collins points
out, for instance, that they need to get the ball over halfcourt
in under ten seconds to avoid a turnover—a rule even rookies don't need to be reminded of.

Collins's overbearing style has driven important players
away, including power forward Otis Thorpe and three-point
threat Terry Mills. Hill has privately grown critical of the
coach and rumors of Collins's impending dismissal are rampant throughout the league. The trade for Stackhouse represents Collins's last-ditch effort to save his job; for his part,
Hill believes that Ratliff, who often found himself in Collins's doghouse, possesses vast untapped potential. And he
doesn't know if the addition of Stackhouse will help. His
game and Stackhouse's, after all, are very similar, though
Hill is the far superior player. Both are slashers, not shooters; both need the ball in their hands to be effective. And

neither can hit threes with any regularity, a gaping hole in the Pistons' offense.

Hill has voiced his concerns quietly, concerned as he is about his image. Throughout the league in the '90s, NBA stars have received increasing criticism for their input into their team's coaching decisions. Last season, for instance, Orlando's Penny Hardaway was instrumental in the team's dismissal of coach Brian Hill. And though the precedent extends at least back to the '80s, when Magic Johnson was reported to have fired Coach Paul Westhead from the Lakers, star players leading internal revolts have become more commonplace, as when Patrick Ewing and John Starks forced Don Nelson from New York in 1995 the year after Webber's showdown with him at Golden State.

Hill doesn't want to be portrayed as one of the growing list of players who chime in on management decisions, but his public silence on Collins's future speaks volumes—which Collins knows. Lately, he and Hill have barely been speaking.

Into this tension comes Stackhouse, who just wants to get through the two games following Indiana: a home-and-home against the 76ers. In the first, in Detroit, Stackhouse, the day after checking into the Hilton Suites just down the road from the Palace of Auburn Hills, scores 20 points as the Pistons blow out the Sixers—and an indecisive, lethargic Iverson—by over 30 points. But before the game's end, Stack feels butterflies. In less than forty-eight hours, he'll be back in Philly's CoreStates Center, but in a different uniform.

Same guy, different shirt, so the fans begin by booing him lustily. Welcome back, Stack. He is nervous from the outset; by game's end, he will accumulate 7 turnovers. When he's taken out for breathers, Collins preaches to him about calming down: "Let the game come to you," he says. "You're trying to do too much."

He misses seven of ten shots, but hits ten of eleven at

the line. In the game's closing moments, the Sixers have the ball, down by two. Rookie Tim Thomas, Stackhouse's replacement in Philly's starting lineup, drives to the basket. Stackhouse skies out of nowhere, rising and rising until, at the last possible instant, he swats the ball away, saving the win as he falls to the floor. He springs to his feet with the widest grin the Philly-less-than-faithful have ever seen from him and sprints to the visitors' locker room, unable to lose the smile.

After showering, he is, as ever, polite and classy—saying all the right things about Brown, Iverson, and Philadelphia. Then, the media dispersing, his new teammate Lindsey Hunter approaches, hands outstretched for a hug.

"Whose house is *this!?!*" Hunter exclaims.

"Stack's house," he responds, beaming but a bit embarrassed. Then he thinks for a moment. "Guess I got the last laugh," he says.

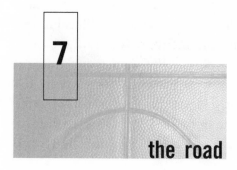

7

the road

"you look like you're in shape. Can you still play?"

Vernon Maxwell nods, though he is stunned. It's his first practice with his new team—the Orlando Magic, with whom he's signed a ten-day contract. All this time he's been sitting out, he's assumed there are no doubts about his game. So why is Coach Daly asking if I can play? he wonders. Is that what these muthafuckas think? Is that going around the league, that I can't play no more?

He fixes Chuck Daly with a hard stare. "Yeah, I can still play," he says. "I can score in my muthafuckin' sleep."

And the next night he proves it. It's just after the New Year when Maxwell plays his first NBA game of the season, the Magic's thirty-fourth, and it is a triumphant return. He leads the injury-depleted Magic over the Toronto Raptors with 18 points in twenty-one minutes, including 9 in a breathtaking fourth-quarter surge in which, it seems, he re-

fuses to let his new team lose, hitting on a series of acro-
batic shots.

It is one of the lead basketball stories on ESPN's
"SportsCenter," complete with footage of Maxwell gasping
for air in the first half and scoring a game-clinching driving
layup in the second. The next day *The Orlando Sentinel* headline reads: "MAD MAX" IS THE ELIXIR FOR THE MAGIC. And in
need of an elixir they are. Before the Toronto game, Daly's
Magic had dropped nine of their last ten and were struggling to score 90 points a game; more players, it seems, are
on the injured list than on his bench. Penny Hardaway,
Mark Price, Gerald Wilkins, and Derek Harper are all hurt,
which prompted the Magic to roll the dice and offer Maxwell a ten-day contract.

"Desperate times call for desperate measures," said Daly
when the signing took place. Few teams, in fact, have embraced "family values" rhetoric more than the Magic, as
Sentinel columnist Brian Schmitz pointed out in a column
headlined MAGIC SIGN A PLAYER WHO IS REAL-LIFE BAD BOY. But
Julius Erving, in his first year as executive vice president of
the Magic, had placed a call to John Lucas in Houston,
where the former San Antonio Spurs and Philadelphia 76ers
coach teaches tennis and, a recovering alcoholic and drug
addict himself, counsels young jocks who struggle with their
own inner demons. Over the years, Lucas had become a
father figure to Maxwell, using a mixture of tough love and
encouragement to cajole him into taking a deep breath once
in a while and to look inward. The word came back to Erving: "Vernon knows this is his last shot. He's got something
to prove."

Bringing Maxwell to Orlando was risky on another level
as well. Throughout his pro career, Maxwell has arguably
been the most booed athlete to visit the O-Rena, where the
Magic play. This is, after all, the Vernon Maxwell who
starred at nearby Bucholz High in Gainesville and then at

the University of Florida, but whose college career ended in controversy and infamy.

For a while in the mid-'80s, Maxwell could do no wrong in Florida. "Walking around with Vernon at U. of F. back in the day was like hanging with Sinatra in Vegas," recalls Todd Boyd, who was called "Real" back then and was Maxwell's resident assistant in the dorms. Boyd, now a professor of critical studies at USC, often had to use his nascent oratorical skills to bail Maxwell out, like the time Max and point guard Andrew Moten beat the paleness off about fifteen white dental school students after the epithet "nigger" was launched during a rough-and-tumble touch football game in the quad. "I remember that meeting with the dean, man," Boyd says. "The dean began by saying that, in a dispute between some ball players and dental students, he had a predisposition to side with the dental students. I went on a riff about the historical implications of that word, you know, how he couldn't understand the violence of that word, despite his efforts to reduce it or simplify it. I was just scared Max or Drew would speak. 'Cause if they did, their contribution to the discourse would have been to tell him to go fuck himself while they slapped his white ass all around his cozy little office."

It was when Maxwell decided to no longer hold his tongue that his time at Florida grew even more controversial. Convinced that Coach Norm Sloan of the Gators leaked to the press the story of his failed drug test during the 1988 NCAA Tournament, Maxwell turned on the program and told about a series of shady dealings, including illegal payments and other recruiting violations, and came clean about his own acceptance of gifts—including a car—from sports agents, a violation of NCAA rules. There was even his immunized testimony at the drug trial of Eric "Ice" Scott when Maxwell was asked how he got the money to buy cocaine from Scott. "I'm sure everybody knows," he said. "The people at the University of Florida paid me. I had a sports agent who paid me." (In the mid-'80s, cocaine was still considered relatively harmless, a rich man's pot: "Vernon and those guys were never really that into blow," recalls Boyd. "They just wanted to smoke weed.")

To folks in Gainesville, Maxwell was a heretic. The University of Florida is a religion: turn on it and you turn on them. The school erased all mention of Maxwell in its record books.

Now, nine years later, here he is, rescuing the local NBA franchise. In the next game, he scores 15 points in twenty-nine minutes, but the Magic lose to the New Jersey Nets. His game is rusty—his outside shooting, in particular, is more inconsistent than ever—but he plays with more energy than anyone on the floor. He signs another ten-day contract and scores 18 points in just fourteen minutes against the Utah Jazz, buzzing past the Jazz's Jeff Hornacek on his way to a perfect eleven for eleven night at the line. Meantime, many of his injured teammates are getting better; after two consecutive ten-days, a team must either sign a player for the duration of the season or cut him. And with Hardaway, Price, and Harper on their way back, it looks like the Magic's backcourt might be too crowded. But Maxwell doesn't care about tomorrow. He likes to boast that he lives in the moment—one late-night barroom soliloquy finds him announcing, "I'm so in the moment, I ain't even here, I'm in the damn future!"—and this moment is particularly sweet. He's back in the league, living the life, doing his thing.

When Alice saw Victor's photo in the paper, she decided to sink her claws into a rich, handsome man just like him. Miguel is in love with Veronica and Neil has fallen for Victoria, who is pregnant. And Michael has donated a lifesaving kidney to Danny. I am told this as background information by Maxwell, whose plot synopsis is critical to my understanding of today's episode of "The Young and the Restless." It is Maxwell's favorite soap, though he's addicted to a number of them.

It is ironic, indeed, that so many NBA players are so hooked on the afternoon soaps, because *their* lives are presented to us as the American male soap opera, much to their own resentment. Women may get engrossed in "The Young and the Restless," but men lose themselves in the sports pages and sports talk radio, a similarly daily narrative of overblown passions, gossip, and cartoonish heroes and villains. Sometimes, as in the network soaps, a bad guy will become good, in the way that Luke Spencer of "General Hospital" evolved from a rapist to all-around good guy. Barkley fits the bill: onetime rebel turned elder statesman. Rodman, thanks to agent Manley's clever cutting-edge marketing, has gone from freak to pop culture antihero. And Maxwell wants to do the same, become someone audiences embrace for a change.

He is lying on the bed of his room at the opulent Grand Bay Hotel in Miami's tony Coconut Grove, a popular village among visiting NBA players. Tomorrow night Maxwell's Magic will face the Heat. For now, he's checking out the soaps when the phone rings. He and a teammate share a laugh over the local groupie—a good-looking black woman in her late twenties who beds at least one NBA player per team per road trip—who has, apparently, fallen into favor with one young star. He'll be bringing her as his date to next month's All-Star Game, oblivious to her, uh, vocation.

"Man, that boy in love," Maxwell says, shaking his head. "These new niggas better learn to be careful."

Maxwell's been around, so he knows the nuances of the sophisticated sexual games that pertain on the road. Many players have a convenient take on the temptations offered to them: They've got their "family girls"—the wives or girlfriends back home, with whom they are legitimately in love—and then there are the "bitches" or "hos" on the road. They are the ones to be wary of.

Players are convinced that throughout the league, there are a handful of women not unlike Alice from "The Young and the Restless," women who, in Maxwell's words, set their sights on "the richest nigga they know" in hopes of hitting it big. Perhaps the best example of this phenomenon is the case of the Dallas Mavericks' A. C. Green, a devout Christian who, at thirty-four, is proud to announce that he is still a virgin. That hasn't stopped four women in search of paydays, he says, from claiming he fathered their babies. So the players share information—like the one recent case buzzing around the league involving a woman who, after a player insisted on wearing a condom, refrigerated the enriched prophylactic immediately after sex in the hopes of artificially inseminating herself.

Now, the show over, Maxwell places a CD in his portable sound system. This is the new Vernon Maxwell. It is an off-night in Miami, in Coconut Grove no less, and he'll stay in the hotel room tonight, listen to CDs, drink some Rémy, maybe watch his bootlegged copy of the movie *Soul Food,* which will put him in mind of the Southern-style foods of his youth.

This is life on the road in the NBA. They are millionaires who stay at the poshest hotels, who have money to burn, but are rarely fully comfortable. Time and again, players will get on an elevator and become acutely aware of a middle-aged white woman clutching her purse. They laugh or stare at the floor numbers going by. "We ain't never not black," says Maxwell with a note of resignation to his voice. They will walk the malls, though the same tensions apply, as when Webber, dressed in sweats, recently entered a Tiffany's. Store security followed him around and asked, more than once, "Are you sure you can afford that?" when his eyes settled on a possible purchase.

Many veterans sequester themselves in their rooms. Grant Hill, for instance, describes himself as a "newsstand junkie" and tends to stay in and read on off-nights. Stackhouse rejoices with teammates when the first of the month rolls around, because that means new titles on the SpectraVision in-room movie menu.

But Maxwell has never been one to hibernate. Like Barkley, he has a passion to be out, to be among people. But this season has seen a newer, calmer Maxwell and he's planning on chillin' tonight. It is the eve of what could be his last game for the Magic. As expected, his minutes have waned in this second ten-day period as other players have returned to the lineup. Worse, he missed practice earlier this week, an event that no doubt had general managers throughout the league shaking their heads.

It was early on an off-night just like this one and he was in his room at the Orlando Marriott. Then some homeys called, guys he used to hang with in Gainesville. The familiar feelings came back. They were going to kick it at some clubs in the 'hood, he was told. His feet started tapping; the hotel room began to feel constricting, suffocating. He could feel that old well of energy starting to surge. If he went out, it'd be an all-nighter.

I gotta do the responsible thing, he thought. He called the airport. Within two hours, he could be with Shel in Alpharetta; they could watch TV together. If he hustled, he could hang with Little V before bedtime. An eight-thirty flight back in the morning would get him to practice in time.

So that's what he did. Shel even remarked how proud she was of him. There was only one hitch: The return flight was delayed on the runway. He called Shell on the cell phone, who called the Magic to warn them he'd miss practice.

It was a classic case of crying wolf. No doubt Erving, Daly, and General Manager John Gabriel all rolled their eyes: We sign this guy for two weeks and he can't even make all our practices? They fined him and he played just sixteen minutes the next game, scoring 9 points.

To Maxwell, it was further proof of a league-wide double

standard. Most coaches hold closed-door practices, after all, not because they think their strategies will be uncovered. Everyone runs the same offense, anyway. No, practices are closed to the media so the fan doesn't learn how often they're blown off by the likes of Michael Jordan. (It is said that Wilt Chamberlain once explained his absence from a game day shootaround by telling his coach, "I'm coming to the arena once in a day. I can come for shootaround or I can come for the game. It's your choice.")

Yet, only those who are portrayed as "bad" in the soap opera–like narrative seem to get publicly nailed for missing practice. When I suggest that it's still not smart to miss practice when you're on a ten-day contract, Maxwell just shrugs. Tupac's "Dear Mama" has come on and he lies there, in a MAGIC T-shirt and sweats, eyes closed, rapping along, *feeling* it.

> *I finally understand*
> *For a woman, it ain't easy*
> *Trying to raise a man*
> *Nobody told us it was fair*
> *No love from my daddy*
> *'Cause the coward wasn't there . . .*
> *They say I'm cold and I'm heartless*
> *But all along I was looking for a father*
> *He was gone*
> *I hung around with the thugs*
> *And even though they sold drugs*
> *They showed a young brother love . . .*

When the song ends, Maxwell shakes his head sadly. "I never got to meet 'Pac," he says. "I always said if I did, we'd have clicked just like this here. We'd have clicked and been hanging out together and shit, just like brothers."

Then he's quiet. It comes as no surprise that he hears his own life story in Tupac's lyrics. Maxwell grew up in

Sugarhill, a small ghetto about ten miles from the college where he'd later become infamous. It was a poor rural place; once a year, the schools administered special shots because so many of the kids were barefoot all day long that their bodies would be invaded by worms under the skin.

There were four kids, two boys and two girls; Vernon was the second-oldest. His mom, Grace, was seventeen when she had Greg, his older brother. Two years later came Vernon. When he was five, his father bolted, never to be heard from again. Grace raised the four kids while working at a juvenile detention center. Soon she married James Camp, who used to haul an eighteen-wheeler. When he hauled turf, he'd keep some for the backyard. That was a highlight. "We always had good grass to play football on," Maxwell recalls.

Today he breaks into a wide grin when he talks about his mama. "That's my girl," he says. He's bought her a house and a Cadillac. "She's let me know she's gonna need a new car soon. I'm gonna take care of that this summer."

But his voice turns cold when he remembers all those birthdays when he'd sprint home from school and, even though he knew presents were waiting inside the house, he'd head straight for the mailbox, checking for a card that would never come. "I love my kids to death, which is why I can't understand how my father could do what he did," he says softly. "Just not do anything for them. Don't send shit for Christmas, don't send a birthday card. I give him the benefit of the doubt. I mean, he lives in Detroit. But still, muthafucka, stop at a mailbox and drop a card for your kid's birthday. If he'd did that, we'd be cool right now. My mom never made him pay his child support for four kids. Never went to the judicial system and said this muthafucka ain't paying. She was too proud."

His voice is rising and he gets off the bed and begins pacing. Maybe this is the root of his peripatetic nature, his immersion in the moment. Moving targets, after all, rarely get hurt. "I hate that muthafucka," he says. "I know I shouldn't hate, but I hate him. I think this is where a lot of my anger comes from, toward my father. The only thing he did good was bring all four of us into the world. That's it. I can't ever see myself doing anything for him. Because he ain't done shit for me. All he had to do was send me a card. He couldn't even do that."

He pauses, flops in a chair. Later, I will learn that his father tried to establish a relationship with him—after Maxwell had a few million-dollar contracts. It was to no avail.

He runs a hand atop his clean-shaven head. "I don't like to talk about this shit," he says. "I get all upset when I talk about that muthafucka."

We make plans to have lunch tomorrow and I leave. At the elevator bank, I hear the opening notes of Tupac, turned up now, loud enough to drown out those decades-old thoughts racing through his head.

Coco Walk, a strip of stores and restaurants in Coconut Grove, is particularly popular among visiting NBA players. At night, there's Paulo Luigi's, an upscale Italian restaurant. During the day, there's the retro diner Johnny Rockets, where Maxwell orders a triple burger with eggs on top, fries, and a milkshake. When his teammate Gerald Wilkins, also at the counter, rises to leave, Maxwell notices the tip Wilkins puts down: a buck.

"C'mon now," he calls out, looking at Wilkins and then back at the dollar while the waitresses look on, giggling.

Wilkins sheepishly digs back into his pocket, emerging with another dollar.

"Now, c'mon, dawg," Maxwell implores him until Wilkins comes through with a five.

We are meeting Gary Grant, a journeyman point guard who played most recently for the Heat and, before that, the Knicks, also under head coach Pat Riley. Like Maxwell until the Magic called, Grant is out of work, waiting for the phone to ring. At thirty-two, he's convinced he's got ball left in him.

As they strut between shops, the two compare notes. "Man, I been watching games at home and I be, like, I know I can bust that nigga," says Grant, dressed in white designer pants and a silk shirt.

"Right, right. Muthafuckas can't play and we be sitting out," Maxwell agrees.

"I don't know if Pat Riley said something about me that blackballed me or what, but nobody been calling," Grant says. "Toronto's got a guy named Garner backing up Stoudamire right now and he ain't doo-doo. And Darrell Walker [the Toronto coach] my man. That's like you getting a head coaching job, V. We were tight. And he says, 'I'm keeping my team the way it is.' "

They amble into a cigar store. A young brunette in a see-through print skirt smiles at them on her way out. "I'm not playing that CBA shit, V," Grant says, pausing to check her out as she walks away. "I'll go and be all-rec in the 'hood before I go to the CBA."

"That's what I'm talking 'bout," Maxwell says.

"Drink my forties and bust ass in the playground," Grant says, laughing. "Be like, 'Bitch, you can't guard me.' "

Maxwell looks at Humidors. Outside, the brunette glides by in a Mercedes and comes to a stop in front of the store. Grant hasn't lost his quickness; he's out the door in a blur and in her passenger seat for a ride around the block. Moments later, the Mercedes pulls up again and Grant emerges, smiling; she blows Maxwell a lascivious kiss and drives off. Grant holds two scraps of paper with her digits, or phone number, on them. One for him, one for Max.

"It's Daddy's car," he says. "She just graduated college. She was like, 'Aren't you Gary Grant?' I may not be in the league, dawg, but I'm still a legend."

They both laugh and simultaneously discard their scraps of paper. Willing women are an everyday sideshow on the road in the NBA—you never have to spend a night (or, for that matter, an afternoon) alone. Getting the digits is the challenge; following through and actually calling, at least after the first couple of years in the life, becomes the exception rather than the rule.

Grant is known as one of the league's premier party animals, but he says it's an overblown rep. "The only difference between the 'good guys' and me and V is they leave the clubs fifteen minutes earlier than we do, right, V?" he says, entering Banana Republic. "They left fifteen minutes ago and we be out there, closing the joint like this."

He sticks his butt out and starts grooving, snapping his fingers in front of him while sensuously rolling his shoulders, right in front of a rack of skirts. Max looks on, as do others, laughing.

"How 'bout this, dawg?" Grant says, laughing now himself. "Talk about your double standards. Barkley tosses a guy through a window and the league tells him to get a bodyguard. Can you imagine if that was us?"

"Shee-it," Maxwell says. "We'd get the chair."

Back outside, an Asian vendor hawking knickknacks asks Maxwell for his autograph. "How's business, dude?" Max asks.

"No good," the man says solemnly.

"It'll pick up, it'll pick up," Maxwell says, stopping in his tracks and staring intently at his newest fan. "Today's Friday. Things'll get better on the weekend. You'll see. Keep your head up."

By now, Grant is up ahead, heading into a shoe store to try on some Calvin Kleins. I join him. When I come back out, Maxwell is still with the despondent vendor, buying some nondescript figurines that will no doubt not make it back to his hotel room and paying with a Benjamin. "Keep the change, baby," he says, patting the man on the back.

*   *   *

Game time and Maxwell gets five minutes in the first half and isn't called off the pine in the second. It is not a good sign.

Still, the benching doesn't stop him from doing his share as a teammate. When Miami center Alonzo Mourning, a behemoth, gets into a shoving match with Magic forward Bo Outlaw, the Magic bench seems nonplussed. All, that is, but Maxwell. Every time Mourning is anywhere within earshot, Max unleashes pearls of invective his way.

" 'Zo, you do all that shit for the cameras, but you and I know what you is," he calls out while teammate Derek Harper, sitting next to him, bursts into laughter. "Ain't nothing but a little bitch!"

Mourning starts to make his way over. "I'm gonna wait for you outside," he says, pointing. "We'll see who's the bitch."

"I be there, nigga, I be there."

After the game, Maxwell knows his run with Orlando is over. "I ain't never played no five minutes," he says, looking at a stat sheet. He consoles himself with the bigger picture: "I did what I had to do here," he says. "I came in for twenty days after not playing for ten months and led them in scoring a bunch of times."

I remind him of Mourning's postgame challenge, fearing a parking lot brawl that could result in injury, not to mention career-ending publicity. He just smiles.

"Aw, that was all just fun, man," he says, packing up his stuff. The trash talk, the ball in his hands at crunch time, the idle hours in cities on the road, it's all part of what he'll miss—again—about the NBA. Tomorrow the Magic will announce that they've decided not to sign him for the balance of the season. Once again, Vernon Maxwell is a former NBA player.

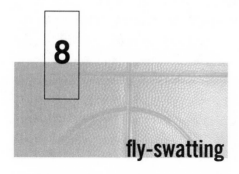

8

fly-swatting

how quickly they forget. In 1993, just six years ago, Charles
Barkley was atop the b-ball world. He was the charismatic
leader of the Phoenix Suns, the team with the NBA's best
regular season record, and the MVP of the league—and Michael hadn't even left yet to play baseball. He was riding
high and living large; tabloids chronicled a fling with Madonna while Phoenix stores sold out of Barkley neckties and
images of his glistening pate adorned city buses.

Prior to '93, there were a host of MVP-caliber seasons in
Philadelphia, like 1990, when he led an undermanned team
to the Atlantic Division title. But now his dominance of the
early '90s feels like a distant memory. If it's remembered
at all.

On this mid-January day after a Rockets practice, Cynthia Cooper comes swaggering into the gym at the Westside
Tennis Center. Cooper is the reigning WNBA MVP, the

leader of the Houston Comets, the league's first champion. Coop—whose charisma evokes Barkley circa 1990 minus the foot-in-mouth tendencies—struts into practice, a gold Nike necklace sparkling as it bounces against her Comets jersey. She is here to plug the just-released Comets schedule for the cameras, though she didn't anticipate a heckling Barkley.

"Hey, girl!" he calls out from his seat on the sideline, where he's gulping mineral water. "I got to call Nike. I don't got that necklace!"

Coop flashes the smile that the WNBA honchos are banking on. "You've got to be MVP first," she says.

Barkley jumps up, animated. "Hey, you know what, who's got the stats about MVP?" he calls out to nobody in particular. "Someone tell Cynthia Cooper I got MVP one year! Been there and done that, baby!"

They share a laugh and then Cooper does her thing for the cameras. Moments later, she is back with Barkley, away from the buzzing media pack that Barkley refers to as "the flies." At thirty-five, he and Cooper are the same age, but they are at vastly different moments. Barkley, who, in addition to missing three games in November with the sports hernia, is just returned after a week laid up with an injured big toe, which, he says, makes him feel "like a big sissy. It's embarrassing." Cooper is shining, reveling in the spotlight that has suddenly found her, basking in it, not unlike the Barkley of the early '90s.

The two huddle together and Barkley admits to the inescapable: He's winding down. "I'm the artist formerly known as Charles Barkley now," he tells Cooper. "I'm just living in his body now. Sometimes I get flashbacks, though, you know?"

Like the one in November, when he went off for 43 points and 15 rebounds at Golden State. Those nights are rarer now, thanks to a rapidly aging body. But the wear and tear has been limited to the physical. His passion for the game—not to mention for the glare of the cameras—is un-

abated. His confab with Cooper over, Barkley heads over to
the flies and sits in the middle of the press pack. Heading
into tomorrow night's game against the Timberwolves, his
Rockets are 18–15 and have been playing without Olajuwon,
whose early season woes were finally attributed to a knee
in need of surgery, and Maloney, whose shooting elbow has
needed rest.

More critical than the injuries, though, is the team's noticeable lack of cohesion, which has Barkley referring to the
Rockets as "Team Turmoil." The buzz is that Drexler and
Barkley are feuding and can no longer play together. Indeed,
they are vastly different: Drexler is, after all, an adherent to
the crossover ethic that Barkley finds so phony. One team
source blames Drexler: "Clyde is jealous," the source says,
pointing out that Barkley's flamboyance naturally overshad-
ows Drexler's quiet, classy demeanor.

Among the press, talk of the Drexler–Barkley spat is a
hot topic. No one reports it, but many see deep meaning in
Drexler's young son's recently yelling at Barkley, "I hate
you! Get away from me, baldy!" But those close to the team,
including Barkley himself, scoff at the idea of significant fric-
tion between the two stars. In other words, it's nothing a
winning streak wouldn't straighten out.

"If I'm on a team that wins, everybody says I have a
great personality," Barkley says. "If it's a team that loses,
people say I cause problems. The public is smarter than
that."

Now, the trading deadline a month away and rumors of
a blockbuster deal rampant, Barkley addresses the state of
the team, which has lost eight of its last twelve, and he talks
about the contract of the Timberwolves' Garnett: "Hey,
when he turned down seventeen million dollars a year, his
exact quote was: 'Call me back when y'all are serious,' "
Barkley says, smiling. "Whoa. I can't speak for the rest of
civilization, but I think seventeen million dollars is pretty

damn serious. And I guess they weren't too serious, since they came back offering more."

But Barkley can't talk hoops for long. "Hey, I got a dish and I was watching, like HBO 10 and I saw *The American President* last night," he announces. "Lemme tell you something: Annette Bening is stunning. What's her guy's name? Warren something? I ain't seen him, man, ain't seen him in a long time. That always makes me nervous, when famous people disappear. Makes you think they got something."

His soliloquy over, Barkley grimaces, slowly rises, and, in a noticeably fragile gait, begins to make his way out of the gym, on his way for therapy on his aching back.

Charles Barkley is realistic about the effects of fourteen years of pounding under the boards. "I'm not a great player, but I'm still a good player," he says. "I think I can go out and get fifteen points and twelve rebounds pretty consistently."

Tellingly, he's beginning to take stock of his career. He's long been tired of the litany of questions about not having won a title, as though leading his '93 Suns to the Finals, where they battled the Bulls in six hotly contested games, was tantamount to failure. In the questions—really, it's one question expertly rephrased again and again—he hears the maddening implication that if his playing days end without a championship, he will be remembered as less of a winner than some of his more hallowed contemporaries. He's begun to think of himself in relation to those who have won rings. "I've never played with a great player in his prime while I've been in my prime," he says. "Michael has had Scottie. Larry had Kevin and Robert Parish. And Magic, shit, Magic had everybody. When I came into the league, Doc and Moses's careers were winding down. And now Hakeem and Clyde, same thing."

It's proffered as a fact, not an excuse. His analysis is on target: He is indeed still a good player who is capable of flashes of brilliance. But there's a danger in that: The limits of his game today can overshadow what he once was. More than a great player, Barkley was a wonder on the court in the same way Jordan still is. You watch and you can't quite comprehend the preternaturalness of the display. He was a six-foot-four jumping jack who was too quick for other power forwards, too strong for small forwards, and too visionary a passer for the double team. In the open floor, he'd rumble the length of the court and bigger men would bail out. Under the boards, he was the quickest jumper, considerable girth and all, this side of Dennis Rodman. And then there was his heart, the way he'd take over in the clutch and stamp his will on a game's outcome.

But, unlike greats ranging from Bird to Malone, he was done in by his supporting casts. The list of so-so teammates is lengthy: His centers were Charles Shackleford, Tim McCormick, Mike Gminski, Mark West, and Oliver Miller. His forwards were Armon Gilliam, Roy Hinson, and Richard Dumas. Among the guards, there were Rickey Green, Scott Brooks, and the often-broken-down Kevin Johnson. There were no Scottie Pippens or James Worthys.

It has become commonplace among the pundits to see great meaning in the absence of a ring on Barkley's finger, as though it says something about his character in contrast to Bird, Johnson, and Jordan. But because Barkley's body has been so beaten down and his spirit so scarred by panic-stricken roster changes around him, any consideration of his on-court legacy requires the effort of memory. To really gauge Barkley, think of your first vision of him. What you saw was the raw heart of a champion.

"I'll never forget the first time I set eyes on him," says Maureen Barkley, Charles's wife of ten years, a former model Barkley met in a Philadelphia area T.G.I. Friday's; when he proposed, he had the waiter at their favorite restaurant pop the question for him. The two separated briefly in 1992 (not coincidentally the same year as reports of a dalliance with Madonna surfaced), but they reconciled and still remain together; Maureen credits Barkley's teammate in Phoenix Danny Ainge (the current coach of the Suns) as a positive influence on Charles and, by extension, their marriage. But even her first impression of Charles was formed by what his on-court persona showed about his makeup. "It was years before I met him. I was watching a college basketball game with my older brother, Ricky. Auburn was playing, Charles's team. And I saw this guy and yelled, 'What is that! He's fat!' I thought it was a joke, like they had a football player on the team. But then we watched him play and I could not believe what I was looking at. I couldn't believe someone that fat could jump that high. And he never shut up; he was always expressing himself. I could tell he was jumping that high just out of desire. He wanted the ball more than anyone else. From then on, my brother and I referred to him as 'that fat kid from Alabama.' "

Of course, the fat kid from Alabama, then nicknamed "the Round Mound of Rebound" or "Boy Gorge," slimmed down after a couple of years in the pros. His prowess surprised even himself. When he was drafted, fifth overall by the 76ers in 1984, his goal was modest; he knew he had the ability and desire to be a successful NBA rebounder and he hoped he could parlay that skill into becoming a consistent 10 points per game scorer. Then as his game developed, far surpassing those initial goals, his personality bloomed. He'd never expected superstardom, and he'd be damned if he wasn't going to revel in it. "We ain't here for a long time, we here for a good time" became his motto.

Throughout the many stages of Barkley, the two constants have been his passion and the palpable work ethic Maureen saw on TV that day. Neither has dissipated since. When Garnett's Timberwolves come in, Barkley is the Sir Charles of old. He plays forty minutes, grabs 9 boards, scores 29 points. As always, he makes for a compelling show. He hits eleven of thirteen shots from the line; when he misses one late in the game, a frustrated fan yells out, "C'mon, Charles!" From the free throw line, he shoots a glare in the fan's direction. "I'm fuckin' *trying!*" he yells, prompting gales of courtside laughter. The Timberwolves win by one in overtime and after the game Barkley looks older than his thirty-five years. The toe is aching, the back is tight, and he's still playing with a hernia—it will require surgery after the season. But two days later, he digs deep again in Chicago, scoring 35 points and pulling down 14 boards in a six-point loss. His team will fall to .500 the next day after losing to Seattle. A clearly weary Barkley hits only four of eleven shots and scores a mere 10 points. The All-Star break is a couple of weeks away and it can't come soon enough for him; in fact, he's making sure the Houston beat writers quote him urging the fans *not* to vote him onto the squad. A long Vegas weekend of gambling and R&R beckons instead.

Just as it's easy to forget the dominant force Barkley was in light of his status today as merely a good player, it's tempting to dismiss his cultural impact of the early '90s given the modern-day kinder, gentler, *Republican* Barkley.

"Man, when he said he was a ' '90s nigga' and when he said he wasn't no role model, my phone didn't stop ringing—I had brothers calling me up from across the country, saying, 'Did you hear what Barkley said?' " recalls Todd Boyd, the USC cultural studies professor who hung with Maxwell back in the day at the University of Florida. "People had been waiting for an athlete to speak up, waiting since Ali, you know? Since then, I think Barkley's been all over the map in what he stands for, but you can't underestimate what he meant back then."

When Nike aired a striking black-and-white commercial of a stern-looking Barkley announcing, "I am not a role model . . . I get paid to wreak havoc on the basketball court . . . not to raise your kids," it sent shock waves through the culture of sports. In reality, Barkley had been

speaking out against the "role model" notion for years, saying as early as 1988 that "I have a sneaker deal myself,
but I don't understand why people would buy one sneaker
endorsed by one player over the other. . . . It's the parents'
job to be the role models. To kids that idolize me, I tell
them, 'Don't do so just because I can dribble a basketball—
that's really sick.' " He wasn't even the first prominent athlete to question role model ideology. In his book *Second
Wind: The Memoirs of an Opinionated Man*, Bill Russell explains his refusal to sign autographs. "During my career,
people would come up to me and say, 'Great game, Bill, I
want my son here to grow up to be just like you,' " he
wrote. "I began to wonder. Those people didn't know a
thing about me personally; for all they know, I might be a
child molester. Yet, here were parents saying they wanted to
model their children after me, instead of after themselves."

But the Nike ad struck a nerve. *Sports Illustrated* published a column by Karl Malone, who was coming under
some fire from the younger generation. Derrick Coleman
called Malone an Uncle Tom around the time that his piece
in *SI* excoriated his friend: "Charles, you can deny being a
role model all you want, but I don't think it's your decision
to make. We don't *choose* to be role models; we are *chosen*."

And that was precisely Barkley's point: Someone was
doing the choosing and it wasn't America's kids. In fact,
kids see through the media role model hype when it comes
to athletes, as evidenced in a 1992 study funded by the Robert Wood Johnson Foundation, not to mention a 1994 Gallup
Poll that asked teens, "Who is your role model?" Nearly
half said they did not have one. Of the rest, nearly three of
four listed their parents, siblings, teachers, or the clergy.
Only 22 percent listed an athlete.

Role model status is conferred by the media, Barkley
realized, which is one reason he purposely harps on "the
flies" so often. It is impossible to disregard the racial implications of the dynamic, given that the term is disproportion-

ately applied to black athletes. "When Warren Moon, an African American quarterback, was accused of wife abuse, many lamented the loss of a role model," writes Todd Crosset, a professor of Sports Studies at the University of Massachusetts. "At about the same time, Bobby Cox, the white manager of the Atlanta Braves, faced similar charges. Few, however, worried if Cox's actions would adversely affect children."

Barkley sensed that "role model" was often used as a racially coded term, not unlike "welfare queen" or "All-American," indirectly conjuring race and racial stereotypes. (A quick Lexis search bears out the suspicion. During a six-week period in 1994, there were 249 mentions of the term just after O. J. Simpson's recent arrest; during the same period, the term appeared in connection with Joe Montana's name four times.) It was conferred by an overwhelmingly white press on those black athletes who, in his words, "played the game" and behaved, who weren't frightening to white America; thus, his pledge to be a " '90s nigga" and "a strong black man."

The " '90s nigga" comment touched an entire generation of young hoopsters, including a lanky high school kid in Detroit named Chris Webber. It was as if Barkley were speaking directly to them; yet, in the mainstream press, it was the same old script: Charles was racist, offensive, outrageous. Yet the context of his outrage was never provided.

On that January 1991 day in Philadelphia, Michael Jordan—who had yet to win his first NBA title—had just led his Bulls to a 103–99 win over Barkley's 76ers. After the game, the media predictably fawned over Jordan, who had, since he entered the league, taken pains to establish himself as the game's role model extraordinaire.

It was a different story in the home team's locker room. Barkley had already been upset for a couple of days by a local article critical of him for missing practice to shoot a Nike commercial. "I had my coach's permission to miss a fifteen-minute walk-through to go make some money," he explained.

When, after the loss to the Bulls, a group of journalists began by questioning his decision to launch a twenty-five-foot three-pointer with twenty-four seconds left and his team down three, Barkley exploded, declaring himself "a '90s nigga. . . . We do what we want to do."

That wasn't all. "Y'all can kiss my black ass," he boomed. "Your lips might stink but you can kiss my black ass. Y'all is just intimidated by a strong black man, you been on my ass all year, and I'm fuckin' sick of it."

Why was Barkley so angry? Partly, it had to do with the complicated dynamic of locker room politics that was playing out that day. He knew the media was there to exploit Jordan's "goodness" against his "badness," and he was offended by the hypocrisy of it: The very guys—and they were all guys—blasting him for making money on a commercial shoot were using Michael and him to produce money-making journalism themselves after all.

But no one asked Barkley why he was angry. Instead, the *Philadelphia Daily News* headline read: OUTRAGEOUS BULL: BARKLEY FOLLOWS ILL-ADVISED SHOT WITH ILL-ADVISED CLAIMS OF RACISM. (One columnist, the normally clear-headed Stan Hochman, responded with a chillingly myopic column detailing his own experiences as a victim of anti-Semitism.) Yet somehow a whole generation of kids—including Webber—knew Barkley wasn't simply pissed off about having his shot selection held up to scrutiny.

"He really helped form who I am, who a lot of us became," says Webber of the player who was his idol when he was a high school star. "I feel like I can say anything today, because I watched him say anything. I feel like you have to respect what I say today, because I watched him demand you respect what he says. The thing about Barkley when I was coming up, man, you'd watch him and you knew it was real. I knew it was real. Now, when he talks, it seems like he's trying to say something to be real like he used to be. But back then, he was the first guy who showed you could keep it real and win, you could be a strong black man and not sell out."

The volume may be down a little, but he's still preaching, still challenging the predilections and prejudices of the men who present him to the world. On this day, post-practice, he sits in front of his locker while the cameramen and writers and talking heads mill about.

I tell him that since I saw him last, I've talked to a couple of his political mentors: Rush Limbaugh and Dan Quayle. Both sang his praises long and loud.

"What they say?" he asks, ignoring the hovering pack.

I read him the quotes. "Charles believes in fundamentally conservative values," said Limbaugh, who has pledged to be Barkley's media adviser come campaign time. The two were introduced by mutual friend Paul Westphal, Barkley's coach in Phoenix. "The first time I heard him speak," Limbaugh continued, "I said, 'I'm listening to myself.' I couldn't deliver the message any better. That's saying something. And he has an innate ability to get people to like him, which is gold in politics. The key for him will be keeping his cool when he enters politics, because his opponents will take a lot of what he's said over the years out of context and use it against him. He's already experienced this with the civil rights community. He talked to Clarence Thomas about what that bunch will do to you if you're not the right kind of black man as they see it."

Barkley acknowledges that he'll suffer some blacklash. It's already come in the form of his former friend Jesse Jackson, whose only public comment to date on Barkley's political future was strikingly dismissive. "He's a basketball star," Jackson said in 1995. And white liberals have already teed off, including a writer for The Village Voice ("Charles wouldn't be the first member of a minority who, once he grew grossly wealthy, just plumb forgot where he came from") and a columnist for *The Arizona Republic*, who lamented, "It's too bad Charles Barkley didn't turn out to be a black man."

But Barkley says he won't get trapped in an argument over labels. "Liberal, conservative—those are just words," he says. In fact, he enters the timeworn debate between the Booker T. Washington and W. E. B. Du Bois factions of black political theory aware of the legacy left by Jackie Robinson, whose political path was eerily similar. Robinson was a militant on civil rights with conservative instincts who allied himself with Nelson Rockefeller's moderate Republicans. Now, more than thirty years later, here comes Barkley insisting that he's entering the Republican Party for the same reasons Robinson and Colin Powell did: to change it and make it more inclusive.

None other than Quayle believes he can do it. "Can you imagine the impact Charles could have?" said Quayle, who has a home in Scottsdale, Arizona, and became acquainted with Barkley there. "Think about what it would mean for his state, our party, and the country to have Charles Barkley as a mentor for guys in the inner city who abandon their families. His is a no-nonsense, tough message: 'Guys, get back home. Be responsible.' I've always thought the second part of his 'I'm not a role model' commercial was the most important—that parents should be role models. It was a family values message."

Now the press approaches his locker en masse, in search of its daily feeding. "Those are great compliments," he says, referring to Quayle's and Limbaugh's comments. "I think Dan Quayle is one of the nicest men I've ever been around. He got a bad rap when he was Vice President. But I'm afraid he might be too nice to be President. In politics, it's a negative if you're not cutthroat and partisan."

He looks up. The microphones are in his face. He has to deal with the flies. But he has some lecturing to do before they can lob their first question at him. He singles out a local TV reporter. "Would you suck a cock for a million dollars?" he asks.

"No," comes the cracked-voice reply while everyone else looks at their shoes.

"A billion?" Barkley won't let it go.

"No" comes the reply, stronger now.

"Well, how much then?"

"I wouldn't do it for anything!"

Barkley grins widely. He's got him. "Well, if you'd do it for free, come on over here, then," he says while nervous laughter fills the air around him. "Tell y'all what, I would. If I was poor, I'd suck a cock for a million dollars."

He pauses and looks at his audience. "And all you muthafuckas would do the same, you just scared to admit it," he says. "Like, remember when that movie *Indecent Proposal* came out? Oprah had on three couples who said they wouldn't let their husband or wife sleep with someone for a million dollars. Couldn't help but notice that they all had money already."

He looks around the room, waiting. Someone asks if the upcoming road trip is crucial to the Rockets' season. He begins by saying, "Every game is critical." Then he's off, talking in basketballspeak, today's lesson plan for the flies completed.

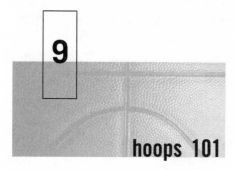

9

hoops 101

"the fat lady is singing. The film is in the apple strudel."

Paul Maloney navigates his way through the crush of bodies at the Green Room, sidles up to this evening's posse—me, Rag, and Ian—and drops the night's code words on us, a self-consciously ironic cue telling us to head for the exits because Matt is outside, waiting. It's a trick Matt learned from Barkley: When seeking to bolt from a crowded social setting, excuse yourself to the bathroom and then proceed outside while your deputy subtly spreads the word to the privileged few tagging along to the next stop. Barkley, who loves attention, uses the system to avoid the long goodbyes that inevitably delay his arrival at the next venue—where all eyes will similarly focus on him. Maloney, so uncomfortable at the center of things, uses it to escape the empty chitchat that makes him so jittery.

And tonight the attention has been on Maloney more

than usual, because, returning after missing his first two games as a pro, he had a good game against the Timberwolves. While Barkley, in Olajuwon and Drexler's absence, was dominating inside, Maloney outplayed Minnesota point guard Stephon Marbury for three quarters, outscoring him 17–10. But the fourth quarter was Marbury's, who scorched the Rockets for 10 points in twelve minutes.

Still, it was Maloney's first solid game in some time. The chips in his elbow have gotten worse—they've begun affecting his shot. Recently, the pain became excruciating upon the full extension of his follow-through, perhaps the most crucial part of shooting technique. Maloney takes roughly five hundred jump shots a day and dissects each one, always making adjustments, always fine-tuning. So he developed a new, more compact follow-through, letting his wrist do more of the work; shortening his extension about an inch was the difference between agony and no pain at all.

Unfortunately, it was also the difference between making and missing shots. Before sitting out the two games, the normally dead-eye Maloney had been ice cold and Houston fans and media were murmuring about the dreaded sophomore jinx. There was the game against Nuggets, where he hit only four of fourteen, including one of seven from behind the three-point line, and the clunker against Webber's Wizards, when he went zero for five in nineteen uninspired minutes. Finally, after hitting only one of ten shots in the two games prior to the Timberwolves' visit, Maloney grudgingly accepted that the only way to return to form was to sit out and let the inflamed tendons heal.

Tonight, the elbow rested, he was the Maloney of old, the guy opposing defenses couldn't leave open, hitting seven of twelve and logging thirty-eight minutes. The swelling had gone down, thanks to the rest and a kick-ass anti-inflammatory drug that will be his new best friend for the rest of the season.

Now all Maloney has in mind is playing pool with the

guys. Outside the Green Room, he's waiting for us in the Navigator and we head to the Ballroom, where Paul has arranged for a private room, complete with pool table and plush sofas. Meanwhile, inside the Green Room, several young women scan the room in search of Maloney. Earlier tonight a stream of them approached while Maloney was plotting his postgame getaway, asking if he *really* planned to show up at the Green Room, searching his eyes for clues because he's been a no-show so many times before. One was, in fact, Nicole Tomjanovich, the coach's twentysomething daughter.

Once at the Ballroom, Maloney is happy to be away from the crowd. And there's something else: "All right! U2!" he exclaims, the most emotion he's shown all night. NBA life normally features a hip-hop soundtrack, so he is relieved that the speakers here blare his kind of music. He gives Paul a high-five. "This was the move! Coming here was the play of the day!"

No one outside the team's inner sanctum knows about Maloney's elbow woes, nor do they know that his solid play tonight is more attributable to matters spiritual than medical. The change began while on the bench during the first of the two games he missed, against Utah. Watching the Jazz on offense and then watching his Rockets with the ball, he didn't so much hear as sense a familiar voice inside his head, the voice of his father, imploring him to not only see what was happening on the court, but to *analyze* it.

It was the same speech Matt grew up hearing in the basement back in Haddonfield, Jim Maloney next to him, remote control in hand, a tape of Mark Price or Maurice Cheeks in the VCR, Jim excitedly showing his progeny how a point guard, more than any other player, can change the course of a game. "See how stagnant the offense has gotten," Jim would point out, freezing the image. "Now watch." And then he'd hit the pause button again and, invariably, the great ones like Price or Cheeks would do something, would take a risk, would drive to the hole and dish or come up with a big steal or knock a bigger player down—all in a part-conscious, part-instinctive effort to jumpstart the game's action.

"Make stuff happen," Jim used to say and, watching Brent Price run the offense, Maloney saw just how plodding and predictable Houston had become with the ball: the guards dump it into the big men and wait around on the perimeter for a three-pointer when the opposition double teams down low.

Maloney knew there wasn't a play in the Rockets' play-book for him, but he decided that didn't matter. When he came back, he'd tell the big guys to come out and screen for him and he'd take it to the basket. *Screw it*, he thought. *I'll tell the big guys to come out and get me, and if it works, nobody can say anything.*

That's what he did tonight, once even crossing Marbury over, freezing one of the quickest guards in the league. He wished Rudy would let him run the pick and roll with his big men, like the Jazz do. The pick and roll might be the most successful play in the history of the sport; if properly executed, a high-percentage shot is virtually guaranteed. It's a very simple concept, really: fifteen or twenty feet from the basket, a big man screens for a guard, who drives while the screener rolls to the hoop. If the defenders switch, the big man has a mismatch down low. If they both drop back, the guard has an open midrange jumper.

But, much to Maloney's consternation, Olajuwon has made it clear he doesn't want to be out high, setting screens. He wants to be jostling for position down low and he wants the guards to get him the ball. If a double team comes, he'll get it back to them—maybe. Even though Olajuwon is still out of the lineup, the playbook is set: No pick and rolls.

It's a particularly frustrating strategy for Maloney be-cause he believes he's made the NBA thanks to his pick and roll prowess during his season in the CBA. "It's why I'm here," he says. Ironically, it's his *defense* of the pick and roll that, as much as his disappointing shooting, has the fans and pundits getting on him this season; they don't know that when Maloney appears to be getting beat by opposing teams running it, he's more the victim of his own team's strategy.

Unlike just about every other team in the league, the Rockets, as Tomjanovich has conceded to Maloney, hang their guards "out to dry" when defending the pick and roll. Players are told not to switch and are to concentrate on denying scoring opportunities to the roller. So Maloney runs around the pick, chasing his man while his larger teammate shadows the opposing big man rolling to the basket. Consequently, because Maloney is always behind his man, chasing him, it appears time and again as though he's been beaten. And since the roller is always covered, the play often ends up with the opposing point guard taking a midrange jump shot while Maloney scrambles to catch up. That was the case in last year's playoffs, when Stockton made a living burying short jumpers off the pick and roll.

The key for Maloney is to anticipate the pick and fight through it quickly so he's not too far behind his man. That requires a heads-up warning from his big man that a pick is being set—"calling out the blues," the Rockets call it. And Barkley is notorious for not talking on defense.

Tonight, coming out of a timeout, in a sign that the dutiful politeness of his rookie year is a thing of the past, Maloney told Barkley in no uncertain terms: Call out the screen. "I know if Bull's or Mario's man is picking me, they'll call it," Maloney said. "I don't know about you, though. I've gotta hear you call the blues." Barkley nodded and the two defended the ensuing play ably, though it still resulted in Marbury draining a twenty-foot jumper.

"I was on Charles all night tonight, 'cause it's me on the line," Maloney says now, putting down his still-untouched shot of peppermint schnapps that Paul ordered—prompting a roll of the eyes from his younger brother—and lining up his shot at the eight ball. "I'm the one who looks like he's getting beat because of the way we defense the pick and roll."

Suddenly there is a matter more pressing than the Rockets' porous defense. One of the girls from the Green Room has shown up here; "All I wanted to do is play pool," Matt mutters, but he asks her to join us because it's the gentlemanly thing. Soon it becomes apparent why these interactions grate on him so, when she corners me.

"I heard Matt has a girlfriend," she says. There's a pause. "Is that true?"

I honestly tell her I don't know. "He's a very private kid," I tell her. The truth is that I'd be surprised; any serious relationship would no doubt jeopardize his legendary single-minded focus. And he's smart enough to recognize that as a risk. Still, there are rumors, all of which make Maloney blush and roll his eyes, which is why I consistently run them by him. (Not too many NBA players blush nowadays.) Like the one that had Pete Sampras's girlfriend, a Houston native, leaving the tennis star for Maloney.

"I was just curious," the girl, who is in her early twenties, says. "Someone told me he has a girlfriend and I was just, like, 'Oh, really?' "

I say nothing and she moves on to Rag and Ian, two of Paul's buddies. Meantime, Matt seems happy the young woman is with us, if only because he's found someone to take his drinks off his hands. Paul orders a round of Purple Hooters, a fruity-tasting shot, saying Matt loves them. "I love them?" he says. "No no no. I *like* that you can't taste the alcohol."

Something occurs to him. Sheepishly, he shares a concern with me. "In your book, you're not going to have a lot of scenes of me, like, drinking in bars, are you?" he asks. "I mean, I don't want my mom to think I'm an alcoholic or something."

"There is no danger of that," I tell him. In fact, on most nights, Maloney stays in. Especially lately, as the season follows a very different script from his storybook rookie year. When things have gotten real tough, when he's been unable to nail what used to be automatic swishes and his elbow has been inflamed and the catcalls from the stands are ringing in his ears, he's sequestered himself in the house he and Paul share in the suburb known as Sugar Land and he pops in a VCR tape that never fails to lift his mood. It took him seven hours to make the tape, a compilation of his favorite clips from his favorite movies, and he sits there, watching these great scenes, holding his stomach and laughing. It's all there: scenes from *Dumb and Dumber, Pure Luck, Ace Ventura: Pet Detective.* He particularly roars when watching Jim Carrey run suicides as a prelude to a pickup basketball game in *The Cable Guy.*

Still, his mother worries that Matt will be somehow corrupted by the NBA lifestyle. At the very least, it changes people; Barkley, after all, was a soft-spoken kid who rarely ventured out of his apartment during his rookie season in Philadelphia, so intimidated was he by the big city. "Matt's always been a very shy boy," says Barbara Maloney. "And that's okay. It's great that he's got this opportunity. He's worked so hard for it. But we don't want him to change."

Now, the evening at the Ballroom winding down, Matt makes a face when he's reminded of his mother's concerns. "My mom just needs something to worry about," he says. "If she's not worried about something, she's worried because she has nothing to worry about."

But Barbara Maloney is more prescient than her son knows. A change is in store for Matt, though it's not necessarily a bad one. It's a change in outlook that more veteran players would say is long overdue.

*   *   *

In the next week, the trade rumors reach a crescendo and virtually all of them involve Maloney. The Rockets say nothing to him. Rudy keeps coaching as if nothing is in the works. Matt scores 13 in twenty-four minutes in a loss to the Sonics and then the story breaks on ESPN and moves across the Associated Press wires, just prior to a Rockets game in New Jersey: The Rockets have traded Maloney, Kevin Willis, Mario Elie, and their number-one 1998 draft pick to Toronto for point guard Damon Stoudamire, the 1995 Rookie of the Year, and two throw-ins, forward Walt Williams and center Zan Tabak. Stoudamire is averaging 19 points and 8.5 assists per game for the Raptors, who have the league's second-worst record.

ESPN reports the deal will be made official within hours. Still, no one says anything to Maloney or the others. Before boarding the Rockets' team bus to take him to what he is convinced will be his last game as a Rocket, Matt calls Barbara Maloney, who had planned to make the two-hour trip up the New Jersey Turnpike for the game.

"Mom, don't bother coming. It looks like I've been traded," Maloney tells her, explaining that he might just get to the arena, be told of the trade, and then have to board a plane for Toronto. At game time, the Houston locker room is eerily silent. Elie blasts team management to the *Chronicle*'s beat writer, but Maloney, in keeping with his trademark equanimity, says nothing. No word comes down before the game and Rudy makes no mention of the impending deal, so Maloney, Willis, and Elie have to go out and play.

Maloney plays inspired. His new "Screw it" attitude has been enhanced, not hindered, by this moment in limbo; time and again, he drives the ball to the basket, and the Nets' Sam Cassell, once a Rocket himself who will express some bitterness toward his former team after the game, seems perplexed by this strangely nonemotive white dude who is lighting it up when everyone expected him to be on his way to Toronto by now. Maloney scores 18 points in forty-one minutes, though the Rockets lose by five.

In the ensuing days, players and fans alike wait for the deal to be announced, but snags are hit. An announcement never comes, though negotiations continue—the trading deadline isn't until after the All-Star break, after all.

So Maloney can only do what he can do: play ball. He goes on a tear, following the Nets game with a 19-point outburst in a loss to the Charlotte Hornets, hitting all seven of his field goals and all four of his foul shots. Then there's 16 points and 4 assists in a win over the Spurs. Many attribute his new aggressive style to the trade that hasn't happened yet, as if it scared him into action. But the inspiration for his renewed play really extends back to the Timberwolves game and that voice inside his head. In the twelve games he's played since then, he's averaged 15.2 points on 51 percent shooting from the floor, including 45 percent of his threes. He's raised his scoring average to double figures and has helped resuscitate a lackadaisical offense, just as his dad would have had it.

Throughout the stretch, no one in Rockets management mentions the trade to any of the players involved. Not Rudy, not anyone. But rumor has it the deal could still go down, so Maloney, Elie, and Willis have to keep playing with it hanging over their heads. So that's how it is, Maloney thinks, recalling how he took less money—considerably less—to come back to Houston this season, out of loyalty to the team that discovered him and gave him his shot. And they don't even pull you aside and talk to you about what they're trying to do? They don't even give you that courtesy?

Screw it, he thinks to himself, a line that increasingly has become his mantra. The Rockets are limping toward the season's midpoint and their starting point guard has finally realized just how much of a business he's really in.

10

the return of the playa-haters

it wasn't supposed to be like this, not this year, but here they come again. Chris Webber recognizes it instantly and braces himself.

It is a phenomenon as old as history itself; only recently, in the subterranean culture of hip-hop, has it been given a name all its own: "playa-hating." And the playa-haters have Chris Webber on their radar screen.

Jealousy, of course, is nothing new. But rappers have spent the better part of the '90s rhyming about a particular kind of envy—that which is aimed at young, black, urban achievers who find alternative ways of making it big. Biggie Smalls sang about it: "There are two kinds of people in this world / We have the playa and we have the playa-haters / Please don't hate me 'cause I'm beautiful, baby." And Puff Daddy has spoken to it, singling out an intellectual elite as its source, when he defined Ph.D. as "playa-hatin' degree."

For young black athletes in the '90s, though, it's not Ph.D.s doing the playa-hating so much as middle-aged, overwhelmingly white sports pundits who live in the suburbs and find it increasingly difficult to understand the newest generation of jocks, those who aren't disciples of the crossover ethic and, thus, are less inclined to parrot back the usual litany of pro-forma quotes once expected of them. In the constant drumbeat of criticism directed their way, athletes like Webber discern a begrudging of their success.

"The media don't like it if you're outspoken," says Derrick Coleman, one of the alleged Gen X bad boys. "They want you to just shut up and do your fuckin' job. Well, we weren't raised like that. When I had a coach, Bill Fitch, who was on a power trip, I spoke out about it. The media don't like that, 'cause they expect you to say what they want, to go along to get along. Well, why do we always have to cross over? Why can't someone cross over to us and understand what's going on in our lives for a change?"*

Lately, singling out Webber and even Coleman as Exhibit A and Exhibit B in an all-that's-wrong-with-sports playa-hating screed has become a thing of the not-so-distant past; they've been replaced by Iverson and, most recently, Sprewell.

The Fab Five and Nelson controversies were long ago, after all, and Webber has since led his team to the playoffs and is having his best year this season, even as his team hovers at the .500 mark: eighth in the league in scoring at nearly 22 points per game, over 9 rebounds a game. It is a foregone conclusion that, though the reserves haven't been

*Perhaps the most comprehensive compendium of playa-hating can be found in writer Mike Lupica's 1996 lament *Mad as Hell: How Sports Got Away from the Fans—And How We Get It Back:* "They don't act like men at all, they act like spoiled, willful children," he writes, providing scant evidence for such sweeping charges. "It's about face. The Pose. The way things look. It's a world that has nothing to do with the fans, or even the games. Just the show one player is putting on for another." Rants like these beg the question: Why not start chronicling something you really *like?*

selected yet, he is about to make his second consecutive All-Star Game appearance, and he will play for USA Basketball in the World Games this summer.

Things should be good, but here he sits, in his home just minutes from the USAir Arena, where the Wizards played their games before the opening of the MCI Center two months ago, and he readies himself for a playa-hating on-slaught. He tries not to read the attacks, but he hears about them. He hears about them in his daily calls home to Detroit, where he talks to everyone in the household and relishes getting caught up to speed on the twists and turns of his brother David's season. A senior at Country Day, Chris's alma mater, David is widely considered one of the best high school point guards in the country. Every week Chris sends him a VCR tape, spliced together by the Wizards' staff, of the best moves laid on the opposition by *his* point guard, Rod Strickland, David's idol. Chris loves these phone calls home, getting to hear David's excited patter about his team, recognizing his brother's ambition and love for the game that—if you're not careful—can get lost at the pro level.

Still, he worries about David, as he has all his life. As the oldest, Webber spent his formative years helping raise his siblings, doing all he could to help out his mom and dad, who were often both exhausted when they weren't working. Growing up, Chris was both protector and caretaker. At an early age, he changed diapers, cooked dinner, shopped for groceries. All five Webber kids often slept in the same bed—until Chris grew to take up an entire one himself—even though they each had their own.

Now, sitting in his living room, the artwork of African American artist Eddie Barnes adorning the walls and his two green tree pythons in an aquarium before him—he bought the snakes to cure his fear of them, and it's worked—he listens to David's breathless play-by-play and worries that his brother might want it all *too* much. When Chris goes home summers, it's all he can do to keep up with David in workouts; he loves that, because his brother's enthusiasm pushes him, too. And he also knows that since he's realized his dream of making it to the pros, he'd give up this life in a heartbeat if it meant David would get his.

Because sometimes the dream isn't all that. Like now, when in one of his conversations with one of his siblings, there's a terse mention of something somebody wrote somewhere about him, and he detects the hurt in the voice of his family member, a resigned tone that he knows all too well.

Now that the playa-haters are on his case again, he knows, his family is in store for more instances where what they read or hear doesn't conform to what they know about him.

It started last month, a couple of weeks before New Year's, when Webber's teammates, Strickland and Tracy Murray, got into a fistfight in a Charlotte hotel lobby after it got back to Strickland, through a female mutual acquaintance, that Murray had called him a "faggot."* The publicity furthered the perception of the Wizards as a collection of dysfunctional malcontents, confirming for many that the team was sorely in need of mature leadership.

The Wizards continued to win nonetheless. A week and a half into the New Year they were on a roll, having won fourteen of twenty and ten of eleven at the MCI Center. With ten seconds left in a close game against Boston, Juwan Howard called timeout—a timeout the Wizards didn't have. The Celtics got a technical foul shot, the ball at midcourt, and a chance to win the game, but first Webber reacted in a way that infuriated those along press row, if not the fans: He broke out laughing. Without having to reference the infamous nonexistent timeout he tried to call at the end of the

*_The Washington Post_, with hardly any internal debate, according to beat writer Ric Bucher, printed Murray's remark as the fight's impetus; when asked whether that constitutes a new policy at the _Post_ regarding publishing speculation about newsmakers' sexual lives, Bucher explained that the charge was really meant as an insult and not as an allegation of fact. Strickland would not speak to Bucher for about a month.

1993 NCAA title game, he said to Howard, "Welcome to the club." Then the two laughed, right there on the court, with the game on the line.

The next day *Washington Post* columnist Thomas Boswell wrote about the scene: "The byplay between Webber and Howard was easy to understand. They acted like high-spirited, cheerful friends teasing each other. They acted like most people would. But should they have acted this way?" He quoted Webber: "I was laughing (because) I knew we were going to win. . . . And it wasn't a championship game." A championship game he lost, it should be remembered, thanks to his own inexcusable mental gaffe.

Boswell's column was nuanced, going on to credit Webber in a number of areas, but he nonetheless questioned whether Webber really learned his lesson from the '93 fiasco. The Wizards' PR office, knowing of Webber's sensitivity on the issue, didn't show him the column. When he was told about it, tears came to his eyes.

"How dare a guy write an article like that," he said, his voice quavering. "How dare he get into that issue, 'cause he wasn't in the locker room that day. That makes me want to just slap him upside the head, 'cause no one knows the seriousness of what I went through. That writer's never been in a position like that, where forty million people saw you make the biggest mistake of your life. I deal with that every day. That's why I want a championship so bad. It all stems from that. Because of all the people I want to say screw you to, who called us underachievers from '93 on. Then, once I win a championship, you watch what happens. These same guys will be like, 'In 1982 Chris helped a little old lady across the street. Isn't he a great guy?' "

Judging by the publicity he's gotten lately, it will be quite a while before he's portrayed as a great guy. It was the story of the day on January 20: Chris Webber's arrest. He was on his way to practice when his Navigator was pulled over in Prince George's County, minutes from his home, for doing 70 miles per hour in a 50 m.p.h. zone. Coincidentally, he was on the phone with his agent, lawyer Fallasha Erwin, at the time. When the officer, a twenty-three-year-old named Raymond Kane, asked for his license and registration, Webber couldn't provide them. He'd left his wallet at home.

"God, that was stupid," Webber says now.

Kane did not recognize Webber. "I'm Chris Webber, I play for the Bullets, and I'm on the way to practice," Webber told him, getting the name of his team wrong—like many, he still had not adjusted to the new moniker. When Kane went back to his squad car to run a check of Webber's Michigan license plates, the registered owners' name came back Mayce Edward Christopher Webber II, Chris's full name. Kane was suspicious enough to order him from the car and advise him that the Navigator would be impounded. Webber asked Erwin if his car could really be impounded for not having his license and registration.

While Webber spoke to his agent, Kane reached through the window and began trying to open the door, which was locked. Webber says that in the process, Kane repeatedly hit him in the thigh. Then Kane reached inside for the lock and opened the door; Webber says he held him off with an outstretched arm while still in his seat belt—as he asked Erwin what he should do. Kane claims Webber slapped him, which Webber denies: "C'mon, at least give me some credit," he says. "Say I stole your gun and threw it into the middle of the highway."

They both agree on what happened next: There came a hissing sound.

"Fallasha, I'm being sprayed! I'm being maced!" Webber yelled, suddenly blinded.

Held for six hours, he was charged with three misdemeanors and six traffic offenses, including resisting arrest, speeding, and driving under the influence of a controlled, dangerous substance: marijuana. (Police dogs would later find a marijuana roach under a seat and "marijuana residue" in the car.) Though Webber passed a Breathalyzer test, someone called a "drug recognition expert"—an officer trained to detect whether one is stoned based on indicators such as pupil dilation—examined Webber and found him to be under the influence of marijuana. Drug recognition experts are, due to the sheer subjectivity of their job, controversial by nature. They rarely, if ever, testify at a trial and are usually a step along the way in pro-forma plea bargainings. But there was little that was run-of-the-mill in this case. Webber says there was good reason for his pupil dilation, bloodshot eyes, and dizziness: He had just been maced.

"It was nine-thirty in the morning and I was on my way to practice," he says. "I wasn't high, I wasn't drunk."

But now the playa-haters had ample ammunition. In the Wizards' next game, a home loss to Portland in which Webber scored 20 points and grabbed 12 boards, he was booed during the introductions.

The condemnation was swift and wide. In the *Post*, Boswell wrote: "What do you call it when Chris Webber is charged with three misdemeanors, plus six more traffic offenses—nine violations—in a single day? A triple-triple." He went on: "When you act like a fake outlaw, you shouldn't be surprised when you're treated like one. If you've got the drugs in the car, if you're way over the speed limit, if you've got an attitude with the cops, how are they supposed to know that you're just a rich young jock who's play-acting until he figures out who he is?" It's a good point, but, as Webber sees it, what makes Boswell's column an illustration of playa-hating is not only the preoccupation with the money he earns, but this: Webber has no idea who Boswell is. To the best of his recollection, they've never spoken, at least not in any meaningful way. "How can Boswell imply he knows about me," Webber argues, "that he knows I'm trying to figure out who I am, when he doesn't have the balls to ask me, man-to-man?"

One of Boswell's colleagues at the *Post*, Michael Wilbon, joined the pile-on, penning a column headlined WIZARDS' BIG THREE ARE A BIG DISAPPOINTMENT that takes Strickland, Howard, and Webber to task because now all three, in the last fourteen months, have been arrested either for driving when intoxicated or driving without a license, a reasonable criticism. But then he descends into playa-hating generalizations: "The culture now surrounding sports encourages more emphasis on driving a 'phat' recreational vehicle than becoming the best basketball player you can be. Living 'Big Willie-style' is more important than taking some extra shots after practice."

It's a critique that cuts to Webber's heart. Now, lounging around the house in his FILA T-shirt and shorts, idly thumbing through a coffee table book entitled *I Dream a World: Portraits of Black Women Who Changed America* that includes one-page profiles of Coretta Scott King, Johnetta Coles, and Barbara Jordan, he speaks in a depressed monotone. "These guys don't know how much I love the game, how much I want to win a championship," he says, noting that he is, in fact, almost always the last guy to leave practice. "Because they don't want to know. They're not interested."

Meantime, nationwide, Webber has rejoined the list of NBA bad boys, back there in the same mentions with Spree and Iverson and Portland's Isaiah Rider, who was convicted last fall of possession of an unregistered cell phone and possession of marijuana.

Missing from the press accounts of Webber's arrest is any attempt, even in passing, to give context to an African American getting arrested in Prince George's County. Webber is convinced he was pulled over because he was a black man driving an expensive sport utility vehicle. (He says he wasn't going twenty miles over the speed limit and that Kane admitted to him that he somehow evaded a radar trap.) Over the last decade, the Prince George's County police have been embroiled in a series of controversies surrounding its treatment of African Americans. There has long been criticism of the force's alleged brutality and alleged quick resort to the use of pepper spray on African Americans.

Webber has been heartened to learn that, though little of this background found its way into the reporting of his arrest, fans—particularly African American fans—know what's up. They come up to him and share their stories, explaining that they too have been pulled over and hassled and sometimes even maced in the same vicinity. They urge him to sue.

He may, he says. Of course, that runs the risk of prolonging bad publicity. But nothing could be worse than letting go unchallenged the new "evidence" play-haters are using against him. Last week, none other than Don Nelson, seizing the moment, got into the act.

"From day one, Chris didn't respect authority," Nelson said after Webber's arrest in widely publicized comments. "He was the number-one pick and he felt everyone should treat him like it regardless. You don't have to like the coach, but you have to respect the uniform. You don't have to like the cop, but you've got to respect the uniform. Chris just doesn't. He measures people's success by their checkbooks. It's sad."

Webber just shakes his head. There's the money thing again—a telltale sign of playa-hating. But Nelson's good. He knows what buttons to push. He knows that Webber prides himself on his love "for the people," on how he'd "rather be a people's champion than a media darling." Painting Webber as some sort of moneyed elitist works on two counts: It needles Webber and carries currency in a press so eager to portray Gen X athletes as valuing nothing but their piles of cash.

Yet it makes Webber angry at himself, not Nelson. The last time the Wizards played at Dallas, Nelson cornered him and extended an olive branch, even told Chris how much he liked him. Now this. Now Webber feels like a sucker. "This just proves that he is a fake man," he says. "I fell for it again and he just had the same agenda. He's going to keep on having that agenda. He's going to hate me for as long as he's in this league."

The conventional wisdom couldn't be more clear about Chris Webber: It's a problem of character. At the same time that the punditocracy is lambasting Webber, Barkley, Maxwell, and others in these most personal of terms, there is an added irony: On one level, behind all the moralistic denunciations, lies a vague insistence that our athletes somehow lead us in moral instruction when, in fact, they are arguably the least equipped among us to do so.

Yes, our athletes make for wonderful metaphor; in every game-winning Jordan jumper, after all, there is a lesson about hard work and perseverance and stirring self-confidence. But in the final analysis, they are prodigies and they come with all the trappings; many have been sheltered and coddled and protected, so it should come as no surprise that the very attribute that allows them to perform at such a high level athletically—their single-mindedness—manifests itself in self-absorption away from the field of play.

And, irony on top of irony, when that rare jock comes along who is willing to take a stand for something beyond the orbit of his own celebrity, be it Ali speaking out against Vietnam or Barkley on the press's role model myopia, he gets derided, not celebrated. Sure, Ali is beloved now, when his voice is silent. But for nearly five years after he changed his name and became Muslim, even the venerable *New York Times*, a supposed bastion of '60s liberalism, referred to him as Cassius Clay.

"It's funny to see how people worship Ali now," says Webber, who, like Barkley, considers the boxing great his hero. "People hated him. They were like, 'He dodged the draft, he's anti-America, he's antiwhite, he believes in Allah.'

Now you realize that he's still a good person, that nothing's changed except the outlook back at that time."

In fact, Webber is a student of the athlete's role in the larger cultural landscape. He is a surprising exception to the self-absorbed jock rule, surprising because, unlike Barkley, he was raised as a prodigy. From eighth grade on, when the first TV news story on him aired, he was recruited by major college coaches. Stardom was expected. Yet he understood early on that life and basketball are not synonomous and he pointedly strove to develop a social conscience, just as his two favorite athletes, Ali and Barkley, had. That this Chris Webber, the one with the passion for social issues, is largely missing from the Chris Webber given to us through the sports media filter is a continuing source of frustration.

Webber's world view is rooted in lessons learned from his mother, his father, his white teacher at Detroit Country Day, and, quite inadvertently, "Doo-Doo Danny."

Doo-Doo Danny was a kid in Doris Webber's daycare, which she ran out of the household between 1979 and 1985. It was there that Chris saw the practical applications of all his mother's church-based aphorisms. Doris's reminders to her children filled the air. "The more you're given, the more that's demanded of you," she'd say. "If God gives you a great blessing, it's a great responsibility." The Webbers weren't wealthy by any stretch of the imagination, but, with both parents working, they were better off than many in their circle and Doris's selflessness left a lasting impression on a ten-year-old Chris.

Doo-Doo Danny got his nickname from the other kids because he smelled. It was a particularly rough winter in Detroit that year and Danny didn't have a coat. Chris had just gotten his first Starter jacket—a white Yankees model. It cost $80 and he had longed for it for years. And Doris gave it to Doo-Doo Danny. Like any ten-year-old, Chris was confused and incensed. But gradually, it started to soak in.

"There were a whole bunch of situations like that, where

I went from being mad to seeing that my mother wasn't slighting us," Webber recalls. "I was, like, 'Hold on. I see. You help others first because you can.' My mother is a church woman and if there was ever a problem in the family of any church member, if a marriage went bad, she'd take in the kids or the wife. My parents are very selfless. I believe God had blessed me with the NBA, fame, and money because of them. Not because of anything I did."

Mayce Webber was born on a plantation in Mississippi, the grandson of a slave. Now fifty-two, he has, throughout the years, been frank with his eldest son about the troubles he's seen, though always with a lack of the bitterness one might expect. He's told stories about dropping out of school in the sixth grade to go to work picking cotton. Slavery might have ended, but Mayce saw its legacy every time the plantation owners disrespected his father in front of his own kids. He's told Chris stories about hearing, as a seven-year-old, the terror-laced whispers that another black man had been hung downtown. He's told stories about the first time he set eyes on an automobile—when he was eighteen and fled Mississippi for Michigan, where he found work at the auto factory.

And he's been careful to convey other lessons, too. About how easy it would be to hate, that not all white people are bad. "I remember my father telling us that there had to be some black people selling us in Africa, too," Chris recalls. "There had to be some black people in Africa who made a deal with somebody, you know? So corruption and immorality know no color."

At Doris's insistence, Chris attended Country Day, where the other kids drove to school in their own Camaros and Porsches. A few black students, mainly athletes, were mixed in, including Chris and Kevin Colson, his point guard in high school and still one of his closest friends today. Doris knew that Chris's basketball future would be better served by playing for an inner-city hoops powerhouse, but academics had always been stressed in the Webber household. And Country Day was a renowned prep school.

It was there that Chris joined Mr. Carlson's Social Awareness Club. After school, he and other students would study and actively debate a host of public issues. Based on information garnered from Amnesty International, they wrote letters to third world dictators who denied human rights and they wrote to governors, mayors, legislators, and parole boards in support of those who the ACLU claimed had been denied their civil liberties. They worked to save the rainforest and embarked upon a local recycling campaign.

And they studied the Holocaust. They went to the National Holocaust Museum just outside of Detroit and visited Jewish cemeteries. Chris was mesmerized when they visited the home of one prominent Jewish philanthropist and saw a collection of photographs of 200,000 charred and emaciated bodies piled one on top of another at the Bitburg cemetery. Chris, recoiling, asked why, why would anyone keep a shrine to such horror in his home? And the answer instantly resonated. "Because these painful memories are really something you have to hold on to. Because they are who I am. Because we can never forget."

It sounded a lot like something Mayce would say about the horrors his own eyes had seen, in this country. From then on, Chris and Mr. Carlson forged a bond; the two stayed in close contact throughout Chris's Fab Five days, often discussing the issues of the world, not basketball. Just after signing his first NBA contract, Webber told Mr. Carlson he was embarking on his own quest to build something out of painful memories, so as to never forget.

He began by buying slave tools in Mississippi, artifacts that had been lying around barns for years but that, a century ago, had been used to pick cotton and plow fields. He found slave shackles and bought them. He purchased a postcard sent by Malcolm X to Alex Haley in 1964 from Mecca. "I think the CIA's watching me," Malcolm wrote.

The collection expanded: There came an original book of writings belonging to inventor Eli Whitney, followed by the handwritten letters of Frederick Douglass.

"One day I'd like to open my own museum or have my own wing in a museum," Webber says. "Or start a traveling museum that can really show kids things, to bring their history to life for them. You know, show them 'Here are some little things about this person, he wasn't perfect, but he did great things, and you can, too.' To show them they have something to be proud of besides athletes and entertainers and drug dealers who drive nice cars. To show them their history is rich. 'Look at these people who are in your blood.' "

As a professional athlete, Webber has looked for ways to live his social vision. Of course, he does the obligatory charity thing, donating a large sum for every rebound this season to children's causes, underwriting scholarships. But that's easy: He has his people write a check for him. The harder part is walking the talk.

Coming out of college, Webber signed a lucrative endorsement deal with Nike, which featured him in a national commercial his rookie year. Nike wasn't particularly pleased with the controversy that characterized that season and Webber wasn't entirely ecstatic about the company's stable of stars in front of him, including Jordan, Barkley, and Penny Hardaway.

So when the initial contract came up for renewal, there were issues of a business nature. But Webber also had an ethical qualm that he announced from the start could be a deal-breaker: the cost of the shoes, which was in the $150 range.

"Man, I can't even afford your shoes," one of his cousins told him. Webber, who often says, "I'm a Pisces, I'm a thinker," typically brooded over the exchange for days. He remembered when his parents couldn't afford the "in" shoe

and he had to play a whole year wearing New Balance.
There was no escaping it: He felt like a hypocrite.

Worse, during that summer of '94, kids in Detroit playgrounds were literally being killed for their Air Jordans and
leather jackets; one Webber acquaintance, Mike Hamm, was
shot and killed for his shoes.

Webber announced he wouldn't re-sign with Nike and
was quoted as saying that the company was exploiting
inner-city black youth. "There was just no way, because of
the way I was raised, that I could have done anything else,"
he says. "And I loved the shoes. And Nike's a great company. And I miss the endorsements. But I had to face
myself."

Nike wasn't happy. "They felt I was trying to tell them
how to run their business, I guess," he says. "I felt they
were trying to tell me how to live my life, what my values
should be."

To Webber, it was one of those instances when he has,
as he puts, consciously chosen to "live the life of Ali." "I
want people to know that I am for them," he says. "The
people knew that Ali would stand up for them. That he was
with them. And I want them to know that about me. And
a lot of times, they can read between the lines."

Like when he snubbed the biggest agents in the business
in favor of Erwin, a black attorney from Detroit who had
never represented a professional athlete. Throughout the
league, black agents are scarce, as more and more players
opt for white—often Jewish—lawyers. (Johnnie Cochran and
rappers Master P and Puff Daddy are beginning to get into
the sports agent business; part of their pitch is keeping the
money in the community.) Webber turned down the likes
of David Falk (Howard's agent), for a principle. "The David
Falks are great agents, but being the number-one pick, I
thought it was my responsibility to put a minority in that
place," he says. "For black lawyers like Fallasha, they must
say, 'I'm never gonna get picked because I'm black.' So I

wanted to give somebody a chance, which would give black lawyers everywhere some encouragement. And it's not like Fallasha isn't good. He's one of the best agents around."

Ever since his arrival on the public stage as a collegian, Chris Webber has spent a good deal of time ruminating on the central paradox of his life, the gulf between his private self—the Chris Webber who speaks so passionately about social problems—and the public image that comes across to the average sports fan.

He has entertained the possibility that it may have something to do with a media that has yet to figure out how to present an educated, middle-class black athlete to us, someone who eschews speaking in the time-honored clichés, someone who has the audacity to comment on matters beyond his sport, someone who defies so many of the stereotypes media has perpetuated. Webber is hardly the only black athlete who gets a warped press: Football's Ricky Watters and baseball's Albert Belle, for example, are also educated, middle-class guys whose questionable behavior has led to a portrait of them as menacing thugs.

Yes, thinking back, Webber recognizes how conventional wisdom gets made. Case in point: one of Webber's first games after his 1997 appearance on an ESPN forum on sports and race, moderated by Ted Koppel, where he acquitted himself admirably, even yelling at one point at football coach Gene Stallings, "The only time you come to the ghetto is to recruit players!"

He'd just had a monster game, but he was still buzzing from talking about race and justice and morality on national television. Somehow, standing in a towel in front of his locker, Webber's comments about the game segued into an observation on racial tolerance. "It's not just about black and white," he said. "We're all afraid of difference. You know, you see an Indian with a dot on his head and you make a joke, instead of asking what that means. Instead of using it as a way to get educated, to learn about somebody else."

He paused. In front of him, the reporters had stopped taking notes. The microcassette recorders were paused. Dumbfounded looks gazed back at him. He wasn't talking jump shots, so the myopic pack, so focused on the ball, wasn't paying attention.

But, ultimately, he knows media-bashing is a copout. More and more lately, when the issue of who he is in the public eye bounces around his head, he cautions himself about pointing fingers. "A lot of it is my fault, too." Webber says now. His personal assistant, Julie, is in the kitchen, putting out a spread of food. "I'm more introverted now, because I feel like if I open up about what I'm really passionate about, it's like throwing my shit in the air so guys can take shots at it on the way down."

He gets up to amble into the kitchen, stretching his long, tired frame. And then he comes back to the point he always returns to. Win and you are free to be yourself. That's why the upcoming All-Star Game will be critical for him; as his second in a row, it will establish him as a legitimate star in this league. A second consecutive trip to the playoffs would cement the deal.

As he sits down to eat, pausing to silently say grace, there is no doubt in Chris Webber's mind that the troubles of this season are behind him. And in the horizon, a lifetime of parlaying his prowess on the court into humanitarian works, the playa-haters be damned.

11

the beast in the 'hood

puffy and Mase are cranked, singing about how more problems tend to come with more money, and everybody is singing along, most of them wildly off-key. Allen is crooning while he cooks up a stir-fry, Fen is howling while he readies the bottle of tequila, and Drake is softly mouthing the lyrics while he wrestles with Rendo. Stack is the one in perfect pitch as he thumbs through a *Sports Illustrated* at the kitchen table in the sprawling home he, Shondra, Jay Alexander, and the posse have just rented in the Detroit suburb of Troy.

"Mo Money, Mo Problems" may be one of the anthems of this NBA season, but, in the month since he was traded to the Pistons, there is a distinct lack of problems in Stack's house. "I got teeth," he announced when I first saw him before last night's game, and, indeed, he has been a perpetual smile ever since. He's starting—thanks, in part, to an injury to Lindsey Hunter—and averaging nearly 19 points per game. Last night, he scored his average in a blowout versus the Spree-less Golden State Warriors, though he shot only five for fourteen.

His shooting has, in fact, dropped off since joining the Pistons, but his scoring has gone up, thanks to the up-tempo game Coach Doug Collins has been preaching. Hill and Stackhouse in the open court are something to behold; last night, Hill had 9 assists and Stackhouse 5, many of those to each other on the fast break. Still, the team is merely .500 since the trade and Hill and Stackhouse haven't meshed yet in the half-court offense.

The Pistons are off today and face the Clippers tomorrow night. So tonight there is a small window of opportunity to celebrate. And there is much to be thankful for. On New Year's Day, a suit from the Pistons' front office came to practice bearing an envelope with Stackhouse's name on it. It was his paycheck. In full.

Stackhouse's contract calls for him to be paid his entire salary—about $3 million this season—on the first of the year. Now he high-fives Allen as he tells his buddy about his favorite practice of the year.

"They had to give me two checks, 'cause that bitch was too big a number for just one check," Stackhouse exclaims, laughing.

This makeshift Stack family—all six of them—has spent the last couple of days moving in. Boxes are strewn throughout the living room. Shondra sets about organizing the place, holding Jay all the while, who sucks on a pacifier and coos at his daddy.

"Talked to my mom," Stack, taking a respite from the jocularity, says to Shondra. "She didn't have a good day yesterday."

The first things unpacked grace the wall and mantel: a portrait of Minnie Stackhouse and a framed photo of Jerry and Minnie. He frowns when he updates Shondra on his mother's health. Should anything happen to her, he knows, it would be the greatest possible test of his taciturn composure. From her, he inherited the quality he likes best about himself: his piety. For more than the last fifteen years, Minnie Stackhouse has been the pastor at Foster Chapel Baptist, a small country church where Jerry perfected his gospel-singing.

From both parents, he learned the value of hard work. Minnie was head cook at the Surf and Turf, where Jerry washed dishes as a teenager, and George spent twenty-six years driving a sanitation truck for the city of Kinston. In countless ways, whether it was George's eloquently dogged example or Minnie's excessive praise for his dishwashing, Jerry got the message from his parents, both children of sharecroppers: There is value in work. He grew up knowing that if he worked at something, they'd support him.

That's why it was a foregone conclusion that his mother would let him leave Kinston High to play his senior year at the fabled Oak Hill Academy, a basketball factory. He'd worked so hard, he deserved to go to the school that would give him with the widest range of options. But then the criticisms—about how he was abandoning his school—came and he can still recall how much it hurt when the school administrator complained that Stackhouse bolting for prep school would cost the public school some $100,000. It was the first time he felt like nothing more than a commodity, but his mother was in his ear the whole time, making sure he knew he was somebody.

And she's continued to be there. During his freshman year at North Carolina, when Coach Dean Smith had a veteran lineup of seniors and was bringing the heralded Stackhouse off the bench, it was his mother who straightened him out when he thought about quitting over playing time, pointing out that he wouldn't want some freshman taking his minutes when *he* became a senior. "You put yourself in those other players' place," she told him.

Three years ago, when her son was a rookie, Minnie was

instrumental in forming the Mothers of Professional Basketball Players, a support group for women whose sons play
in the NBA. The idea came out of a lunch Minnie had with
the mothers of a handful of other NBA players—there was
Shawn Kemp's mother, Gary Payton's, Jason Kidd's; Charlotte Brandon, Terrell's mother, became MPBP president.
Also active in the group are Doris Webber; Janet Hill,
Grant's mom; and Lucille Harrison, Shaquille O'Neal's
mother. When their famous young sons are on the road,
they commiserate over the risks and pitfalls. Plus, no matter
where Jerry is, Minnie knows he is just a phone call away
from a home-cooked meal and a de facto mom.

The posse, though widely derided, is another form of
support. It has become something of a phenomenon in the
'90s: NBA players traveling with entourages. But, given that
Stack has felt like a commodity since high school, given that
he's rarely met anyone in the last five years who didn't want
something from him, it makes sense that he'd surround himself with the guys who knew him before he was a star. The
same is true of Webber, who hangs with Kevin Colson, or
Maloney, who knows his brother is watching his back. But
when it's a white athlete, the practice isn't so loudly
condemned.

"If [Philadelphia hockey star] Eric Lindros hangs with a
few of his friends, it's Eric and his buddies," Stack said
after the reports of a posse fight between the Stackhouse
and Iverson camps appeared. "If it's a couple of my friends
or relatives, wearing their caps backward, it's a posse, like
they're thugs. I think that's racist."

Webber, who has taken his share of posse-directed barbs,
adds, "What people need to realize is that a guy like Jerry
is going to get married someday soon. He's just living with
some guys right now. You know, you can't go grocery-shop-
ping for yourself. And especially the first couple of years,
it's lonely. I know I needed somebody my first two seasons."

Indeed, Allen, Fen, and Drake perform innumerable services for Stack. Tomorrow, for instance, someone will get groceries, someone will get Jerry's Rolex repaired, and someone—probably Shondra—will find a pediatrician. Most important, he can talk hoops with them and get his ego stroked, as when talk turns to the upcoming All-Star Game fan balloting. In the East, Jordan, of course, has one guard spot locked up. The leading vote-getter at the other guard position is Penny Hardaway, even though he's been sidelined with an injury all season.

"It's all a popularity contest," Stackhouse says. "You talk to anyone who tries to guard him and they'll tell you that Rod Strickland can bust anybody's ass—"

"And he ain't gettin' no votes," barks Allen.

"Rodman too, man," chimes in Fen. "That nigga can ball."

"That's what I'm saying, it don't matter if you can ball or not," Stackhouse says. "It's easier to make it if you're a guard out West, because you've got Michael and Penny in the East. And just judging by his statistics this year, Grant probably doesn't deserve to make it."

It's 6 P.M. Time to do some shots. There's a bottle of Rémy, but Fen has opened the tequila. We each do two throat-burning, tear-inducing shots. Though the group is ecstatic about being in Detroit, my presence seems to have prompted some reconsideration of Stackhouse's time in Philly.

"I'm rooting for them not to win another game, man," Stackhouse says. "Not because of the guys on the team. I love those guys. But for how they let my shit drag on. I was being traded for a year and a half. No one in my class had to go through what I went through. I mean, even now, Joe Smith might get traded from Golden State, but that's a new thing. He didn't have to live with that uncertainty. You know what I'm saying?"

One of the guys mumbles something about Larry Brown, who, just before the trade, announced his surprise that Stack

had a post-up game. Yet when he was hired, he claimed to
have watched hours of footage of Stackhouse's game his first
two seasons, when some argued he posted up *too* much. To
Stack's support group, it was just more proof that Brown
didn't deal with their man straight-up.

"But Brown is getting great press in Philly," I counter.

"You know why?" Stack jumps in, eager to have the last
word on the coach who, he claims, barely acknowledged
his mother when Minnie Stackhouse visited Philadelphia.
" 'Cause he's an arrogant asshole, just like them in the
media. Yeah, he knows his X's and O's, but coaches don't
play the game. The best coach I've had so far was Luke
[John Lucas], because you could talk to him and he'd listen.
Right now, I'd say Pat Riley is the only one who makes a
difference, 'cause he runs his own ship, does things his way,
and he wins."

Stack takes one more shot. Then he makes a phone call
and changes into a PELLE PELLE sweatshirt and jeans while
the fellas put on their Tommy Gear hats, an elastic, stock-
inglike cap that is all the rage this winter. Shondra affection-
ately runs her hands over Stack's scalp, but he pulls away,
trying to look cool in front of the guys. He kisses Jay and
we're out, on our way to the 'hood.

After he was the first pick in the 1990 NBA draft and
signed a multimillion-dollar contract with the New Jersey
Nets, Derrick Coleman made a decision: Just because he suddenly had money, that didn't mean he'd be wanted in the
suburbs. So he did the next best thing: He told his mother
he'd bring the burbs to her. He bought a few of the houses
on the block where he grew up on Detroit's West Side, at
12 Street and Rosa Parks Boulevard, renovated them for
himself and his mother—"my inspiration," he calls her—
and his extended family, including Po, his stocky, gregarious cousin.

From the outside, the Coleman inner-city estate looks

like any other series of modest row houses on this inner-
city block. Except, that is, for the three-foot-high gate in front
that seems to be an urban approximation of the stereotypical
picket fence—"Man, this be like a gated community," Fen
says—and the full-size basketball court at the end of the
driveway, behind the houses, complete with the finest in
backboards and breakaway rims. It is for neighborhood use
and its condition is eye-opening; no graffiti, no mess.

"Yo, Stack!" Po calls, rushing outside. "D.C. told me to
look out for you, man. How you been?"

Inside, immaculately modern furnishings give off the feel
of new money. The living room has black and white leather
sofas and chairs and mirrored walls. Every item looks
brand-new, polished, and placed just so. Downstairs, in the
basement, leather coats are piled in the corner, on sale, Po
says, for $300 each. There are about fifteen guys milling
about, some watching the movie *Face-Off* on the big-screen
TV while a few of us head into the sauna to smoke a blunt,
a cigar packed full of marijuana. Stack sees a ball and grabs
it, idly dribbling, while Po begins telling hoop tales of his
neighborhood.

There are a few renowned basketball neighborhoods in
America, and Detroit's West Side is one of them. These very
streets have produced, among others, Coleman, Webber,
Howard, Jalen Rose, and Steve Smith. Nearby is St. Cecilia's
gym, where all these players return in the summers to go
to war, often joined by the likes of Magic Johnson (who
played pickup ball on these streets as a boy growing up in
Lansing, Michigan) and Isiah Thomas; the summer games
in St. Cecilia's shoebox of a gym are local legend, complete
with trash-talking and hard fouls far rougher than those in
the NBA.

Yes, the guys here in the 'hood can only laugh when
they read the so-called experts whining that Coleman or
Webber care only about the money and not about compet-
ing. They laugh because they've been there, packed tightly

into St. Cecilia's, where there are no cameras or writers and where they've seen both guys dive for loose balls and bang so hard they've almost come to blows, and then, afterward, they've seen them return to Coleman's house, where his mother will feed the lot of them. Not caring? Hell, they remember when Webber was in high school and Coleman was in college and D.C. stopped speaking to his protégé— for two years. It wasn't until both were stars in the NBA that Coleman explained he was starting to like Webber too much and didn't want anything—even friendship—to jeopardize their intense competition against one another.

Today, though, they remember the guys who didn't make it out. "Man, there are about five guys in this neighborhood that could be balling in the NBA right now," says Po. They all start naming names and the stories start flying. The kid who went to Norfolk State, who hurdled guys when they tried to draw charges. The dude from around the block who was crossing guys over before anyone called it a crossover. The point guard from down the boulevard who was more of a blur than Iverson. None of them made it; some got hurt, some got waylaid by drugs, some couldn't make the grades.

Stack is wandering around the basement, still dribbling, when Allen and Fen start talking about their own hometown legend who didn't make the NBA: T.D., as in Tony Dawson, Stackhouse's older brother. Fen nods toward Stack. "Why you think he became the Beast?" he says. "He had a brother who was the Beast!"

"There's not nobody in this league that can stop him from scoring," Stack says, overhearing. "My bro was the best scorer I knew, growing up. He got those ten-day contracts here and there, but it was always a situation where they had to let somebody go and he was the last one brought on, you know what I'm saying?"

He pauses, thinking back to all those moves his older brother put on him, how automatic he could be. He smiles when he thinks of the family reunions when all the brothers would ball up and he'd get a chance to show what he could do, a chance to show what his brothers had taught him. But then a glance at his watch breaks his reverie. It's nine-thirty. Time for detox to start.

"Can I interest you in a bottle of champagne?" our waitress asks.

We're at Ruth's Chris Steak House for dinner, half an hour after bolting Po's. Stack loves champagne, but he solemnly shakes his head no. So do Allen, Fen, and Drake. The shootaround is at eleven tomorrow morning and the game is at seven, so this is it. He's allowed himself four hours of partying. "My detox has started," Stack says.

Stackhouse orders the Porterhouse steak for two, a Fred Flintstone–type slab of meat that he slathers in tabasco and Worcestershire sauce. "I like flavor," he explains.

Meantime, his pals start doing impressions of one of their marble-mouthed high school coaches, who used to complain about them farting on the "raggedy-ass van" they'd take to games. "I'm gonna turn this muthafucka around!" Allen says in an exaggerated Southern drawl and Stackhouse laughs so hard steak hangs from his mouth as he holds his stomach.

The next night he and Hill are in synch on the fast break. Stack scores 20 points on six or thirteen shooting and dishes out 8 assists; Hill goes for 33 points, 10 rebounds, and 6 assists. They beat the lowly Clippers by twenty-eight.

But it doesn't matter. The whispers along press row are about when—not if—Doug Collins will be let go. He's lost both Hill and Dumars and the Stackhouse acquisition hasn't made a drastic enough impact on the bottom line to compensate. Quite remarkably, any day now, Stackhouse could find himself introduced to his fifth pro coach in a career that is but two and a half years old.

After the game, though, he is feeling good. We reminisce

about his first extended road trip in the NBA, about how wide-eyed he was, how he'd wade for hours through the autograph-seekers, how he fed off the adulation. "I'm getting back to that joyousness now," he says, his face lighting up. "Back to having fun and playing basketball. For a long time, I lost that feeling of having fun on the basketball court. I forgot that a game is supposed to be fun. This feels good."

As he's talking, a gaunt and pale Doug Collins scurries past, looking tense. He doesn't seem like a coach who has just won a basketball game. As Jerry Stackhouse elaborates on his soaring mood, it becomes clear: Its greatest exacerbater might just be the fate of his coach.

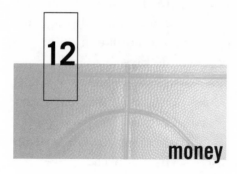

12

money

it's nine days till All-Star weekend and there is a consensus among players around the league on one thing: The break can't come soon enough. By now, the average NBA player has logged some 25,000 miles of air travel and accumulated more aches and bruises than the rest of us experience in a lifetime. The jump shots are starting to hit the front rim, a sign of weary legs, and concentration lags are leading to an upsurge in turnovers, a sign of mental fatigue.

No wonder Barkley publicly—and successfully—campaigned for the fans to leave him off their ballots. The days between February 5 and 10 are the grind's only respite. Still, Chris Webber would trade all of the rest that the All-Star weekend promises for the chance to play in the game.

On the day that the reserves are named, Webber is in Indiana to play the Pacers. He's still confident he'll make it—his numbers are impeccable—but a momentary doubt crosses his mind when he boards the team bus at 6 P.M. en route to Market Square Arena. He settles into his seat and has just put his headphones on when Nicole Addison of the Wizards' PR office approaches.

"Chris, I don't know if you heard," she says softly, pausing to gauge whether this is old news to him by now. She can't tell. "But you didn't make it."

There is silence as Webber sits there, impassive. After a moment, he speaks. "Well," he says, in an even, stoic tone. "At least Rod made it."

Nicole, in her first year on the job, feels a lump forming in her throat. "No, Rod didn't make it either," she says. Later, she will recall that her voice cracked delivering this news.

Webber shakes his head, puts his headphones back on. By the end of the bus ride, he's given himself a pep talk, already beginning the process of turning the slight to his advantage. Even through his shock, he knows what this is: something to make him mad for next year, something to use in those workouts where it gets to the point he doesn't even enjoy it anymore, but he keeps on going, thinking of the gas this type of dis gives him to keep pushing.

When the Wizards arrive at the arena, they find that Indiana center Rik Smits, despite numbers clearly inferior to Webber's, has made the All-Star team. In part, Smits's selection might stem from the Pacers' stellar midseason record, second in the East to the Bulls. But many league observers believe Webber's arrest kept him off the team, just as Strickland's arrest last year, coupled with this season's fistfight with a teammate, did him in. Tonight Webber scores 18 points and grabs 11 rebounds in a one-point loss. After the game, he talks to his family and makes arrangements to visit them over the break.

Six days later, the Charlotte Hornets and Boston Celtics are tied at 86 with 1:04 left in the game. Following a timeout,

Coach Dave Cowens inserts the newest Hornet into the game, a guy his general manager, Bob Bass, just signed to a ten-day at shootaround this morning: Vernon Maxwell.

Maxwell has already scored 12 points in this game, meeting the approval of the boisterous Charlotte crowd. He has penetrated, played active defense, made things happen. Now, with ten seconds left on the shot clock, Maxwell dribbles the ball just beyond the top of the key.

"Money! Money!" Cowens yells, the team's warning for the shot clock winding down. To Maxwell, the word means nothing—he's not yet tuned into his new team's vocabulary.

Not that it matters. The crowd is getting louder, so Maxwell knows it's about time to shoot. And there's no way he's giving up this ball. His whole life, the big shot has been his. Other guys—even some All-Stars—hide from crunch time. As Maxwell proved in Houston, where he drained clutch jumper after clutch jumper, he wants the ball with the game on the line. In fact, according to Houston talk radio personalities John Granato and Lance Zierlein, a recent informal poll asked NBA players to name the players they least wanted to guard in the final seconds of a tight game. Jordan, naturally, was number one, followed by Reggie Miller. Then came Maxwell, who attributes his clutch play to a unique mindset: "It's 'cause I don't give a fuck," he once explained. "I'm gonna be a hero or I'm gonna be a zero. Fuck it. As soon as I realize them's my two options, I'm home-free. Ain't no pressure."

Now, with the crowd screaming and Cowens wildly gesticulating on the sidelines, the pressure is palpable—but Maxwell is oblivious. He stutter-steps, then fires an off-balance twenty-five-footer that backspins high through the air in a tantalizing arc before splashing through. The Hornets win. Maxwell has logged twenty-seven minutes, hitting five of twelve shots for 15 points, grabbed 5 rebounds, handed out 3 assists. All this after signing on just nine hours ago.

After the game, Coach Rick Pitino of the Celtics can't

believe it. "We got beat by a very difficult shot by a guy they just picked up," he says more than once.

"It looks like I might have found a home," Maxwell says after the game. The Hornets, winners of five of their last six, have suffered a rash of injuries lately, particularly at guard. Starters David Wesley and Bobby Phills are both out, as are reserves Dell Curry—a popular shooting guard who has played his entire career in Charlotte—and Corey Beck. Maxwell should see a lot of minutes in the games to come.

He just wishes the All-Star weekend wasn't so near. He's had enough time to chill. He wants to play.

On the very morning that his friend Maxwell signs with Charlotte, Jerry Stackhouse's upbeat mood takes a hit. Yesterday, as expected, the axe fell on coach Doug Collins. Now, in Washington, D.C., for a game against Webber's Wizards, Alvin Gentry, the interim coach who had been Collins's assistant, pulls Stackhouse aside as the team gathers for shootaround at the MCI Center.

Gentry explains that Lindsey Hunter, who has been hurt, can play tonight and that a team rule prohibits a player from losing his starting job due to injury. While Gentry speaks, it dawns on Stackhouse: He's being pulled from the starting lineup. He's never heard of such a team rule. Besides, he's been averaging almost 19 points a game since Collins made him a starter. But he says none of this. He simply nods and decides to keep it all in. While the other players seem relieved that Collins is finally gone, Stackhouse—though used to dealing with coaching changes by now—realizes that little good can come of this switch for him.

Come game time, Stackhouse plays twenty-seven minutes, about five less than he was averaging as a starter, and scores 22 points. But Webber scores 23 and grabs 12 rebounds in a 113–101 Wizards win. Late in the game, Webber reinjures his chronic shoulder injury and he will be out for three weeks, a further blow to the Wizards' chances of putting together an extended run this season and which makes his desire to play in the All-Star Game moot.

Meantime, Stack is given cause to worry through the long All-Star weekend when Gentry plays him only nineteen minutes three nights later against the Rockets. Things were going so well. And now this.

On the eve of his game against Stackhouse's Pistons, Matt Maloney sacks out on the sofa of his room at the Hilton Suites to watch "SportsCenter." His elbow is still aching, his team is still struggling (they are .500 heading into their final game of the season's first half), and the fans and media are still squawking about him. His recent play should have silenced the critics; instead, they've continued to single him out when pinpointing the Rockets' woes, ignoring the obvious: The big three—Olajuwon, Drexler, and Barkley—have played only a handful of games together. And Olajuwon has been out since November.

Maybe it's the nature of his game that sets Maloney up as a convenient target. He's a decent athlete—as Barkley says, "He's quick enough"—but does nothing, save hit open threes, spectacularly. When his spectacular teammates are missing from the lineup, his limitations are more obvious.

So the digs at his game come. Three nights ago, while he scored 16 points and dished out 7 assists in a 110–97 win over the Grizzlies, TNT announcer Reggie Theus diagnosed the Rockets' maladies this season: "Maloney has disappeared," he said. "Remember when we thought he was a good player? He's back to being Maloney."

"Man, that just proves that unless you're part of a team, you shouldn't be on the air talking about it," Maloney says now, upon hearing of Theus's comments. "Reggie Theus is a jackass."

He can't wait for the break. His elbow needs the rest and his mind needs a diversion. He and Paul are accompanying Barkley to Las Vegas; there Matt and his brother will play blackjack, craps, and roulette. Barkley will take a break from his gambling to have dinner with Dennis Rodman, who was also left off the All-Star team.

For Maloney, it will be a chance to get away, to shed some of the hard feelings engendered by the trade that never happened. "It just showed me that you don't trust anybody in this league," he says. "You just go out and play. What you do in the off-season doesn't matter. What you do off the court doesn't matter. And it doesn't even matter what you do on court. If you're playing good, you're trade bait. If you're playing bad, you're trade bait."

Ironically, this newfound realism has liberated Maloney on the court. He's still heeding the lesson learned from watching the games he sat out a month ago, the lesson his father used to preach: Make stuff happen. He's driving to the basket, creating, sometimes deviating from the set offense. Why not? The worst has already happened. "What are they going to do? Trade me?" he says, laughing.

Against the Pistons, a 104–92 loss, he plays forty minutes and scores 14 points on five of eight shooting. Barkley goes for 26 points and 10 rebounds. After the game, both agree: Vegas beckons, and it couldn't come soon enough.

HALFTIME:
ALL-STAR WEEKEND

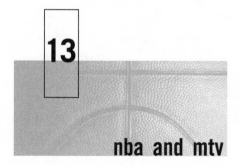

13

nba and mtv

it's bedlam. The NBA All-Stars are seated at separate tables throughout a midtown Manhattan ballroom for the weekend's media availability session, and, although the table of Coach Larry Bird of the East is nearby and reigning MVP Karl Malone holds court some fifty feet away, the media pack is swarming around the story of this midseason: Kobe Bryant. He's the youngest player ever to start an NBA All-Star Game, and he's not even a starter on his own team.

Jordan is a no-show. He's in his hotel suite, battling the flu, though indications are he'll play tomorrow. That makes Kobe the man for now, and scribes and TV guys battle for position around him like big men under the boards. The same question, in countless incarnations, keeps coming Kobe's way: "How does it feel to be considered the next Jordan at nineteen years old?"

He responds patiently, softly, that it's a tremendous compliment, but his mind is focused on just being Kobe. He repeats it like a mantra. He might even repeat it if someone had the creativity to ask a different question. Each time he does, the scribes dutifully write it down while the cameras keep rolling.

Suddenly there is a commotion and a burst of energy among the pack. Someone with a camera and a boom mike is elbowing his way in, grabbing a chair, and sitting alongside Kobe. "Man, I can be rude," MTV's Bill Bellamy will say once he gets what he needs from Kobe and elbows his way back out of the throng.

But for the moment Kobe beams, relieved to see a familiar face, someone he can speak to. "Yo, Kobe, man," Bellamy asks. "What's bumping in your trunk?" Some scribes looked puzzled, others roll their eyes or grumble to each other. But all notice Kobe's voice finds a groove that is far more engaged than it was moments ago. He looks into MTV's camera and smiles. "Fugees, man," he says, turning on the charm. " 'Ready or Not.' "

The beat writers and talking heads stand idly by while Bellamy draws Kobe out on his taste in music and asks if he'd ever imagine he'd be starting in the game he used to watch his idol, Magic Johnson, play in. The question prompts Kobe to share a memory from when he was twelve, wearing his Lakers number 32 jersey, watching Magic run the open floor while Isiah Thomas and Larry Bird tried to defend. Five minutes later, Kobe and the MTV veejay bump fists and Bellamy begins making his way to the next All-Star. He's barely free of the crush when he can hear the predictable questions start again—someone asks Bryant if he'll be nervous guarding Jordan.

"You gotta talk to these guys like they're people, man," Bellamy says, spying Atlanta's Steve Smith across the floor and nodding for his crew to follow. "The advantage I have is that they know me. I'm on TV every day and they watch me when they're working out."

Bellamy, host of MTV's "MTV Jams," is also a stand-up comic and actor, starring in 1997's *How to Be a Player* and *Love Jones*. Throughout the media availability session, his résumé helps him, as player after player opens up to him, abandoning the clichéd, monotonic replies reserved for the pack of flies.

When he gets to Smith, he begins by asking, "Yo, wassup with this," while making a knife-twisting motion to his heart. It's one of Smith's signature showboat moves—in fact, he used it on his Detroit homey Webber a couple of weeks ago after Atlanta beat the Wizards. Smith laughs and explains: "The twisting means there ain't no life left in you, it's *really* over," he says while Bellamy gives him a high-five.

For those who have long covered the NBA, glorifying trash-talking and unsportsmanlike conduct is precisely what's wrong with the league. It is a prime example of the generation gap between today's players and those who comment on their play. Smith, Webber, and Bellamy—who is black *and* in his late twenties—see antics like on-court motions of knife-twisting as theater, as entertainment. Old school types see it as a symbol of the oncoming extinction of class, as though hoops were once some elegantly choreographed, gentlemanly competition. And they hate the encroachment onto their turf by the likes of Bellamy, viewing such cameos as nothing but photo opportunities built on softball questions (as if constantly asking Bryant about replacing Jordan is somehow hard-hitting).

"See, if people would just sit down and talk to these guys, you'd learn what a serious job, what a serious life they have," Bellamy says. "We watch the games on TNT and think these guys are machines, but when you hear their different perspectives, when you sit down and kick it with them, when you hear how hard it is to stay in the league, how hard it is to score, that's some other shit right there."

Bellamy has gotten tight with a number of NBA stars, like Shaquille O'Neal, who has made the transition from basketball star to multimedia entertainer by cutting rap CDs and making movies. (Interestingly, O'Neal's rap career has come under fire for being a distracting outside interest, while Grant Hill's classical piano playing has been widely lauded, indicating that the true objection is to the nature of Shaq's interest—rap—rather than its mere existence.)

"If you're not tapped into this life, then you're just standing around on the outside, going, 'Damn, what the hell does all this mean?' " Bellamy says, before running off to find Gary Payton, with whom he's played pool in the All-Star's Seattle home.

Bellamy's point is that, in order to understand a culture, one must first decode its language. And the language of the NBA is, increasingly, hip-hop. Tonight he and Puff Daddy will cohost the MTV "All-Star Jam," featuring live performances by Sugar Ray and Mase, rap's rising star and a one-time New York City hoops phenom who, in high school, once lit up Stephon Marbury for 32 points. Garnett, Jayson Williams, Ray Allen, and Spike Lee—promoting his soon-to-be released *He Got Game*, which stars Allen—will all be there. But Bellamy will be the only member of the media at the "Jam" who also attended the availability session.

The media throng comes out en masse the next day for Commissioner David Stern's state of the league press conference, however. Like a smooth politician, Commissioner Stern knows how to stay on message. He is clearly setting the stage for the upcoming labor dispute, repeating time and again his position that "revenues are rising, profitability is declining, and ticket prices are going up. . . . The paradox is that as the dollars have increased, so have the percentage of those dollars that are paid out." Of course, this is a paradox only an owner or league suit could appreciate, as opposed to the players, whose skills the owners use to justify the increased revenue.

In March the owners will vote whether to reopen collective bargaining. The vote will be a formality, though Stern won't admit that now. The 1995 agreement will be reopened and a lockout will jeopardize the 1998–99 season.

The critical provision of the last agreement centered on the players' share of league revenues, defined as "basketball-related income." If the share exceeded 52 percent, the owners reserved the right to reopen and amend the numbers, by adjusting or, they hoped, obliterating the "Larry Bird exception," which allows a team to re-sign its own player to any sum regardless of cap room. In addition, they hoped to lengthen the three-year term of the capped rookie contract, so players like Stackhouse and Garnett will no longer have their eyes on long-term, multimillion-dollar deals midway through their second seasons.

According to Stern and Deputy Commissioner Russ Granik, the players are currently getting over 57 percent and some thirteen teams are losing money. The players don't buy it. As Barkley has been pointing out all season, Stern and the owners have been crying poor despite the windfall from a whopping $2.64 billion TV contract from NBC and TNT. (Barkley recently chided Stern about the commissioner's $9 million (!) annual salary: "Have you ever heard the words 'salary cap'?"). Most ominous is that next season the NBA will get that TV money whether there is a season or not, providing Stern and the owners with the wherewithal to maintain a hard-line stand.

The issue really comes down to defining league revenues. Last season, Granik says, the players received 55 percent of "basketball-related income, which now basically includes the kitchen sink."

Not quite. Basketball-related income doesn't include the bulk of money generated by luxury seating or arena signage, for example. Wizards' owner Abe Pollin, for instance, who owns the teams *and* the arena they play in, can assign revenue generated by naming rights, premium seating, signage, concessions, and parking to his building management corporation, thereby protecting that money from being shared with the players. In Florida, after all, Wayne Huizenga, owner of baseball's world champion Marlins, cleverly credited his team's revenues to his many related businesses, making it seem like the team lost money.

But Stern is smart and he knows one thing: In the court of public opinion, there will be scant sympathy for multimillionaire athletes seeking more money—even if in-depth analysis proves their demands are fair—and there will be even less sympathy if so many of the younger guys keep getting in trouble. Just this morning, in fact, it was announced that Charlotte Hornets star Anthony Mason is being questioned about statutory rape—one more alleged transgression that sets the players' bargaining position back. (Mason would plead guilty to two counts of endangering the welfare of a child and be sentenced to 200 hours of community service.)

A serious risk, however, resides in Stern's hard line, and it is evident in his final response at today's conference. When he's asked to predict the effect of Jordan's retiring—as he's said he would if the Bulls don't bring back his coach, Phil Jackson—Stern offered, "Can a league like ours say that losing the greatest player of all time perhaps in any sport will not have some negative impact? I'm not going to stand here to fool you. Of course it will. But I'm comfortable, as were Time Warner and General Electric, when they agreed to pay us $2.7 billion against a certainty that at least half and probably three-quarters of that contract would be post-Michael, that our business . . . will continue to grow."

There hangs the league's Sword of Damocles. The dawn of the post-Michael period would be the worst of all possible times for a bloody labor war.

Despite the two previous days, despite the Kobe buzz and Stern's pronouncements, Jordan is the story of the All-Star Game itself, scoring 23 points, leading the East to a 135–114 victory, capturing another All-Star Game MVP

Award. The reigning regular season MVP, Malone, gets pissed and sulks when the ultrahyped Bryant waves him away as he's setting a screen; to the oversensitive Malone, Bryant's message—"I don't need you, I can take this guy myself"—is a sign of disrespect.

But the move of the game does belong to Kobe, who, on a fast break, whips the ball around his back, seemingly about to throw a behind-the-back pass to a teammate. Only he doesn't release the ball and, instead, wraps it all the way around his body, bouncing it to his free hand, freezing the opposition and everyone in Madison Square Garden, before exploding to the basket unimpeded for a lay-in while the crowd goes apoplectic.

In the age of the ubiquitous highlight, it is rare to be surprised by a move, but Bryant has done it. What's more, the move isn't the product of some spontaneous burst of creativity. It's come from countless hours of rehearsal on the court and it's a point *The New York Times* would be well served to notice.

On game day, the paper's front page features a piece by Mike Wise headlined: AS THE NBA'S STARS SOAR, THE QUALITY OF PLAY FALLS OFF. "The game—the nuts-and-bolts skills of the players as well as the ability to create the sublime choreography of teamwork—is ailing," Wise writes. He cites a 3 percent decline in field goal shooting percentage over ten years—the difference of one or two shots a game—and a drop of about 7 assists per game over the same time span as proof that the game is in trouble. He even quotes Jordan concurring: "I guess some of this crept in because of myself and Charles Barkley," Jordan said. "With our ability to take over a game and sell ourselves as individuals, we have infected the game as much as we've helped it."

But Wise misses his point. Jordan's quote pertains to something off the court—the effects of the NBA's rapid climb to the pinnacle of America's commodity culture. Besides, he and Barkley and Malone and Magic Johnson *and*

Stern (everyone, it seems, but the ever-progressive Larry Bird) are all on the same page when it comes to heaping scorn on the newer generation of players.

When it comes to matters *on* the court, Wise's article pines for the good old days—an era that never was. Its best refutation can be seen on ESPN's Classic Sports Channel, which is currently showing game six of the 1977 NBA Finals, pitting the Philadelphia 76ers versus the Portland Trail Blazers. Watching it, one sees why scoring is down in the modern-day NBA: because defense is up. NBA basketball in the '70s was rife with wide-open scoring chances; the reason so few backdoor plays work now is that today's player is too quick to let his man beat him to the basket.

Those players of yesteryear whose games are so heralded now can't compare to the players of today, who are bigger, stronger, faster, and more conscious of taking care of their bodies, thanks in part to advances in nutrition and medicine and to the incentive provided by big-time contracts. That '77 series proves this, too: There's not one small forward in today's NBA that chicken-armed Portland starter Bobby Gross could play against effectively.

Yes, the type of preparation that went into Bryant's seemingly spontaneous All-Star move, the countless hours in gyms and weight rooms, might just exemplify the NBA's best-kept secret: It isn't just Jordan who works his ass off, contrary to the widespread deification of him following his virtuoso All-Star appearance. And there is something else that all of it, from the awestruck game stories to the weepy *Sports Illustrated* cover story begging him not to quit, ignores. Jordan is a good example of work ethic, but his greatest legacy has nothing to do with the game itself.

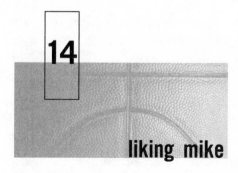

14

liking mike

worry is in the air. There's Lupica, frowning. There's the fat guy from WFAN, looking fretful. There's Vecsey, mouth twisted in a perpetual snarl. Everywhere you look, you see dour faces. This might be it for Mike.

Michael Jordan is at the podium before them, saying all the right things as usual. He is graceful when queried about Bryant, who was held out of the fourth quarter by Coach George Karl of the West lest he—God forbid—score more points than Jordan and steal an MVP Award otherwise destined for the deity. Jordan reiterates his position about his future, linking it to Jackson's. The adoring pack watches the Alpha-Male, but doesn't necessarily listen. No, those who have turned into an art form the tendency to deride today's player in light of Jordan's work ethic are busy worrying about what life might be like once he hangs up his Nikes.

They are right to laud Jordan, as his performance just

confirmed once again. But when their praise degenerates into condemnation of those who would follow, they miss an obvious point: The real lesson of Jordan's success is not lost on the very guys they critique.

Today's player has read what we've read about Jordan's never-before-seen obsessive work ethic and an indomitable (some would say unhealthy) competitive streak. Today's player knows Jordan was cut from his varsity team his sophomore year in high school and that, when teammate Dickie Simpkins beat him at Ping-Pong, Jordan bought a Ping-Pong table and didn't rest until he'd become better than everyone else on the team. Stories of his need to dominate at golf, at cards, and at business have become the stuff of legend. And around the league, that pack listens—and takes notes.

"Even today he still beats you with the basics we learned years ago in summer camp," says Webber. "Then when you start watching out for the basics, that's when he kills you with the spectacular. He's like that rare kid in college who would be mad if he got a B."

Maxwell says, "I did all right against him until one summer, when the rest of us were playing golf, and he added that little turnaround jumper to his game. It was all over for me after that."

Throughout the NBA, player after player attests that what sets Jordan apart is his mental approach to the game. His preparation is overtly intellectual. Witness his theory of hitting a baseball, which he explained to writer Bob Greene during his brief baseball career. "What I need to do is get the feeling of what a hit feels like and store it in my mind. . . . If I can put that in my mind, then the next time maybe I can call all of that information up without having to consciously think about it. Obviously, I did it in basketball." (He was starting to do that on the diamond as well. Although widely portrayed as a bust for the Birmingham Barons, he hit a respectable .260 over the last month of his season and was fifth in the Southern League in stolen bases with 30.)

Ironically, though, unlike Bird and Magic Johnson, who brought passing back into vogue, Jordan will leave the game as he found it, in large part because he is inimitable. No one can do what he does: No one can fly like he's flown and no one can work as hard as he's worked and no one can compete as fiercely. That's why we've lived through a laundry list of "next Jordans," none of whom could possibly measure up: Hill, Penny Hardaway, Stackhouse, now Bryant. When will the punditocracy so worried about life without Mike throw up its hands and admit Jordan is, and always will be, one of a kind?

Jordan may not have revolutionized the game, but he's changed his culture in a way no other athlete has since Ali. There his real legacy lies. An icon, he long ago ceased being just a basketball player in the same way that he ceased being just a black man and so showed us the power of transcendence. For what has he done other than to shed all the uniforms of team and race and class we would dress him in and clothe himself instead in the suit of America's foremost working capitalist? And all the while he was remaking fashion as well: That herd of geeky white guys with shaved heads (read: yours truly) would be geeky white guys *with hair* were it not for him.

His legacy took hold when, as a twenty-year-old rookie, with a curious amalgamation of instinct and vision, Jordan reinvented the realm of athlete endorsements. Then there's his status as the preeminent crossover role model, a status he has used in decidedly, albeit subtle, political ways. In his obsessive construction of a Rockefeller-like empire and his (some would say) uppity presumption of partnership with the NBA powers-that-be, Jordan has become the walking embodiment of Malcolm X's rhetoric: He is a multimillion-dollar black-run business unto himself. And don't let his crossover politeness fool you: Time and again, Jordan has stood up to authority, serving as a sort of one-on-all empow-

erment initiative, ironically making the landscape safe for a
new generation of ballplayers—the hip-hoppers—to confront
white mainstream taste much more openly.

The Derrick Colemans, Chris Webbers, Latrell Sprewells,
and Allen Iversons can all "keep it real" because there came
before them Michael Jordan, whose story is a classic triumph
of the workingman.

Were it not for a sporting press blinded by a too-keen
focus on merely basketball, the Michael Jordan story would
read like accounts we get of the meteoric rise of Bill Gates,
complete with glowing tales of hard work and vision. You
want vision? Try this: A twenty-year-old kid leaves the University of North Carolina in 1984 and somehow senses that
the black sports icons of the past—guys like Jackie Robinson
and Ali—were the perfect heroes for the modernist moment.
They got caught up in the social movements of their time
and would forever be linked to them: Robinson would always be the catalyst of the civil rights struggle, Ali always
the most eloquent anti-Vietnam crusader ("I ain't got no
quarrel with them Viet Cong"). But this kid senses that he's
emerging on a decidedly postmodern stage, an era dominated by the power of imagery. And so he inundates us
with images of himself: flying through the air, playing with
kids, smiling joyously, dressed in impeccably tailored, big-
shouldered suits.

You want vision? He aligns himself with only the most
blue chip of companies. He wears Nike and Hanes, drinks
Gatorade, and eats Wheaties for breakfast and McDonald's
for dinner—a flawlessly put together portfolio that rivals the
stock picks of Warren Buffett, the world's best evaluator of
company performance.

No matter the company, Jordan has enriched its bottom
line. His partnership with Nike (and its cutting-edge ad
agency, Wieden & Kennedy) has become the consummate
example of "win-win" business deals, with Nike selling over

$200 million in Air Jordans the past eight years. And we
never get tired of the avalanche of imagery because he has,
in his way, kept it real. We've been fed a true American
myth in the Michael Jordan story, a narrative that begins
with hard work and culminates in an empire of wealth.

Along the way, there were countless other examples of
that vision. Even at twenty, for instance, he was aware that
this century is replete with cases of African American sports
heroes going broke. Joe Louis died penniless, Ali lost a fortune, Kareem Abdul-Jabbar went bankrupt. Thus Jordan has
worked hard to make himself into a refutation of the "nigger-
rich" stereotype that other athletes' business failings have
long been lampooned to support.

In fact, has anyone countered as many stereotypes as
Jordan? It's now impossible, after all, to stereotype jocks as
dim-witted, unfeeling, macho bullies, not after we watched
this graceful man take flight and especially not after we
grieved with him over his murdered father. (Imagine: a jock
sobbing on television!)

And he's no aberration, not anymore. Jordan's success
off the court has spawned a whole generation of athletes
who see themselves as businessmen and entertainers. Webber, for instance, has started Humility Records, a hip-hop,
jazz, and R&B record label in his hometown of Detroit, and
has bought a Gold's Gym franchise. "I wouldn't have started
these businesses if I hadn't watched Michael these past few
years," he says. "He's showed me I can be more than just
an athlete."

Similarly, Grant Hill has dumped his management company and taken matters into his own hands, starting Gran-
Hco Enterprises. Rather than relying on an agent to secure
him endorsement deals, Hill now meets a payroll and em-
ploys people. "Michael's led the way for what I'm doing
now," he says. And Stackhouse takes business courses during the summer at the University of North Carolina, so in-

tent is he on building something long-lasting out of basketball.

And do you believe for a moment that, before each and every business decision, Tiger Woods doesn't wonder, What would Mike do?

But not everybody wants the youth of America to be like Mike. There has long been a Jordan backlash, particularly among the liberal and civil rights communities. Jordan doesn't speak out on social issues, the complaint goes. He doesn't "give back." In short, he's not black enough.

Jim Brown, the former NFL great who works with inner-city gang youth, has voiced the criticism. Jesse Jackson has hinted about it. "In some ways, I can't understand it," Jordan told *Playboy* in 1992. "Because here we are striving for equality and people are going to say I'm not black enough? At a time when actually I thought I was trying to be equal? I try to be a role model for black kids, white kids, yellow kids, green kids. . . . Don't knock me off that pedestal that you wanted me to get on to."

In fact, the record indicates Jordan has taken political stands, albeit cleverly and sometimes covertly. When he failed to join his teammates at the White House for a post-championship photo op with President Bush, many in the black community saw it as a distinctly political snub. (Last year, adding fuel to the suspicion, he did attend a similar function with President Clinton.) That same year he began wearing an x cap well before Spike Lee's *Malcolm X* hit theaters, creating a style craze that helped mainstream the once-verboten name.

And when it comes to the NBA, Jordan has flexed his muscles in a way no other star has—not Erving, not even Barkley. Three years ago, for instance, he led the ultimately doomed attempt to decertify the Players' Association. It was a surreal moment: The owners, all of whom had made fortunes as capitalists, wanted a salary cap, an artificial restriction on their laborers' earnings. Jordan, their top worker, cemented his place as a working-class capitalist by arguing for a free market.

But Jordan's most stunning act is the one he's closing with. If he does retire, it will be because Bulls ownership refused to bring back his coach and spiritual counterpart, Phil Jackson. "If Phil goes, I go," he's said time and again. Think of it for a moment: What other worker in this economy has had the balls to tell the owner he's walking if management doesn't bring back his supervisor? The underlying rationale is a distinctly American one about merit: "We deserve to run this thing out," he's said many times in reference to his team's string of championships.

Still, there are valid criticisms. Nike's use of third world labor is troubling; so was Jordan's silence when Senator Jesse Helms fought off a challenge from a formidable black candidate, Harvey Gantt, in Jordan's home state of North Carolina. (Jordan did send Gantt a private donation.) "That Gantt campaign was a moment when he could have made a big difference," says Ken Shropshire, a professor at the University of Pennsylvania's Wharton School and author of *In Black and White: Race and Sports in America.* "But you have to be careful of putting too much on one man. The problem is, there's only one Michael Jordan. If there were ten or twelve—and maybe Tiger Woods will soon approach that stature—then Michael's silence wouldn't mean a thing."

Those who condemn Jordan for not speaking out curiously refrain from demanding that, say, Gates endorse candidates for office. (As if he could deliver the geek vote.) Nor have they castigated Arnold Palmer or Jack Nicklaus for their silence on restrictive country club memberships. Even Jordan's well-intentioned critics hold him to a higher standard of social responsibility simply because of his skin color—a subtle racism in itself.

Moreover, they overlook Jordan's postmodernism: What he represents matters much more than what he says. That was the case with Jackie Robinson as well. He broke baseball's color line—he didn't need to hold a press conference, too. Jesse Jackson is fond of saying, "There are tree-shakers, and there are jelly-makers." Isn't it enough that Jordan makes the best jelly, refuting time-worn stereotypes all the while, and has left in his wake a whole new generation of kids who can take the next step?

THIRD QUARTER

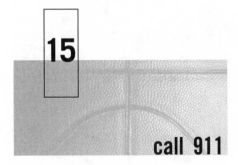

15

call 911

he comes sweeping through the doors of Mickey Mantle's restaurant on Central Park South like he owns the joint. New York is like him: fast-paced, loud, always in motion. He heads straight for the bar and orders a round of Rémys with Bud chasers. Vernon Maxwell is back in the Big Apple, which always rekindles memories of his greatest moment: the 1994 NBA Finals.

Maxwell's Hornets play the Knicks tomorrow night, the first game of the second half of the season for both teams. And he is psyched, having just checked into the Plaza, the hotel where he had four rooms throughout those '94 Finals for him and his fellas, and what a party it was. Every night he got in after sunrise, and he still went out and kicked the ass of his nemesis, Knicks shooting guard John Starks. The one thing Vernon Maxwell has always understood is his body; he knows, for instance, that he requires only about two hours of sleep a night. Eight hours leaves him too keyed up to play.

Yes, Maxwell is psyched to be back in New York, not to mention back in the league for one more chance, this time with a playoff-bound team. "I know people don't believe me, but I really am changing," he says, throwing back a shot of Rémy while motioning for another round. "I gotta. Little V is twelve now, man, and he be reading the sports section of the paper every morning. So if I fuck up, he be reading about it. Which means all the kids at school be knowing about it, too. I can't be doing what I used to do. Now that Little V reads, man, it's time to change."

Vernon's cousin Steven Maxwell comes in, wearing a stylish burgundy overcoat, holding a cell phone. Another cousin, DeJuan, waits outside in the car. We're going exploring, Max-style. As Maxwell begins to make his way through the restaurant's doors, he spins around, hearing a familiar voice. It's coming from the TV above the bar. There, on the screen, is John Starks's sweaty face, offering up some sound bites about the Knicks' chances in the season's second half without their injured leader, Patrick Ewing.

A group of patrons want to get in, but Maxwell blocks the entranceway, focusing on Starks. "C'mon, boy! Bring that over here!" he starts yelping in a high-pitched voice that carries. "C'mon, boy! Bring that shit my way! You mine, boy! You mine!" And then he turns into the New York night.

On our way to the Shark Bar, a popular soul food restaurant among NBA players, Maxwell is his usual passionate self. "Shark Bar's my favorite spot," he says, fiddling with the radio of his cousin's ride, settling on Hot 97, "Where Hip-Hop Lives," and LL Cool J's hit "Phenomenon." "Everything at Shark Bar is fresh, man. Everything be fresh."

"No doubt, no doubt, cuz," Steven shouts over the music. "Not like Sylvia's, fast-food soul food."

In his lap, Steven nimbly rolls a blunt. This season Ver-

non has made great inroads into cutting down his intake of
marijuana; he no longer is an All-Star on the All-Cannabis
team. In part, that's because it's too risky. Any day now,
the Supreme Court of the United States will agree to either
hear his appeal or let stand his 1995 Houston conviction for
possession of less than a joint of smoke. The appeal is based
on a claim of ineffective counsel, an argument the Court
rarely agrees to hear. Either way, another bust might jeopardize not only the rest of his season, but his future in the
league.

Maxwell is growing up, too. He's discovered a new drug:
his family. Gone are the days of the early '90s when Shel
would hire a private eye to tail him and then file for divorce
before the inevitable tearful reconciliation. They've been
through too much together to give up now. That's right,
Vernon Maxwell has become the NBA's least likely exemplar
of family values. For years, only loving pulls on fat blunts
could soothe his raging hyperactivity, but now the stability
of his home life, particularly his closeness with Little V, has
become the impetus for slowing himself down when the
rush of old demons make themselves known.

But this is New York, and one hit would make him nice
for the night. Besides, Steven's got some Chronic, an expensive, exotic, imported variety of pot. "We gonna smoke before tomorrow?" Vernon says from the front seat to his
cousin. "I can't wait to wrap my lips 'round that thing."

"I'm working on it, cuz," Steven says. "This is a tedious procedure."

Vernon's head whips around. " *Tedious procedure*'? What
the fuck you saying?" he says, wearing a look of mock puz-
zlement. "Since when did you go and get all white on us,
muthafucka?"

Steven laughs, bringing the blunt to his lips. After I've
had a few hits, my jaw locks. I manage to say, "Good shit"
and then I'm useless the rest of the night. True to his word,
Maxwell takes one long pull and he's done, too.

This year, more than in the past, pot in the NBA has become a hot media topic. It began on the eve of the season with the *New York Times* piece that estimated 70 percent of the league smoked. And the issue is related to the upcoming labor strife as well. It turns out that the NBA is the only one of the four major pro sports leagues that doesn't list marijuana as a prohibited substance. (In part, that's because the NBA drug policy was drafted fifteen years ago, when marijuana use was a lowly misdemeanor in a number of NBA cities, a crime on a par with getting a parking ticket.) As a result, the spate of recent pot-related arrests, further fueling antiplayer resentment among fans, plays right into management's hands during collective bargaining.

In the *Times* piece, Stern sounded the anticipated notes of alarm. "There is the issue of muscle deterioration that could come with the retention of substances like marijuana in the body and concerns about the recovery time of injuries that might be lengthened by marijuana," he said.

But the *Times's* writer, Selena Roberts, failed to question Stern's self-serving medical opinion. "Wow, that's the first time I've ever heard that," responded Lynn Zimmer, Ph.D., associate professor of sociology at Queens College in New York and coauthor with Dr. John P. Morgan of *Marijuana Myths, Marijuana Facts: A Review of the Scientific Evidence,* when told of Stern's remarks. "There's not one single basis in fact in that statement. In fact, what's clear is that marijuana is a muscle relaxant. Far from leading to deteriorating muscles, it can actually give sore muscles much-needed relief."

NBA players have spent their entire lives in constant conversation with their physical selves, aware of every twinge, every ache. Consequently, they can instinctively see through the hyperbole surrounding pot even faster than most American twentysomethings. (Indeed, it can be argued that the *Reefer Madness*–like rhetoric of the drug war's campaign against pot erodes the credibility of its much more

accurate and important messages against cocaine and heroin—two drugs virtually absent from NBA culture.) The fact
is, Stern's wannabe diagnosis notwithstanding, every time a
nonpartisan commission of experts has been formed within
the last 100 years to study marijuana there has been widespread agreement: The drug has no proven ill consequences.

For example, Richard Nixon's own National Commission
on Marihuana and Drug Abuse found unanimously in 1972
that "marihuana [sic] use is not such a grave problem that
individuals who smoke marihuana, or possess it for that
purpose, should be subject to criminal procedures." In 1969
the British *Wootten Report* found that "the long-term con-
sumption of cannabis in moderate doses has no harmful effect." A 1982 National Academy of Sciences report
concurred: "Over the past forty years, marijuana has been
accused of causing an array of antisocial effects,
including . . . provoking crime and violence, . . . leading to
heroin addiction, . . . and destroying the American work
ethic in young people. [These] beliefs . . . have not been
substantiated by scientific evidence."

In all, ten nonpartisan commissions since 1894 have
reached the same conclusion about marijuana. Yet modern-
day American athletes are still held to a standard when it
comes to the drug that doesn't even apply to other celebri-
ties in the same culture. A month before Maxwell wraps his
lips around the blunt before we go into the Shark Bar, *Details
Magazine* ran a profile of actress Bridget Fonda, who joked
about how she discussed her role in the film *Jackie Brown*
with director Quentin Tarantino while they munched on pot
brownies. If she were an athlete, the outrage would be deafening: guilty of conduct unbecoming a role model.

"That's what I'm saying," Maxwell says when I tell him
this as we're shown to our table at the Shark Bar. "We're
entertainers, too, just like Bridget Fonda. There shouldn't be
no difference in how people look at us."

Maxwell waves across the room to his teammate, J. R.

Reid, who is in the corner with a female companion. When our food comes, Maxwell starts moaning and groaning in pleasure, attacking his fried chicken, collard greens, and mac & cheese with a singular intensity. Between mouthfuls, he and his cousins reminisce about '94.

"You was with me that night up at Madonna's place, remember, cuz?" he says to Steven, who smiles knowingly. It was after her tryst with Barkley and prior to her relationship with Rodman. That night, at her place on the Upper West Side, she invited Maxwell to go with her on tour in Europe. He said he'd never been overseas.

"That's when she told me I needed to broaden my horizons 'cause I ain't never been to Europe," he recalls now, smiling. "Man, what the fuck I wanna go to Europe for? I still got her phone number somewhere."

"Man, '94 was seriously off-the-hook," says Steven.

It was the year of Jordan's baseball sabbatical. The Knicks were led by Ewing, Starks, and Maxwell's current teammate Mason. With Maxwell on the Rockets were Olajuwon, Cassell, Kenny Smith, Robert Horry, and Mario Elie. After Houston's hard-fought seven-game victory, Olajuwon was given the MVP Award for the series, though some felt Maxwell was just as deserving.

The series boiled down to a war between Starks and Maxwell, two strikingly similar players. Both were, and still are, great athletes, strong defenders, and streak shooters capable of busting games open. Moreover, both play with a fiery, demonstrative passion. In the seventh game, Maxwell got the better of his rival. Starks shot just two for eighteen, continually forcing shots with Maxwell draped all over him. Maxwell scored 21 points, including the clutch three-pointer that sealed for Houston its first NBA title.

"I love Starks," Maxwell says now, conjuring up the respect old warriors tend to have for one another. "He's my nigga. I ain't never seen another dude play just like me. Our games be, like, identical."

We order another round of Rémy. Our waitress is light-skinned and attractive, which Maxwell, between bites, notices. "Baby, this gonna happen?" he says.

She looks at him and fights back a smile.

"Us, baby. We gonna happen?" he says in his best Barry White approximation.

She can't help it; a grin escapes. "I hear there's some big basketball star here," she says. "And I don't date athletes or entertainers and I don't like waiting for the phone to ring."

"Aw, baby, you hurtin' me," Maxwell says. "Why you think I'm an athlete? There are three other guys here, you know."

"I could be wrong, but I'm thinking you're the athlete and he's your manager," she says, nodding my way.

Maxwell doesn't miss a beat. "Baby, I used to be an entertainer, but now I'm a producer," he says as she raises her eyebrows as if to say "Uh-huh" before walking away, beaming. Moments later, a large man leads his date out of the restaurant. On their way past us, unbeknownst to the guy, his date subtly drops a scrap of paper on our table. DeJuan passes it to Vernon.

"I see you already got a phone number tonight," our waitress says, back now and leaning over Maxwell's shoulder.

"Aw, man." He laughs before ripping it up.

When she's gone again, it's time for Vernon, the relatively worldly older cousin, to lecture Steven and DeJuan about the byplay just completed, to make clear that he's learned the hard way to keep this type of flirting all in good fun. "See, you dudes never did learn," he says. "There be all types of bitches out here who'll want to mess with you. You gotta be careful. They all want you to fall in love with them. See, I learned. I love Shel like a muthafucka, you know what I'm saying? 'Cause she know me. These others, they don't know me."

Steven and DeJuan nod, not bothering to point out that

they wouldn't mind having as many chances as Vernon to learn their lessons. Though they are his cousins, they didn't grow up knowing Vernon. Steven's mother is Vernon's father's sister, and DeJuan's mother is Vernon's father's other sister. It wasn't until Vernon was playing for the Rockets that Steven showed up one day at a Rockets practice. He ended up spending six months in Houston with his new-found relative. Despite Vernon's disdain for his father and despite what he knows about long-lost relatives and old friends emerging from the proverbial woodwork once you've hit it big, Vernon embraced the cousin he never knew, much to the chagrin of members of his own family, who didn't want to see his kindness exploited.

"Vernon Maxwell!! Winning games now for Charlotte!!"

A tall figure dressed in sweats stands on the balcony of a Teaneck, New Jersey, condo, the site of our next stop, yelling in a deep baritone. It's Sam Cassell, Maxwell's former teammate and best friend on the Rockets, now averaging 19 points per game for the New Jersey Nets.

It's an off-night for Cassell, who is hanging at home, playing pool with his posse, guys Maxwell knows from their time together in Houston. "I talked to Penny," Sam says. "He wanted you to stay in Orlando."

"I know. He told them that," Maxwell says. "But they had fourteen guaranteed contracts ahead of me. That's okay. I'm in a good situation now."

The first thing a visitor to the Cassell abode sees is a pool table and Maxwell instantly grabs a cue. Before he can begin play, though, Sam asks how Little V is doing. Everyone gathers around while the proud papa starts riffing, gesticulating with the pool cue.

"Man, that muthafucka had twelve touchdowns in eight games," he says.

"For real?"

"I was proud as a muthafucka," Maxwell says. "I didn't

know he could play football like that. I be on the sideline, holding the down marker; that's how into this shit I was."

Everyone laughs at this image of Mad Max as a hip-hop Robert Young.

"I'm serious, man, I was like, 'That's my boy,' you know what I'm saying?" he says. Later, he will acknowledge that, standing there, holding the down marker, pulling for his son, he realized that he'd never played a single game of anything in front of his own father. But there is no room for sentimentality now. "Then one game he got hit by this big cracker, the dude just laid him out real good and here comes Little V over to me all wobbly and shit, runnin' my way, *crying!* 'I quit' he said. I said, 'Muthafucka, you a Maxwell, get yo ass back out there,' and he went, man. He went."

The guys are doubled over, laughing, as Maxwell shakes his head proudly at the memory of his son's guts. "That cracker did hit him a good one, too," he says.

Cassell leans closer. "Max, you talk to Peanut?" he says, referring to their old Houston homey, who Maxwell blames for the 1997 pistol-whipping.

Maxwell says nothing. He stares straight ahead, watching Steven rack the balls.

"Call Peanut, man," Cassell says, not taking his eyes from Maxwell. "Give him a call, man."

Maxwell says nothing.

"V?" Cassell says.

It's time for Vernon to break. Before he does, without looking at Cassell, he says simply, "I don't fuck with Peanut no more."

For the rest of the night, playing eight ball, each player gets a turn to try and run the table. Most times it comes down to a showdown between Cassell and Maxwell, not coincidentally the two most competitive guys in the room. When Maxwell goes on a run, he doesn't stop talking, just like when he's in the zone on the court. "I can play anything, hear me!" he shouts, smacking a ball into the corner pocket. "I love challenges!" Smack, Side pocket. "I can do this!" Smack. Other side. "I'm a scorer, this is what I do, I score!" Smack. Far corner. "Maxwells always give ourselves a chance!" Smack. "Don't ever count a Maxwell out!" Smack. He's left with the eight ball in a tough position. He goes for the far corner and barely misses, prompting a celebratory dance by Cassell.

When it's Cassell's turn, Maxwell still can't shut up. Every time Cassell bends to shoot, Max starts jawing: "Uh-oh, you in trouble now!" Smack. Side pocket. "What you gonna do now? It's over baby, it's over!"

The intensity of this late-night pool game is characteristic of just how competitive most pro athletes are; they've spent their lives defining themselves and being defined by wins and losses. Playing a game "just for fun," without regard to its outcome, is a foreign notion. So this impromptu pool rivalry continues past midnight, both guys feeding off going against the other, just like Rockets' practices back in '94. Before he leaves, Cassell asks Maxwell if he's heard from any of the other guys they used to hang with in Houston. "What about Cowboy? You hear from him?"

"Cowboy's inside for good," Maxwell says matter-of-factly. "He ain't coming out."

Cassell frowns. "So you got Starks tomorrow night, huh?" he says, walking Maxwell to the door.

"Gotta make a move and go on that nigga," Maxwell says. "Know what I'm saying? You can't make a move and hesitate, 'cause he'll recover. I gotta remember that."

They embrace. By one-thirty, Maxwell is back at the Plaza, dreaming, no doubt, of John Starks.

Just prior to game time, Assistant Coach Tom Thibodeau of the Knicks knows a war is imminent. Thibodeau was John Lucas's assistant coach in Philadelphia, where Vernon played the 1995–96 season as a point guard, scoring 16 points a game. Thibodeau knows what Maxwell is capable of when he gets those competitive fires burning. When he hears that Maxwell was back in his hotel room by one-thirty last night, he knows.

"Damn," he says. "For Vernon, that's like staying in."

Every time Coach Jeff Van Gundy of the Knicks brings Starks in, Cowens counters with Maxwell. Through three quarters, Maxwell has outscored Starks, 12–9, while talking to him the whole time. The game is seesawing as the fourth quarter begins, and both Maxwell and Starks raise their level of play. First, it's Maxwell's turn. He drives the baseline on Starks, who gives him the slimmest of openings; finding himself trapped under the basket, he jumps back into the lane, double-clutches, and somehow spins the ball off the glass and in while Starks hacks his arm. Good and a foul.

Next trip down it's Maxwell lining up a three and hitting. Moments later, he pulls up for three and it goes, too. Getting back on defense, he makes a beeline for Spike Lee and comedian Richard Lewis, both in their usual courtside seats. "Spike! Spike!" Maxwell calls. "Call 911, baby, 'cause this muthafucka is on fire!" Lewis and Lee both burst out in laughter.

Five minutes into the fourth quarter, Maxwell has scored 10 points, giving him 22 for the game. For some reason, though, the Hornets offense forgets about him the rest of the way and grows stagnant.

Starks, meanwhile, heats up. Tonight's game is a sign of just how much he has matured since his collapse against Maxwell in the '94 Finals. Then, his confidence shaky, Starks wilted before Maxwell's tenacious defense and nonstop trash-talking. Tonight he shrugs off Maxwell's scoring and boasting and scores the Knicks' final 10 points on open jumpers after Maxwell leaves him to help out teammates by double-teaming down low. The Knicks win, 99–91, but Maxwell has shown again that he can still score, hitting eight of twelve shots for 22 points in thirty minutes.

After the game, Knicks point guard Chris Childs is amazed at the battle between Starks and Maxwell. "It was like they were playing their own private game of horse out there," he says.

Ewing, his injured wrist in a cast, comes into the Hornets' locker room to hug Maxwell. Meantime, the media swarms all over Mason, who is dealing with the statutory rape investigation. "Man, I'm sure glad I'm on the other side of what Mase is going through," Maxwell says, pulling on a plaid Ralph Lauren shirt. "I told him if he needs a friend, I'm here, you know."

A handful of reporters approach Maxwell's locker. But they don't want to talk about his game tonight or the rivalry with Starks. Instead, they want a comment about the Sprewell case; over the All-Star Weekend, arbitrator John Feerick heard from both sides and will announce his finding in three weeks, on March 4. But Maxwell will have none of it.

"Man, I ain't got no comment about that," he says. "That doesn't involve me. The arbitrator's going to do his thing." He shakes his head and turns away.

But not even the playa-haters in the press can darken Maxwell's mood for long. The next night he shoots just one of seven against the Bulls, but he finds himself with the ball and his team down one with seconds left. He lofts a prayer that looks good all the way, hitting the backboard, then one side of the rim, then the other, bouncing softly around before falling off the lip of the basket. Hero or zero.

Two nights later, the Sixers come to town. Maxwell still harbors ill will toward them because the Sixers didn't re-sign him in 1996. Instead, they gave Lucious Harris, now riding the pine for the Nets, $1.5 million a year for seven years—"They gave him my money," Maxwell says. This 76er team, though, is coached by Larry Brown, who was Maxwell's first pro coach in San Antonio. He likes and re-spects Brown, but that doesn't stop him from riddling the

76ers defense while talking all the while not to any opposing player, but to Brown himself.

"I was available, Lar-ry, I was available," he shouts at Brown, who can't help but smile slightly after Maxwell drains one of his 5 three-pointers in seven attempts. In twenty-four minutes, he scores 19 points on six of eleven shooting, keying a Hornets 103–96 win. In five games, he's averaging 13 points on 44 percent shooting, good enough for the Hornets to sign him to a prorated minimum salary for the rest of the year—roughly $120,000—and for Cowens to remark that, when his injured players return, Maxwell will still be a part of the regular playing rotation.

How happy is he? The Supreme Court has decided against hearing his appeal, but that doesn't ruin his mood. His conviction in Houston stands. Of course, it's a misdemeanor, so Maxwell and his Houston-based lawyer, State Representative Ron Wilson, assume he'll do some community service in the off-season. So he doesn't give it a second thought. Why should he? He's back in the NBA, for a play-off contender, no less.

16

taking the baton

"let's check out God for a second."

Chris Webber, son of a God-fearing church woman, was raised to be a person of faith. But he has gotten even more spiritual of late, as his season has progressed according to some higher power's plan. He's currently reading a book entitled *The Seven Spiritual Laws*, for instance, because he's convinced that his astrologically dictated nature as a ponderer has kept him from attaining his destiny, prevented him from, in his words, "going with my first mind, following my heart."

He is standing in front of the wall-sized window on the top floor of Velocity Grille, the restaurant and bar in the MCI Center, and he is looking down at the practice court where his injury-depleted team just finished scrimmaging. And he is watching God. God Shammgod, that is, Webber's teammate, who is working out on his own, trying to come back from a knee injury. He's nailing jumpers and Webber smiles.

"That's good to see," he says. "It would be better if that was Juwan, though."

As Webber and his teammates expected since training camp, Muresan has never come back. "We're not counting on Gheorghe," Webber says. And the Wizards' front line has been especially depleted of late, as Howard has been out with an ankle sprain. Moments ago, one of the beat writers asked Webber what he does to take his friend's mind off the fact that he's not playing. "Well, really, I just try to be lighthearted," he said. "It's really eating him up, so I just try to be there for him. You know, go over his house, crack jokes, that type of thing. He's definitely one of the keys to us making the playoffs."

Just a little over a week ago, Webber returned from an eight-game, three-week absence due to the shoulder injury he sustained against the Pistons just before the break. The Wizards went 3–5 in that time, while Webber rehabbed both his body and his snubbed All-Star spirit.

"I don't know if I can explain where I'm at, mentally," he says, sitting down and ordering a barbecue chicken sandwich while a handful of fans come by to offer their best wishes. Interestingly, during games, there is still a smattering of boos when Webber's name is announced during the player introductions, the residual fallout of his arrest. Yet in person, Webber receives nothing but kindness from the fans. "See, a lot of times, I plan too much. Really, what I want to get out of this book *The Seven Spiritual Laws* is peace and relaxation, almost in a meditative way. To feel confident in my dreams again, to deal with those feelings that you have but that don't really make any sense."

And Webber does seem more relaxed. Partially, that's due to yesterday's big win, a 96–86 drubbing of the Lakers that put the Wizards' record at 30–29. Webber was huge: forty-six minutes, 31 points, 10 rebounds, 8 assists. Most impressively, he hit eight of his ten foul shots, his game's Achilles' heel. (Like Shaquille O'Neal, Webber hovers around an abysmal 50 to 60 percent from the line.)

Indeed, he's been on a tear in the four games since he came back; not coincidentally, the Wizards have won three of the four. Also not coincidentally, his return to the court took place against Barkley and the Rockets.

By all accounts, Chris Webber was an impressionable kid. Among his influences were his parents; his high school teacher Mr. Carlson; Muhammad Ali; and Spike Lee, who would speak to the kids each summer at the Nike basketball camp. Webber would pay rapt attention. "He was saying, 'You guys, you better not sell out when you get big'," Webber recalls. "This was back when he'd just made *Do the Right Thing* and I'm sitting there, thinking, 'Man, if Spike can go out there and do it and be black and maintain his identity and still be respected and loved, I can do the same thing.' "

It was the highlight of each summer for three straight years—going up to Spike and introducing himself, shaking his hand. That thrill was exceeded only by what awaited him upon his return to Detroit after playing in the McDonald's high school All-America game when he was seventeen. At Rick Mahorn's summer camp at Country Day, he met his idol, Charles Barkley, for the first time.

Barkley posed for a photo with the young, highly touted Webber, who was wearing his MCDONALD's jersey, a hightop 'do, and a wide grin. When he got the photo, Webber had it blown up to six feet, framed it, and kept it in his room. It's still there now, back in Detroit: Charles and Chris, smiling for the camera.

Webber would soak up everything he could get his hands on about Barkley: magazine profiles, videos, the infamous Barkley autobiography, *Outrageous*, in which Barkley later disavowed some of his own comments about his teammates, claiming he was misquoted. Misquoted in your own autobiography? That was Charles. Turned out he'd never read the galleys sent to him by the publisher.

Barkley was widely ridiculed for the book, as well as countless other controversies, but that was part of what resonated so deeply with a young Webber. Barkley was about the truth. "If you asked him something, he would not look away from you," Webber says. "That attracted me to him. His physical play. The fact that they said he was overweight. The fact that Bobby Knight cut him from the Olympic team. The way he used to dunk on people. His shoes, the Air Force Ones. He was who I wanted to be. An aggressive power forward. He was six-foot-four and dunking on bigger guys. I just loved that about him. He's a guy who would get mad or cry, depending on the moment you caught him at. That's what I am; I've let my weaknesses be out there to everybody, man. Where it's just the truth, you know?"

Once Webber turned pro, Barkley taught him a lesson in the playoffs of his rookie season. Barkley's Suns swept the Warriors in the first round, and Barkley went off, torching Webber for 56 points in one game. Webber took his medicine and vowed to get over his awe.

Now, nearly five years later, their relationship is strained, much to Webber's regret. Clyde Drexler has told Webber that anytime his name comes up in the Houston locker room, Barkley disparges him. "I hear all the time that Barkley says stuff about me and it hurts," Webber says.

"I haven't said anything about Chris Webber," Barkley responds tersely when I broach the subject with him. "I *haven't* said anything about Chris Webber." Something in his tone suggests he doesn't wish to discuss the matter further, but there are those close to him who confirm, in fact, that Barkley, while not holding anything against Webber personally, sees him as the embodiment of much that has gone wrong in the league. He's critical of all the showboating, posturing, and flexing for the cameras, all from a guy who hasn't won a damn thing, who has made the playoffs only twice—last season and his rookie year—and who barely accomplished that.

The criticisms have found their way to Webber through back-channel sources, including Drexler, who has his own issues with Barkley. Whether the shoulder was ready or not—and there was some question about its status—there was no way Webber was going to miss Barkley's only trip to the MCI Center on February 24.

The Rockets came limping into Washington having lost two in a row. In a sign of just how quickly things can change in the NBA, the Rockets had thought they were finally on a roll only a week before. Barkley hit a game-clinching baseline jumper on national TV against the Lakers, giving him 26 points for the game. Olajuwon was finally back and, before that game, Barkley tried to inspire his team. He told Tomjanovich that Kevin Willis had done such a superb job filling in for Dream that he didn't deserve to lose his starting spot. Saying he had "checked my ego at the door," he volunteered to be the team's new sixth man off the bench. Then he went a step further: He told NBC that he had a drinking problem and wouldn't drink again for the rest of the season. Like many of his antics, it was calculated. Privately, Barkley admitted he wasn't in danger of becoming an alcoholic (though he is a legendary drinker). Frustrated that his teammates, particularly Dream and Clyde, who already had their rings, didn't seem to share his hunger for a championship, he wanted to demonstrate his willingness to sacrifice in order to win. Few recognized it as such, but, together, both moves were textbook illustrations of leadership by example.

The win over the Lakers put the Rockets' record at 25–25 and was their third in four games, a streak that included a 97–83 drubbing of Seattle in which Barkley hauled down 21 rebounds. After beating the Lakers, the Rockets blew out the Clippers behind Barkley's 22 and then the Pistons by ten. Five wins in their last six outings, Olajuwon's return, Maloney's improved play, and Barkley's selfless leadership prompted some optimism in Houston.

But then the Timberwolves downed them, 100–95, and the Knicks destroyed them, 92–74, exposing Houston's old and tired legs. Barkley, in particular, looked like a fragment of the player he had been in Los Angeles just a week before. In the two games, he made just seven of twenty-five shots, scoring 18 points, and collected only 3 assists. Worse, the games themselves told a more distressing story than the stat sheets. Barkley was often trailing the play, seemingly worn-down.

He was ripe for Webber's return. From the outset, Webber was possessed, taking the ball strong to the basket. Barkley was reduced to fouling him and Webber made nine of his thirteen free throws. The Wizards won by twelve, and Webber received a roar of approval from the home crowd: He'd played forty-four minutes, hit thirteen of twenty-four shots, grabbed 13 rebounds, scored 36 points. Barkley, on the other hand, scored 16 points and had 7 rebounds.

In the game's waning moments, when it was clear the Wizards had won, Barkley flagrantly fouled Webber from behind. It was his sixth personal foul and the technical was his second—so he was, in effect, ejected from the game twice on the same play.

After the flagrant foul, Webber wheeled around and took a hard and purposeful step toward Barkley, towering over him. Webber's teammate Calbert Cheaney stepped between the two.

"He's not going to do anything," Barkley said to Cheaney while the two men glared at one another.

Without taking his eyes from his onetime idol, in a smooth voice that masked the roiling emotions within, Webber said: "I'm you now, Barkley."

As if the crowd had heard the trash talk, there were deafening cheers when Barkley turned and exited the court.

The adrenaline of that moment may be gone, but Webber

is still basking in the moment, seeing it as an important coming-of-age step. "I don't think a lot of people realize it, but us younger guys have already taken the baton," he says. "You don't have to give it to us—we've taken it. 'I'll hit you with it, too, Barkley, if you want to fight about it.' See, I can disagree with him, but I can still step outside of myself and I know what he formed for me, I know what he's done."

Still, the criticism from Barkley and others in the older generation rankles. "You know, someone like Barkley should realize he was young once, too," Webber says. "I mean, all I can say to him is: 'Weren't you having dinner with Jesse Jackson and now you're best friends with Rush Limbaugh?' I can definitely see how he's grown and evolved."

Webber laughs when I tell him how Barkley's criticisms of the younger guys echo Julius Erving's hand-wringings, who has gone so far as to lambast Jordan for occasionally shooting free throws with his eyes closed. "A lot of these are our own hangups, man," Webber says. "I love that Michael does that. It's entertaining. He never does it at crunch time. And if he didn't have five championships, maybe he shouldn't do it. I shouldn't do it. I haven't gotten to the point yet where I can shoot free throws with my eyes closed. But, man, these guys are taking themselves too seriously when they talk about this stuff. Look at Dr. J. He used to play with a gold chain on. How much more ghetto you gonna get? He was in *The Fish That Saved Pittsburgh*, with that big Afro. It hurts to hear the older guys talk about us. 'Cause I guarantee you, Dr. J wouldn't change any of that stuff he did. He wouldn't lose the Afro and Charles wouldn't stop being so expressive on the court. Why should I?"

Webber pauses to down a glass of cranapple juice. "That's why I want to win a championship so bad," he says, putting the issue to rest. "Right now, Barkley and I have the same number of rings. I'm going to get mine before he gets his."

*   *   *

His Barkley rant notwithstanding, Webber is in a distinctly more relaxed mood. Maybe it's the winning, maybe it's *The Seven Spiritual Laws,* maybe it's simply that the All-Star slight has been absorbed, dealt with, tucked away. As a result of all these factors, he's not obsessing solely on all matters Webber. The best prescription when adversity hits, he's realized, is to get out of your own head. Consequently, his conversational gamut runs far and wide. On this day, he's particularly perturbed by the witchhunt of President Clinton. The Clinton–Monica Lewinsky story is a mere few weeks old and Webber's already had enough. "It's getting ridiculous," he says. "I like Clinton. I met him when I was thirteen and I slept over Grant Hill's house when we played on the same AAU team. He was governor of Arkansas then. I remember being a shy little kid, talking to this guy who was a big sports fan and the governor of Arkansas. I always thought that was Clinton, but last year I said to my mother, 'Mom, next time you talk to Mrs. Hill, could you ask her if I met the President in 1989 at her house?' My mom was, like, 'Oh, Chris you didn't meet the President.' And then he came here for a game just recently, and before I could say anything he said, 'I remember meeting you. Grant Hill's father introduced us.' I couldn't believe it. His aides must have reminded him or something."

Also on his mind of late is the continuing exploitation of college basketball players. It was the reason he left Michigan and the Fab Five after two years; he was getting tired of seeing the school and the Big Ten and the TV stations literally take in millions of dollars because of him while he couldn't afford a pizza for dinner. It became such a negative experience: two straight appearances in the NCAA championship game, yet labeled underachievers and awash in a sea of hype and pressure, the game had ceased to be fun. They were subject to NBA-like scrutiny, but without the compensation.

That's why he tries to talk publicly about the Webber Plan, his panacea for college basketball, as much as he can. The NCAA will soon make modest stipends available to scholarships basketball and football players, which he opposes. The great thing about college sports is the joy that flows from its amateur status, he argues; rather than start down the slippery slope of turning the collegiate game professional, the Webber Plan would have universities do the right thing, long-term.

"Colleges should set aside a fund that the players could take from when they graduate, to help get them started," he says. "For instance, take Michael Talley from my team. He was a highly recruited high school player; he gave Michigan everything he had; took them to a Final Four, which made the school a lot of money; and then five freshmen—me and Jalen and Juwan and Jimmy and Ray—come along and he loses his spot. That changed his whole life. I think, since he did take the school to a Final Four before we got there, there could have been ten thousand dollars put away for him to use once he graduated. It's a way to help players help themselves, while keeping the game played by amateurs."

He looks at his watch. He's been lost in a welcome discussion of issues for hours, a nice break from one of the unexpected pitfalls of his job: You're often either talking or thinking about yourself. But tomorrow night the Knicks come in. For tonight, it's dinner with his buddy Kevin Colson in Georgetown.

And tomorrow night the roll will continue. The Wizards beat the Knicks by thirteen behind Webbers's 26 points, 7 rebounds, and 6 assists. A ten-point loss to the Celtics follows, but the Wizards rebound by beating the 76ers and Bucks. That makes six wins in the eight games since Webber's return.

Maybe God is righting this ship, after all, Webber thinks after his 24 points downs the Bucks.

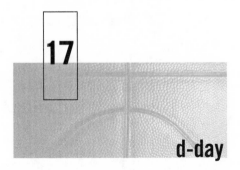

17

d-day

jerry Stackhouse keeps thinking, Maybe something will break tomorrow. It's twenty-four hours until the trading deadline, almost three weeks after he lost his starting position and six games since the coaching change. During these games, Stackhouse has watched his minutes get cut by eight per game, down to twenty-four. In this stretch, he's averaging a mere 12 points per game.

Now he flops down on his bed in the Four Seasons Hotel in downtown Houston, where the Pistons will take on the Rockets tomorrow night. But he can't stop thinking about last night, when he played 24 minutes, scoring all of 8 points on three for nine shooting, in a 95–94 heartbreaking loss at San Antonio that dropped the Pistons to 23–28. With six minutes to go, he hit a three-pointer and then dunked one on the fast break to give his team a 90–84 lead. But Gentry *still* removed him from the game. Granted, Malik Sealy was

having a good game—he'd finish with 13 points—but getting pulled characterized this stretch of games under Gentry
for Stackhouse: He feels like no matter what he does, it
won't be enough to pick up his minutes.

So now he's holding out hope that tomorrow will bring
him good news. His minutes and shots were there, after all,
when Lindsey Hunter was out of the lineup and the hot
rumor yesterday was that Hunter will be moved tomorrow.
Earlier today, however, team brass pulled out of a deal with
Toronto that would have sent Hunter, Jerome Williams, Don
Reid, and Grant Long for Kenny Anderson—who was
traded by Portland for Damon Stoudamire but has since refused to report to the Raptors—and Zan Tabak, Shawn
Respert, and Chris Garner. In effect, it would have been a
Hunter for Anderson deal, but the Pistons withdrew.

Still, Stackhouse entertains the notion that Hunter's upsurge in minutes is all about the team's desire to trade him,
to showcase him. But Stackhouse also knows that his problems go beyond losing minutes. When Gentry does play
him, it seems he's often frozen out of the offense.

"Anyone can see it," he says. "When I do get in, they've
got me just standing in the corner. They run something for
me every once in a while, like they're trying to pacify me."

It would be funny, really, if this weren't such a critical
time for him. Yesterday at shootaround, Gentry acknowledged as much. "I know I've got to get you some minutes,"
Gentry told him. "I know this is a big year for you."

In other words, this is Stackhouse's "Show me the
money" moment. As a free agent once this season ends, he's
got to finish strong if he hopes to sign somewhere for the
$10 million per year he believes he's worth. He's watched
other guys, guys he came into the NBA with, like Garnett,
get theirs. If Garnett's worth twenty million dollars, I'm
worth half that, he reasons.

Panic has taken hold. Just a month ago, he was a scoring
machine and looking at a big enough payday at the end

of the season for Fila to finally begin production of a new Stackhouse commercial for the Stack III. It would be footage of Stackhouse in his Piston uniform soaring through the air, while his voiceover intones: "The only competition is you."

But lately, Stackhouse hasn't taken his own commercial's advice to heart. He's pressing and it shows. "I've got this sense of urgency when I get into the game, 'cause I still want to maintain what I do, how I've been scoring the ball," he says. "Damn, I gotta get it done. I'm not gonna let my scoring fall off 'cause of what he's doing."

"He" is Gentry, who is immersed in his own big moment. This is Gentry's second go-round as an NBA interim coach. Last time, he took over for Kevin Loughery in Miami, compiling a 15–21 record, and then the Heat went out and hired Pat Riley away from the New York Knicks. Head coaching chances don't come along often in this league and now, suddenly, Gentry finds himself with another opportunity.

He has taken over a team with arguably more individual talent than last year's, which won 54 games under Collins. That Piston team had mainstays Hill and Dumars, but didn't have center Brian Williams, who is averaging 18 points and 8 rebounds a game, or Stackhouse or Sealy. Yet last year's team was more of a *team.*

No one knows this better than Hill, who is finally starting to say what he really feels about his team. He's been publicly bemoaning the loss of past Pistons, including Allan Houston, Terry Mills, Otis Thorpe, Michael Curry, and now Theo Ratliff. "It pained me to see Theo Ratliff leave," he told *The Detroit News.* "I wasn't for the trade. Theo can block shots, hit little jump shots, and now that Doug is gone, I know he would be playing with a lot of energy. Not that I don't like the guys who are with me now, but those others are guys I have been in the trenches with. I mean, there's no guarantee the guys on the team now are going to be here next year."

Gentry has been around the league, so he knows that the mindset of his superstar is as important to his future as his team's performance. If Hill's disapprobation led to Collins's dismissal, it stands to reason that Hill's support couldn't hurt his candidacy for full-time status once the season concludes.

Stackhouse understands this, too. When asked to explain why Gentry is cutting his minutes, he clearly refers to Hill when he replies, "I think he's just trying to get in with certain guys on the team." Then, when asked point-blank whether he was bothered by Hill's public denunciation of the trade, he says a bit naively, "I don't give a damn what he thinks. He don't sign my check."

The next day at noon the Pistons still have not made a move. Six hours remain until the deadline. After shootaround, Stackhouse meets his first pro coach, John Lucas, for lunch and a needed pep talk.

Since being dismissed by new ownership in Philadelphia in 1996, Lucas has taught tennis at the Westside Tennis Center and continued his customary good works by preaching the gospel of Twelve Step recovery to athletes who, like himself a generation ago, achieved too much too soon and lost themselves to drugs and alcohol.

But he's kept in touch with the NBA game and recognizes what he sees in Stackhouse, his first-round draft pick in 1995. "You're putting undue pressure on yourself to be successful," Lucas tells Stackhouse as they sit down to eat at Cleburne Cafeteria, a popular Southern-style restaurant in the shadow of Houston's Compaq Center. "You look like a player who's rushing."

Lucas goes on to explain that he's been where Stackhouse is now—playing for a contract, playing for a new team after being traded. He knows what it's like to see your peers—like Garnett, ever the benchmark—get their money, while question marks still surround your game. No one in the macho atmosphere of the NBA will talk about the effects, Lucas knows. They won't use phrases like "low self-esteem," because that wouldn't be manly. But he realizes from his own recovery and from, in his words, "looking deeper than the surface" when evaluating the modern-day athlete that Stackhouse is suffering a crisis of confidence.

"When you're traded, your mind starts playing tricks on you," Lucas tells him. "It's like you're not wanted. Your self-worth goes down."

He pauses. Stackhouse nods, picks at his fried chicken, doesn't open up. Still, Lucas sees he's on the right track. He remembers how his former coach here in Houston, Tom Nissalke, used to tell him to "quit running for class president." Lucas knows now what Nissalke was driving at; he'd been trying too hard and had to let up a bit and let the game flow to him.

"Life is nothing but a lot of new beginnings, Jerry," he says. "Relax and enjoy the ride. Whatever the money will be, it'll be."

Lucas understands what few insiders will admit: The hours before the trading deadline are an emotionally perilous time in the NBA season. General managers and players alike wax philosophic about the game really being a business, but they ignore the very human turmoil that characterizes this day. Getting traded is like getting dumped in a relationship; Lucas has seen firsthand how, as is the case in so many romantic uncouplings, players never recover from the rejection they feel when the team that drafted them, that made all sorts of commitments to them, then tells them, "We're moving on without you."

Dealing with personal issues is Lucas's strength and, in his mind, his efforts during this lunch are the literal definition of coaching. His job today is, in effect, to mend a quietly broken heart by convincing Stackhouse that his troubles are about nothing other than practical matters. "You were always going to be a late bloomer," Lucas tells him. "Remember, you changed positions when you came into the league. You played power forward in college."

Everything Stackhouse has gone through, Lucas tells him, ought not to be viewed as a referendum on his worth as a basketball player. The 76ers had to jettison him, after all, lest they lose him to free agency. And, as Lucas's last top draft pick, he belonged to the old regime; Iverson is the poster boy of Philadelphia's new owners. And now, in Detroit, his minutes have become linked with the job fortunes of an interim head coach. Like a mantra, he keeps telling Stackhouse, whose eyes search his former coach's for calming wisdom, that all of life is a series of new beginnings. "So enjoy the moment," Lucas says. "You're free to start over."

Phil Jackson's use of Zen philosophy to motivate his players, even Jordan, has been well publicized. When Jordan speaks of "being in the moment," as he often does, it **echoes** Jackson's preachings, gleaned from the writings of Thích Nhât Hanh or Shunryu Suzuki, to surrender ego and quiet the distractions of the interfering mind. "If you are too clever, you can miss the point entirely" goes the old Tibetan saying. Zen practitioners might call the resulting mindset nirvana; athletes call it the Zone.

Lucas's Twelve Step rap is essentially the same philosophy with a different lexicon. The first step, of course, is admitting you have a problem and recognizing a higher power: relinquishing ego, that chattering soundtrack inside your head. "You've got to get past all the pressure your mind is putting on yourself," he tells Stackhouse. "It's about letting go of the pressure."

When they part, Stackhouse seems lighter in spirit. Ever since his entry into the league, Stackhouse has had to wage war against his own inner thoughts. There's nothing wrong with the form of his jump shot, puzzled afficionados will tell you, before pointing to their head, as if to say. "This is where the problem resides. Too much thinking."

That's why, for three years now, Stackhouse has been in

the care of Taaj Jaharah, a licensed massage therapist and New Age guru who spent close to twenty years working with Kareem Abdul-Jabbar and treats dozens of pro and college athletes today with a comprehensive, holistic mind-body approach. "I train their biomechanical structure for efficiency to create a more durable and injury-free athlete," she explains. At the same time, she uses hypnotic language to rid athletes of the type of "limiting thoughts" Lucas observed Stackhouse having. "Limiting thoughts are actually distortions guys make up," she says. "I try to get them to realize the world is actually awash in nurturing possibilities."

Just a few hours after Lucas's talk recalled much of Jaharah's preachings in Stackhouse's mind, some players are crying in their beers like jilted lovers, wondering how the team that drafted and promoted them in the most hyperbolic of terms could be giving up on them now. Others—like Maloney—are exhaling, their fates secure for at least the balance of the season. Like the Rockets, the Pistons stand pat, rampant rumors notwithstanding. The Celtics get Kenny Anderson and give up Chauncey Billups, the Heat trade Isaac Austin for Brent Barry, the Bulls send Jason Caffey to the Golden State Warriors for forward David Vaughn, and the 76ers' Jimmy Jackson and Clarence Weatherspoon head to Golden State for Joe Smith and Brian Shaw.

Come game time, the Rockets beat the Pistons by ten. Barkley scores 14 and grabs 14 boards; Maloney shoots one for six, but hands out 7 assists. And Stackhouse gets twenty-six minutes and scores 13 points, hitting five of ten shots as his first pro coach watches the game. Afterward, an ever-reflective Stackhouse is amused when he realizes that it was only two years ago that he was playing for Lucas and being touted as the latest savior of the 76ers. He's now on his fifth coach and has saved none of them or their teams. He wonders, When will I stop being tested?

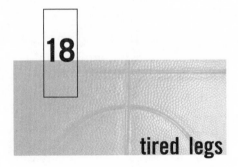

18

tired legs

since the loss at Washington that saw Barkley ejected after being abused by Webber, the Rockets have won six of nine, losing twice to the Jazz and once to Pat Riley's Heat. They've beaten Barkley's former team, the Suns, on the road, with Barkley getting 15 points and 12 rebounds, right around his season average.

But they haven't caught fire and it's coming down to crunch time. There's a little over a month to go in the regular season and the Rockets will likely be seeded eighth in the playoffs, thus facing Utah in the first round. Of course, being the seventh seed doesn't look any better: The Lakers or Supersonics would likely await.

And the fans are getting impatient. This is, after all, a team with three bona-fide Hall of Famers. But instead of Hall of Fame ball, the fans have gotten only small bursts of tantalizing play followed by stretches of no-help defenses, lackluster turnovers, and shoulder-shrugging body language. It is the age-old characteristic of a too-old team: worldbeaters one night, has-beens the next.

His whole career, Charles Barkley has been able to use his mental toughness to compensate for his physical shortcomings. He has excelled through sheer force of will and nothing has changed this season, save the result. He can't turn it on and take over like he once could. But what is even more frustrating is that his teammates don't even seem to share his desire; his team is complacent and even his bold moves a month ago—removing himself from the starting lineup, giving up drinking—hasn't changed that.

Tonight the Milwaukee Bucks come to town and the Compaq Center is abuzz with a bombshell of a report: Clyde Drexler is about to be named the new head coach of the University of Houston, his alma mater, effective at the close of this NBA season. He won't comment because there will be a press conference tomorrow, but some Rockets observers nod knowingly. Drexler has never been known as a locker room leader, but his equanimity this season in the face of his team's struggles has been particularly noticeable. "Now," some along press row mutter, "it makes sense." He'd checked out of this season long ago, concentrating instead on securing his next professional challenge.

The Rockets beat the Bucks, raising their record to 34–31. After the game, Barkley sits at his locker, a towel draped around his waist, reading the paper. The media mills about, waiting for Drexler to emerge from the shower so he can continue deflecting the barrage of questions until tomorrow's press conference.

Meantime, Barkley is expressing his distress over last night's episode of "60 Minutes," which featured Ed Bradley questioning Katherine Willey, another Clinton accuser. "I think the whole thing is stupid," he says.

"I agree," I say. "But—"

"No, if you agree with me, then that's it, right there." He

cuts me off, debating Barkley-style: smash-mouth political discourse. "It's a disgrace that the politicians are wasting the American people's money on something that's never going to come to fruition. It's disgraceful. That's why America is never gonna be successful, because we're all just little pawns in a big game. They're not going to do anything to Bill Clinton, because he didn't do anything wrong. That's why I hate the media so much. They're letting our money be wasted by this thing. Forty million dollars on Whitewater, another twenty million dollars on this."

He shakes his head before burying it back in the paper. Drexler emerges from the shower.

"Coach Drexler!" Barkley exclaims.

"Governor Barkley, what's up now?" Drexler replies.

Barkley is reading about a sexual and racial harassment suit brought against the Rockets' front office. "Man, I don't know about this racial stuff, so I can't comment on that, but all this sexual harassment stuff is getting absurd," he says, ostensibly to Drexler, but really for the ears of anyone remotely nearby. "Let's tell it like it is. Now. Man, Paula Jones be lucky if someone wanted to touch her ugly ass."

There is laughter and Drexler raises an eyebrow in surprise before seeming to inch farther into his locker. They are, in many ways, mirror images of the other. Drexler is a cultivated art collector, a Renaissance man who always plays his hand close to his vest—witness the secrecy of his year-long negotiations with the University of Houston. Barkley, of course, is Barkley—never an unexpressed thought. And he's not through now.

"Man, this whole Olympic thing; they're acting like they burned down a whole city," he says, pausing for a Drexler response. None comes.

"Can you believe that?" Barkley tries. Drexler doesn't know that Barkley's referring to the myriad press reports on the U.S. hockey team's destroying hotel rooms; he just has the look of someone who'd say anything if it facilitated a speedy escape.

"If they had won the gold medal and caused three thousand dollars' worth of damage, nobody would say a damned thing," Barkley says. "They just want to harass them guys. You guys in the media are making a mountain out of a mole hill. I'll give y'all three thousand dollars to let it die. What the players should have done was send a letter that said, "Kiss my ass, here's three thousand dollars." That would be the correct way to handle it. Right, Coach Drexler?"

Drexler smiles while hurriedly dressing.

"Man, making a big deal out of three thousand dollars' worth of damage," Barkley continues. "I'd pay three thousand dollars to see two dogs fuck."

After politely declining to respond to questions about his impending announcement, Drexler is out the door.

In the age of Iverson, Sprewell, Webber, et al., the qualities that make for a successful coach have come under review. It used to be that a coach's authority, by dint of the position, was questioned, if at all, only privately. The military model held: The coach, clipboard in hand, was the commanding officer, devising strategy, barking orders, and the players asked, "How high?" when told to jump.

No longer. Now such a coach would be seen as the Great Santini. "Look at Rudy," Barkley says at practice the day after the win over the Bucks. "He's a terrific coach because he's not an ego fanatic. It's not an ego trip, where it's his way or the highway. I compare him to Phil Jackson. Phil works with his players. He didn't try to change Dennis Rodman. He tries to work with him. And God knows Rudy's got some working to do with the players around here."

The skills most in demand of today's coach are people skills, which is what makes Drexler a strange choice as a head coach: someone who, while always pleasant and "classy," has always been guarded and aloof. Doomed are coaches who eschew the personal for the technical—all those chalkboard scrawls, detailing intricate X's and O's. The beat writers love to talk strategy, which explains all the hype about Bulls Assistant Coach Tex Winter's "triangle offense."* But students of the game know that chalkboard diagramming pales in comparison to getting guys to respect you and to play.

Indeed, there is a set of criteria emerging for coaching in the new NBA. Part of it has to do with an ability to remain cool under pressure; the high-strung coaches who seem to panic during games—the Carlesimos, the Collinses—tend to elicit impatient eye rolls from their charges rather than undying loyalty. And there is the issue of dress code: Coaches who dress with a *GQ* sense of style—Riley, Chuck Daly—start out with a baseline of respect from players; it's not purely coincidental that Carlesimo, compared to other coaches around the league, would make Blackwell's worst-dressed list if he were well enough known.

"I would make a great coach," Barkley says, noting that college teams, including Auburn, his alma mater, have sounded him out about coaching. "But I have other plans once I'm done playing."

Coach Barkley might seem almost as incredible as Governor Barkley, but there are those who think it makes perfect sense. "Charles *would* make a great coach," says John Lucas. "Forget all the X's and O's. The guy knows people. And he does a lot of his explaining and criticizing through humor, which players appreciate. It's not threatening and it's not embarrassing, but it is awakening."

Lucas should know. After his dismissal from Philadelphia, Lucas's stock as an up-and-coming coach dropped. But

*The hype is interesting on a number of levels; as USC Professor Todd Boyd points out, far too much credit for the Bulls' success has been given to a seventy-year-old white assistant coach, for an offense they don't even run when the game is on the line.

that shouldn't diminish what he did, first in San Antonio, then in Philly. With the Spurs, he allowed his players to conduct their own huddles, "empowering" them, giving them a "sense of ownership," and they had two highly successful seasons, going deep into the playoffs. He reached Rodman by treating him like a professional. The media blasted Lucas for establishing separate rules for the free spirit, but Lucas persisted: When Rodman offered that he didn't want to partake in the pregame layup drills, Lucas acquiesced, noting that Rodman rarely shot the ball anyway. Instead, Rodman rode a stationary bike for hours, right up until tipoff. "He was more prepared to play than anybody on our team," Lucas recalls.

In Philly, he put together a ragtag team that, in his second season there, won only 18 games. A year later, most of his players would be out of the NBA. (In fact, the next season, with the addition of Rookie of the Year Iverson and a healthy Derrick Coleman, the 76ers would win only four more games than the year before.) Yet when then-76er owner Harold Katz contemplated firing Lucas at midseason, Coleman, Maxwell, and Stackhouse all spoke out, saying, in effect, "If he goes, we go." Jordan's loyalty to Jackson, while stunning, is easier to comprehend, given their run of championships.

"Coaching is about finding what hoops guys will jump through for themselves," Lucas says. Indeed, much has been made this season of Rodman's good behavior and credit for it given to his incentive-laden contract. But the threat of losing money by itself doesn't motivate Rodman.

"Most athletes are addictive personalities, just like most high-powered executives," Lucas says. "And a contract like Dennis's says 'You can't' when addictive personalities operate under the assumption 'I can do anything.' If you're telling me I can't do it, I have to prove to you that I can. The contract is a challenge."

Similarly sophisticated coaching is on display this season

by Larry Bird in Indiana and Danny Ainge in Phoenix. When Robert Horry threw a towel in Ainge's face, the coach restrained his ego and used the incident to secure the respect of players league-wide. By far, the majority of those who will be free agents next season want to play for the Suns—in part because of the Phoenix weather and the Suns' considerable room under the salary cap, but mostly because they want to play for Ainge.*

And Bird's confident countenance has inspired a team that under old school tactician Larry Brown had been on the downswing. Bird's players have embraced him—in player jargon, they'll "run through walls" for him—because, at every opportunity, he demonstrates his respect for them, as when asked recently about his coaching future, he responded in a way Brown rarely did: "At the end of the year, if guys like Reggie [Miller] and Mark [Jackson] come to me and say, 'Coach, we respect you, but it's not working out,' I'd shake their hands and move on," he said. "It would hurt my pride, but these guys' careers are winding down and I'd want to make sure this is still fun for them."

Of course, if he is interested in a coaching career, Barkley is unlikely to ever get the chance, given his well-deserved reputation as a loose cannon. To many, he is a force of nature that needs to be handled; lost in the bigness of his persona, however, is Charles's deepest secret: He is *nice*.

"Charles is the exact opposite of most modern athletes," David Coskey, director of communications for the Philadelphia 76ers and a Barkley confidant—Charles is the godfather of one of Coskey's boys—once told *The New York Times Magazine*. "Most of these guys are jerks who want you to think

---

*It wasn't so long ago that Ainge was one of the league's bad boys. As a starter for the Boston Celtics, he went so far as to bite the venerable Dr. J during a melee. While punished and widely criticized, the angel-faced Mormon experienced little of the vitriol reserved today for the likes of Sprewell, Iverson, and Maxwell.

they're nice guys. But Charles is a genuinely nice guy who wants you to think he's a jerk."

Even after his metamorphosis into NBA elder statesman, casual pop culture observers know Barkley as the brute who spit on a fan and who has been arrested for fighting outside a Milwaukee bar and for throwing a heckler through a plate-glass window in Orlando.

But such run-ins are the price paid for Barkley's brand of populism. Unlike Jordan, who conducts his social life within the mysterious contours of clubs' VIP rooms, Barkley mingles. Consequently, once in a while, there will be some "nitwit," as he puts it, intent on tempting Barkley into providing fodder for a payday.

That's what happened outside the bar in Milwaukee, when three guys surrounded Barkley and a female companion late at night. It was the dead of winter, but, in an attempt to intimidate them, Barkley took off his jacket and shirt and starting improvising karate moves while emitting the piercing wails he'd heard in B-grade martial arts movies. "I wanted them to think I was crazy," he'd recall later, admitting that he knows nothing about karate. Approaching the middle assailant, he threw one punch to the nose and dropped the guy. The other two took off. "He was a big guy, but he was a bleeder," Barkley told David Letterman shortly thereafter.

The truth is, these infrequent run-ins notwithstanding, Barkley is one of the nation's most approachable star jocks. He's never turned an autograph-seeking kid away. "Charles has a heart the size of New Jersey," says his wife, Maureen. "Of course, he's got a butt the size of New Jersey, too. But it's amazing, the way he reacts to people in a restaurant, taking the time to speak to every single person who comes up to him."

Barkley is particularly touched by kids, which is why the infamous "spitting incident"—in which he inadvertently spat on a little girl sitting courtside during a game at the

Meadowlands—hurt him so deeply. What few know is that he struck up a close friendship with the little girl and her family in the aftermath of the incident.

When he and Maureen first had Christiana, Mo would laugh at how often Charles would sneak into his daughter's room at night to put his ear to the baby's chest, making sure the child was still breathing. Driving by a playground of kids hooping it up, he's been known to stop and get in the game. He makes regular visits to children's hospitals, always insisting that no media chronicle his good works.

He argues that seeking publicity for charity cheapens the act and calls into question the motivation. But it may go deeper than that: As Coskey implies, Barkley is aware that the moment he is known as a sentimental softie is the moment he loses a large part of his mystique.

"Charles can also be very defensive, so there's a lot about himself he doesn't want to let out," says Maureen. "He grew up in a situation where he was just so unsure of everything. They didn't have a lot of money, he didn't have a father. I guess it forces you to build a glass wall around yourself. There are people who are nice to him today who wouldn't give him the time of day if he weren't Charles Barkley."

His mother agrees. Charcy Glenn told *PhillySport Magazine* in 1988 that her son changed once he became a pro athlete. "Leeds is a small town where people wave to you when you pass their house," she said. "Charles was raised to trust people. He was very naive when he moved to Philadelphia. Here in Leeds, white and black work very well together. We still leave our door open. Charles used to think everyone was nice. He's learned a lot lately. He's growing up."

So the tough-guy posturing masks a soft heart; but it's such a thin veil, those who know him see right through it. "People have one impression of Charles because they see him on the court, slam-dunking," says former Vice President

Dan Quayle. "But, personally, he's quite a soft guy. He's big-hearted and really cares about people. It's remarkable to watch him interact with kids."

Call it the Barkley m.o.: gentle giant with kids, patient celebrity with respectful fans, marauding terrorist on the court and with the media. The terrorist, of course, makes for the better copy, which Barkley knows all too well.

On March 19, the Rockets beat the Celtics, 105–96, upping their record to 35–31. Maybe they're starting a roll that will carry into the postseason. The win is their fifth in a row, although they're all against teams they are expected to beat. Perhaps most significantly, the big three are back in the lineup together, and Olajuwon might finally be returning to form. Tonight he hit fifteen of twenty shots for a game-high 33 points.

But the team's fortunes are still overshadowed by the Drexler announcement, which is starting to sink in. The morning after the win over the Celtics Drexler's retirement has prompted some Barkley soul-searching.

Seven years ago, when he was twenty-eight and getting badly battered under the boards night after night, a doctor told him he had the body of a thirty-five-year-old. He said then he'd play only three or four more years. Maureen said then that her husband wouldn't play much longer, because he wouldn't be able to tolerate any deterioration in his skills. "He has too much pride," she said.

Now here he is, still playing. The loss of skill that creeps up on athletes at his age is something he thinks about, though. He was there when the home crowd booed Dr. J in 1987, his final season. He remembers how Bird couldn't walk at the end. It's tricky, knowing when to go.

"The fans and the media are selfish and unrealistic," he says now. "Guys deteriorate. It makes me sad that fans are so stupid that they don't want guys to retire. I look at retirement as a great thing. It's great to be successful for a long period of time, retire, and be happy ever after. The fans want you to keep playing. For what?"

He looks tired. Back therapy beckons, and there is a touch of envy in his voice when he talks about Drexler, who has finally set for himself an end to the grind. A friend suggests that it's nice that the fans want him to keep playing, that all they want is for him to give back to the game and to keep entertaining them.

"Hey, you've given to the game," Barkley says. "See all those kids with your jersey on? You've given way more than you've received. And you can't give them entertainment anymore. There comes a point where you can't give it anymore."

Just in case anyone thinks he's using the second person to talk about his teammate, Barkley rises with a groan and repeats himself. "You just can't give it anymore," he says.

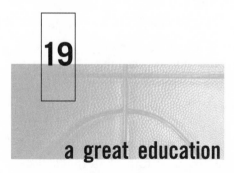

19

a great education

as he makes his way off the floor after his team's win over the Celtics, Matt Maloney is vaguely aware of a tall blonde woman making her way through the crowd toward him. As always, he averts his eyes.

"Matt! Matt!" she calls.

He looks up but doesn't slow down. She says nothing. Just gazes at him and forces an envelope into his hand. Safely in the runway, he opens it and his placid demeanor is suddenly gone; eyes bulging, face reddening, he looks at a naked photo of the woman, on her knees, smiling for the camera. On the back is scrawled: THINKING OF YOU, ROBYN.

"Oh, man," he says, shaking his head. "I've gotta show this to Brent."

Once in the locker room, he sees Price. "Hey, check this out," he says.

When someone comments that, having gone through all

the trouble to get to him, you'd think she'd have left her phone number, Maloney is clearly shocked.

"You don't think I'd ever *call* her, do you?" he says.

Others are titillated by the photo. Shaking his head as they pass it around, he seems a little freaked out by it.

"There are some strange people out there," he mutters.

Maloney, who had 19 points against the Bucks two nights ago, scored 10 tonight, making his last four shots from the floor after missing his first four. Later, it's those first four he can't get out of his mind, sitting with Paul, Nicole Tomjanovich, and Robin, a pretty blonde from the Rockets' community relations office, at the Volcano, a Houston bar.

Shooters live in fear of the same thing: the almost imperceptible foul on the all-important follow-through after the ball's been released. It's rarely called, because most refs consider the shooter fair game once the ball's out of his hands. That's what Matt claims happened tonight on his first four attempts. Defensive players running at him nicked his hands—maybe even his fingertips—on his extension after he'd launched the shots. Refs discount the shooters who complain of such seemingly incidental contact; indeed, most chalk it up to the softness of shooters, assuming that those content to stand outside and drain jump shots have an aversion to physical contact.

But that doesn't hold true in Maloney's case. He's a big point guard—six-foot-three, but, more important, a solidly built 200 pounds—who actually likes to guard his man down low. He doesn't mind being banged around while being run through picks—as he exhibited in last year's playoffs, when Stockton had him charging into roadblock after roadblock. No, Maloney can bear that. He can't stomach the fouls that the refs consider ticky-tack but that he knows mean the difference between a made and missed shot. Tonight the refs cost him maybe 6 or 9 more points. It's not fair, he argues: There is a boxscore after games that reviews how players have performed, but nothing that indicates what kind of game the refs have had.

So tonight, after getting whacked following his fourth straight miss, he had to speak his mind.

"I haven't gotten a call since I've been in this league," he called to the ref, who just shrugged.

"Well, last year, you were a rookie," Paul says now. Everyone knows that rookies get no breaks.

"But it's no different this year and it happens to other guys I talk to," Matt says. "The truth is that white guys get porked in the NBA. I'm telling you, it's prejudice. Brent and Mark Price have experienced the same thing. We don't get the calls."

It is not that radical a thesis. White players, a small minority in the NBA, believe they suffer from a preconceived perception of slow-footedness. Calling fouls on their quicker defenders concedes that the defender was himself out of position, something most refs—not to mention coaches and broadcasters—are loath to recognize, given the preconception.

In fact, in a culture that finds the majority—whites—complaining about how often blacks think and talk about race, it should come as no surprise that, in turn, Maloney and other white basketball players—the league's minority—see racial implications where others don't. After all, fewer than 15 percent of the NBA starters are white; Maloney has had to overcome prejudice just to get where he is.

"Granted, only a small percentage of guys from the inner city make it, but the chances are greater that someone from there will make it than someone from Haddonfield, New Jersey," he says. "So my situation is almost the reverse of what you would think. It's like a black guy from the inner city becoming CEO of a Fortune 500 company."

And as a minority, Maloney says his eyes are opened every day. "This is a great education," says the history major who posted a 3.0 GPA at Penn. In the CBA, for in-

stance, he roomed with Cuonzo Martin, a six-foot-six black
man from East St. Louis. "Basketball made it possible for a
kid from the ghetto in St. Louis and a kid from Haddonfield
to become best friends," he says. "I don't know where else
that happens. I guess the Army. And what was cool was
that neither of us are sensitive about our differences. So we'd
bust on each other all the time. I'd get on him about rap
music."

Indeed, it is one of the great paradoxes of sports' place
in popular culture. Those who chronicle sport may lag behind the cultural zeitgeist—witness *The New York Times*'s
insistence on calling Ali "Cassius Clay" for years after his
name change—but sport itself has long served as an egalitar-
ian model. The civil rights movement, after all, didn't start
with *Brown vs. Board of Ed.*; it started with Jackie Robinson.

And as Maloney knows, with the possible exception of
the military, professional sports in America is a shining example of meritocracy in action. "The best thing about sports
is that it's color-blind," Barkley often observes. "In the
locker room, we're all the same. Sports brings us together.
I mean, if you can play, you gonna play, no matter what
color you are."

As Barkley suggests, unlike most of the American workplace, discrimination isn't an impediment to opportunity in
sports. Partly that's because performance in sports can be so
easily measured: If you can score 20 points and make half
your shots, there's an NBA roster spot for you. Whites like
Maloney still have to counter misperceptions, but they nonetheless get the opportunity. If they perform, they're in; if
not, it will have nothing to do with pigmentation. Yet subtle
racial preferences do exist—off the court, especially when it
comes to the game's marketing. How else to explain New
Jersey's Keith Van Horn, the league's latest "Great White
Hope"—a good player whose hype is overshadowing fellow
rookie Tim Duncan, a *great* player who happens to be black?

For his part, Maloney gets frustrated at the repeated la-

beling of him that has racial roots: "heady," "slow," "soft."
But at least he's here, countering the stereotypes, night after
night. And he's open to alternative views. Now, for instance,
still ruminating on those first four shots tonight, he entertains factors besides race for the silent whistles. "The only
other thing I can think of is that I'm stronger than a lot of
point guards, so that when I get fouled, if I don't flop
around, it may look like incidental contact," he offers with
a shrug.

It is mid-March. A little over two weeks ago, arbitrator
John Feerick, dean of Fordham Law School, ruled on the
Sprewell case, reinstating the final two years of his contract,
worth $17.3 million, and reducing the NBA-imposed suspen-
sion by five months, making Sprewell eligible to play—
under contract to the Warriors—next season. In effect, Feerick found there was no precedent in league annals for the
severity of Sprewell's punishment.

Now Sprewell has embarked on a publicity campaign to
repair his image. Maloney watched him on "60 Minutes"
and was struck by a fact Sprewell has been trumpeting as
proof of his overall good character: He's had only a handful
of technical fouls called on him in his entire NBA career.

"I was, like, 'Wow, I've gotten, like, nine technicals already,' " Maloney says. Last week against the Nets, for instance, he approached a ref after a foul had been called on
him. "You called that?" he said. "Man, you're having a bad
night." It was said conversationally—without the histrionics
that are intended to show up the ref and that qualify as
automatic T's—but he got whistled nonetheless. Then there
was the game at Portland, when, trapped in the corner by
a double team, Maloney tried to call timeout, but the ref
was out of earshot.

"I didn't hear you," the ref explained when, after a turnover, Maloney protested.

"Don't you think it's your job to get in position to be
able to hear me?" Maloney asked. The ref's response: a T.

Granted, there is something of the Ivy League in the way Maloney questions calls. His Socratic method differs from, say, Maxwell's style. Last week, Maxwell was given a quick T upon entering a game simply for mumbling the phrase "What a shitty call." Immediately after the whistle, he stormed the ref. "Muthafucka, you shoulda died when you was a baby," he said, earning an immediate ejection.

Maloney's increasing decibel level on the court is a testament to his growth since entering the league. With Olajuwon's return to the lineup, his scoring chances have dropped off, but the new, aggressive Matt who emerged after resting his elbow in mid-January appears to be here to stay.

It's evident in his demeanor. When, two weeks ago, Heat point guard Tim Hardaway was raining in jumpers off pick and rolls while the Heat battered the Rockets, the home fans started calling for Maloney's exit from the game. Tomjanovich complied, bringing in rookie Rodrick Rhodes to try and contain Hardaway.

But the opposite happened: Hardaway broke the rookie down, crossing him over, scoring at will. Against Maloney, at least, the scoring was within the Heat's offensive flow, as a result of pick and rolls, and Hardaway was being kept from the lane and forced to knock down outside shots. As it became clear that the crowd's desired change wasn't working, a disgusted Maloney, on the bench, held his arms in the air, palms upraised, while surveying the crowd, as if to say, "Okay, smart guys, what now?" It was a seemingly out-of-character moment.

Gone is the rah-rah, wide-eyed rookie. "These people don't like to hear this," he says, sweeping the barroom with a wave of his hand. "But after they tried to trade me, I realized I have to care more about whether I get my numbers or not. I've got to look out for number one, which isn't to say I still don't want to win or that I don't root for Brent when he's in there. But that's the biggest difference between me last year and this year. They've shown me that this is a business, plain and simple."

We get another pitcher of beer while he confers with Paul about the upcoming labor strife. "It seems to me, if the players are getting about half the money, or a little over half, what's wrong with that?"

Paul cautions him to think about his own situation. For two years now, Matt has been vastly underpaid for a starter: $247,000 his rookie year, $320,000 this season. One of the union's goals in negotiations will be to up the minimum salary into the $500,000 range, because the escalating salaries at the star level—Garnett, Garnett, Garnett—have had a re-verse trickle-down effect, creating a gulf between the ultra-elite players and the increasing number of players stuck with the minimum. In effect, the big salaries are contributing to the extinction of a middle class in the league, a class Malo-ney aspires to.

Finally Maloney turns to the women and says he wants to go to the Vapor Room, a trendy martini lounge with good music. They're all for it. It's about 1 A.M. now; I ask if it isn't past his bedtime. "I figure in sixty or a hundred years, no one will remember any of this," he says, referring to his season, his elbow, the Rockets' record, the labor dispute. "They'll remember we had a president who some people tried to impeach and failed. That's all. So I figure we may as well have some laughs."

Paul is good for laughs. At the Vapor Room, there is an eye-level mirror next to the bar. "Hey, look, they owe me royalties," he blurts out, pointing at his reflection as his brother makes his way over. "See? They've got my photo on the wall!"

Matt laughs so hard he grabs his stomach and pushes his brother out of the way. "That's a good one!" he says, now standing in front of the mirror himself and flapping his arms. "Hey, look at this, Paul," he says. "It's a video of me!"

Paul and Matt puff cigars purchased at the bar and sit down, cosmopolitans in tow. The sound of "In the Name of Love," U2's tribute to Martin Luther King, Jr., fills the air, and soon Matt is crooning right along with Bono. Music is the other passion of Matt Maloney. Back in Haddonfield, when he wasn't on the court he was playing guitar in a typical suburban garage band or writing music and lyrics. Just recently, he made his own CD in a Houston recording studio, playing every instrument, singing his own tunes. Paul wants to market the CD locally. "The teenyboppers around here will go for it in a second," he says.

There is, of course, precedent for NBA players crossing over into other forms of entertainment. Shaq has his rap CDs and Waymon Tisdale has released jazz recordings. Maloney's music is eerily similar to U2, one of his favorite bands. His voice, in fact, is a cross between Bono and another favorite, Morrisey, the brooding lyricist who sings earnestly of his devoutness and celibacy and place in the world. Maloney's lyrics, in fact, are similarly self-revealing. He sings about loneliness, heartbreak, alienation.

"Matthew reminds me so much of my dad, it's scary," says Nicole Tomjanovich, who sits across from Matt as he and Bono continue their duet. She's an attractive woman in her early twenties, about to start medical school, who is thankful the deal that would have sent her friend to Toronto fell through. "Like Mathew, my dad is really, really sensitive. He just loves his players so much. He tries to please them all, but you can't, not always. I know he was having a real hard time when Matthew was almost traded. They are so much alike. My dad is always reading, just like Matt. Self-help books, philosophy books. And my dad is a wonderful musician, too. He writes music and plays music. I'm always finding him relaxing listening to John Lennon music. It's like his therapy."

She's watching her friend Matthew as the U2 song ends.

"How 'bout that song?" he says, smiling at Nicole. "MLK, baby."

"Yeah, my dad and Matthew are both sensitive, caring, and musical," she says. It's 2 A.M. Matt Maloney, cigar in mouth, taps his foot to the music while nursing a drink. He is loosening up.

The next night Maloney scores 19 points in a win at Dallas, and the Rockets up their record to 36–31. With fifteen games left, it appears they are about to close out the season with a run, maybe establish some momentum, maybe move up a spot or two in the standings.

Barkley, for one, is worried. He doesn't want to face the Lakers in the first round—his slow-footed, aging Rockets versus the fleet Lakers presents too many matchup problems.

Maloney doesn't care who he plays. He just wants to rest his elbow. He's icing it every day, trying to keep the swelling down after taking hundreds of shots. "I wish I could take a couple of games off, like I did before, to get it ready for the playoffs," he says. "But that's not going to happen."

20

don't get vernon mad

"man, he ain't lost it."

That was Gary Payton's verdict two night ago, after Vernon Maxwell befuddled one of the league's best defensive players—they don't call Payton "the Glove" for nothing—to lead the Hornets to a 104–98 win over the mighty Super-Sonics. Maxwell exploded off the bench for 22 points, on eight of fourteen shooting, in twenty minutes. The Sonics tried everything to stop him, from shooting guard Hersey Hawkins to Payton to their trademark defensive traps, but Maxwell kept draining threes—five of nine—and driving into the lane.

There was motivation aplenty for Max. Of course, the Sonics are one of the league's elite teams—and Maxwell lives to show up the best. More important, he had lobbied Payton in the off-season to secure him a deal on George Karl's team. Hawkins, after all, is a serviceable shooting guard, but he doesn't have Maxwell's fire, defensive quickness, or championship experience. Payton told Maxwell he'd see what he could do, but that was the last Max had heard from his friend.

It was payback time. Luckily for Maxwell, he hit his first couple of shots, insuring against a quick hook. One thing Maxwell has learned in his sixteen games as a Hornet is that Cowens isn't naturally inclined to give his bench a lot of minutes. Maxwell knows that to get his time, he has to light it up immediately when he gets in.

"I love Dave, I really do," he says of his coach now, four days after his heroics versus the Sonics. He is huddled over a shot of Courvoisier at Charlotte's Scoreboard Sports Bar, where they are out of Rémy, V.S.O.P., thanks to his recent visits. "But there ain't no rhyme or reason to when you gonna play here. This place is so fucking wishy-washy."

Indeed, two nights ago, his stellar game against Payton and Hawkins was followed by just twelve minutes and 2 points in a win over the Nets. In Cowens's defense, however, his team is the hottest in the league—winners of eight in a row with the Knicks due in tomorrow night—and they are starting to get healthy again. Starting shooting guard Bobby Phills is back and Dell Curry is getting close to returning. "When Dell gets back, I don't know if there'll be any minutes for me," Maxwell says.

The fact is that, though the NBA is a shining example of meritocracy, like every other workplace, job performance doesn't necessarily account for everything. The Hornets invested heavily in this season's starting backcourt: Phills and David Wesley. Both received multiyear, multimillion-dollar contracts, and both have been mild disappointments. But no matter how well Maxwell or the other guards—Curry, Corey Beck, B. J. Armstrong—play, there will be no unseating of the starting twosome and nary a dip in their minutes, because of the sizable investment made in them.

Nonetheless, despite a staggering spate of injuries, the

Hornets have gone on this winning streak, thanks largely to Maxwell. This morning at practice General Manager Bob Bass, perhaps sensing that Maxwell's minutes would be curtailed as other players return to the lineup, made sure Maxwell knew that he recognized his contribution. "I'd say you've won four games for us since you've been here," Bass told him.

Now Maxwell orders another round. His cousin Steven is in town and they are joined by Aaron Wingate, cousin of the Sonics' veteran David Wingate, Maxwell's teammate eight years ago in San Antonio. Ron Herbert, a white restaurateur and Wingate's buddy, is also in the house; earlier tonight we ate at Herbert's place, Red Rocks Cafe, where Herbert is adding "Vernon's Meat Loaf Sandwich" to the menu. During the meal, it became clear that the curvy blonde hostess had her sights on Maxwell—and that Herbert had his on her. "I think we watching 'The Jerry Springer Show,' " Steven said between mouthfuls of his barbequed beef sandwich. "A fuckin' love triangle, man."

But there was no harm, so no foul. It's a couple of hours later, and a deep frown crosses Maxwell's brow when, on the big screen in front of him, the Spurs are taking on the Nets. When the camera finds his autocratic coach of last season, the Spurs' Greg Popovich, Maxwell shakes his head sadly. "Fuckin' Grand Dragon," he says of the man who, according to a teammate he trusted, referred to him as a "rebellious nigger." "All that dude's missing is the white sheet, man."

And, it could be argued, all Popovich's team is missing is Maxwell. With surefire Rookie of the Year Tim Duncan and a rejuvenated David Robinson leading the way, the Spurs have one of the game's best front lines but, as has been the case for years, their backcourt—Avery Johnson and Vinny Del Negro—is sorely lacking.

Maxwell watches the game and roots against his old team, but Herbert won't let him watch in peace. He is a

buzzing ball of energy, a nonstop, rapid-fire conver-
sationalist.

"Who do you think is better, you or Dale Ellis, huh?"
Herbert asks.

Maxwell looks up. "One-on-one?"

"Shooting."

"Shit, Dale is a shooter," Maxwell says. "I'm a scorer.
We play one-on-one, he won't score off me."

Herbert's train of thought cannot be derailed. "Best
shooter I've ever seen, Dale Ellis. Whaddya think of that,
Vernon, Dale Ellis?" Herbert pumps out. "I mean, that guy
can shoot. You know, I love you, but—"

Maxwell cuts off his new friend. "You gotta realize, I
don't want a lot of folk loving me," he says. "I like 'em to
fear me. I like 'em to think I'm a bad muthafucka."

Minutes. Throughout his pro career, Vernon Maxwell
has had a tempestuous relationship with minutes. When he
gets his, when he knows he'll have time to settle into a
rhythm, all is well with the world. When they aren't there,
when, for whatever reason, his thirty-five minutes have been
cut or are suddenly being distributed unpredictably, he is
on edge, he is moody, he is angry.

Ever since he was a kid, Vernon Maxwell has been unable to sit still. It is torturous: sitting on the bench, watching
a guy score who you know you can shut down. He'll drape
a towel over his head or glare at his coach or, when it all
gets to be too much, start cursing out the coach to his teammates. All because he wants to play so badly, to be in control, to win.

It is the one major regret of his career: the power his
minutes hold over him. It's what did him in in Houston.

The beginning of Maxwell's end in a Rockets uniform
came on February 6, 1995, less than eight months after the
'94 title win over the Knicks. That was the night that Maxwell charged into the stands after the fan who was heckling

him about his stillborn daughter. "When Maxwell drew a ten-game suspension from the NBA, that got us thinking about the stability of our starting shooting guard," Tomjanovich later wrote in his book, *A Rocket at Heart: My Life and My Team*. "What could we expect from Max? He was a fiery guy who had had his share of incidents on and off the court. In a year when we were struggling, putting your team in that kind of jeopardy really got me thinking about making a deal."

So the Rockets traded for Drexler, a hometown hero, while Maxwell was suspended. Even with Clyde, the Rockets continued to struggle, limping into the playoffs as the number-six seed. Meantime, Maxwell was sulking about diminished playing time. Tomjanovich's plan was to gradually move Maxwell to point guard; a backcourt of Maxwell and Drexler would be particularly imposing.

But he underestimated the emotional powder keg that is Maxwell. Tomjanovich introduced Drexler to the team with the warning that everyone would have to sacrifice in order to accommodate their newest teammate. From Maxwell's perspective, only his minutes were drastically reduced. In the team's first-round playoff game against Utah, Maxwell played just 16 minutes, but Tomjanovich still had enough confidence in him to run the last play his way, with the Jazz up 102–100 and a couple of seconds remaining. Maxwell fired up a three—trying for the win—that bounced off the rim. It would be his final shot as a Rocket, because, the next day, Maxwell did the unthinkable and quit the team.

The Rockets went on to win another title and Maxwell signed the next season with Philadelphia. He and Tomjanovich patched things up when Maxwell, wearing a 76ers uniform, visited Houston. Before the game, Tomjanovich shared nothing but fond memories of his six years with Maxwell. "He was a special-type guy—a warrior," he told the *Houston Chronicle*.

Now it's three years since he bolted Houston, and here

he is, in Charlotte, his minutes being cut again. Curry is healthy, which means he'll see even less playing time in the weeks ahead. "That's okay, that's okay, I learned, man," he says now, in the front passenger seat of his Range Rover as Aaron drives back to the two-bedroom condo Maxwell has just moved into for the balance of the season. "This ain't Houston in '95, know what I'm saying? I gotta be realistic. I'm not in the same situation now. There I was starting and getting, like, thirty-five minutes a night. I'm not in that situation now. Here I just had to show I could still ball so somebody will take care of me next year. Give me some minutes, let me be a sixth man. It's like my mom is always saying: 'You made your own bed. You reap what you sow.' I made my bed when I left Houston. So now I gotta do this, you know? Show I can still play and that I want it."

He leans forward and cranks the stereo—it's Mase, singing "Tell Me What You Want." The Knicks are due in tomorrow. No wonder he's thinking about Houston.

Maxwell is first off Cowens's bench against the Knicks and he hits an apparent buzzer-beater from halfcourt at the close of the first quarter, but it is erroneously disallowed by the officials.

At halftime, the Hornets lead, 47–43, but Anthony Mason rips into his teammates in the locker room, reserving much of his ire for the guards—Wesley, Phills, Maxwell, and Beck—who, he claims, are not fighting through picks. Mason, of course, carries a special vendetta against the Knicks, the team that traded him away for Larry Johnson. Maxwell, noting that Johnson, who Mason is guarding, leads all scorers with 15 points, is the only one to respond to Mason's diatribe.

"This is the fuckin' NBA, man. Picks happen," he yells. "Just do your job—your man's got fifteen muthafuckin' points!"

As the Hornets emerge from their locker room, Maxwell

and Mason carry their confrontation into the layup line. They continue jawing at one another, neither man willing to allow the other the final word, much to the delight of teammates J. R. Reid, Corey Beck, and Travis Williams, who laugh their way through the drill.

In the second half, neither Starks nor Maxwell is a factor. Cowens hardly goes to his bench at all and the Hornets win, 85–78, raising their record to 39–23, behind Glen Rice's 22 points and Mason's 21 points and 5 assists.

It's 2 A.M. and the night is just beginning. The Hornets arrived back from Orlando two hours ago after a 100–82 win—number ten in a row.

The NBA is quite naturally a nocturnal league. Games end at ten or eleven at night, leaving players too keyed up to simply head home for "SportsCenter." So they go out: Tonight the destination is Stayin' Alive, an all-black Charlotte dance club.

Maxwell is in a good mood, despite seeing only five minutes of action earlier tonight. Curry got some time as did, quite inexplicably, B. J. Armstrong, who has been riding the bench a lot lately but who played with energy when called upon tonight.

On the plane ride home, Maxwell won $200 playing cards and is certain that he's on his way to a bigger payday. He and Mason bet $2,000 on whether Houston had the home-court advantage throughout the '94 playoffs. Mason says they did, Maxwell says they didn't. Maxwell knows he's right.

But Maxwell's happiest about the arrival tonight of his older brother Greg, who is in town with their fast-talking, gregarious brother-in-law Jesse James Armstrong. Greg, two years Vernon's senior, is bulky and imposing and, just as when they were kids, always watching his little brother's back. When he hears that their cousin Steven was in town until earlier today, for instance, Greg rolls his eyes.

"I'm glad Steven left," he says. "See, Vernon's too good to people and sometimes he gets used. Like with Aaron [Wingate, who picked Greg and Jesse up at the airport]. He seems like a cool guy, but all Vernon knows is that he's Wingate's cousin, so he gives him the keys to the apartment and the Range Rover. People think Vernon's a bad guy, but his biggest problem is that he's too nice."

Greg and Jesse, who is married to Vernon and Greg's sister Shauna, both live in Gainesville, where Greg was recently laid off from his job as a baggage handler at American Airlines. Where Jesse is wild and comical, Greg is laid-back and serious, the result of a lifetime spent looking out for younger siblings.

We leave a message for Webber and Strickland, whose Wizards are tomorrow's opponent. Meantime, as the night wears on, more and more Hornets show up. At one point, I spot Vernon, Greg, Beck, and Travis Williams, all at the bar laughing at me—the club's lone white guy, drink in hand, politely paralyzed as they send woman after woman my way, undulating before me, trying to entice me to bust a move. The guys think I don't see them.

At about 3 A.M., Mason, wearing a lime green shirt and pink designer blazer, glides in with his posse and settles in at the bar with a nod to Maxwell. He sends over a bottle of Moët to Vernon, who responds in kind with Rémy. They are teammates, after all. Over the sound system, the deejay welcomes Mason to the club and congratulates the Hornets on winning their ninth in a row.

"Now, I had something to do with some of them wins," Maxwell says, leaning against the bar. "But that's okay. That's what fucked me up in Houston. Everywhere I went, it was 'Hey Max, yo Max,' and that shit messed with my head. This is better. I don't want to be that visible. I just want to play ball."

Jesse is buzzing around the bar. "Can you believe I let

my sister marry that fool?" Maxwell says as he watches
Jesse. "I can't help it, though. I love that fool."

Suddenly his expression changes as he looks me in the
eye, down at my drink, then at me again. I've been nursing
my drink and now I'm busted. Maxwell grabs a promotional
flyer off the bar and hands it to me. "See this? This here a
bitch card," he says. "It means you a bitch, 'less you down
that and do some serious drinking."

Fearful of the bitch card, I tell him to order shots and
line 'em up. It's going to be a long night.

With roughly six weeks left until the end of the regular
season, competition on and off the court is heating up. Off
court, the players know that a new fashion season is upon
them—five-button single-breasted suits with butterfly collar
shirts are all the rage—and it's time to place orders for their
spring duds.

Over the past ten years or so, a cottage industry has
sprouted up in the shadow of the NBA: custom-made clothing. For NBA players, buying off the rack has always been
problematic. Any choice, after all, is bound to require extensive tailoring, and browsing in crowded men's stores often
results in unwanted attention or, at least, gawking.

Enter the clothiers who cater to the NBA. There are a
handful of them, and their competition can be as intense as
what transpires on the court. They can be seen in hotel lob-
bies on the road, eagerly testing out fabrics and patterns on
clients and would-be clients alike. Foremost among them is
Cary Mitchell of Charlotte, with over sixty players, including
Barkley, Stackhouse, Grant Hill, and Tim Duncan. He convinced Larry Johnson, who is color-blind, to give up his
penchant for bright orange suits and even organized the
Knicks star's closet by shirt, tie, and suit so that putting
together a matching outfit would no longer be a challenge.
Over the last four years, Mitchell estimates that Johnson has
bought over 150 custom-made suits at an average cost of

about $850 each. Others order a complete wardrobe at upward of $50,000.

On this day, after watching the NCAA Tournament and eating take-out barbeque for lunch at Maxwell's new digs—a six-pack has the refrigerator all to itself—it's time to get dressed for the game against the Wizards. Maxwell pulls out a sleek black suit from his closet, designed by Jonathan Smith, whose company, Bespoke Carolina, is based in Myrtle Beach, South Carolina.

Smith outfits a number of the Hornets and takes particular pride in the sartorial stylings of center Matt Geiger. "Matt was your typical big bald-headed white guy when I first met him," says Smith. "He always wanted to dress well, but never found his identity. Now he's one of the best-dressed guys in the league. He's considered very avant-garde."

Maxwell takes an iron to a white silk shirt and says, "I hate getting all dressed up just to go the arena and get undressed again."

Once at the arena, he might have wondered why he bothered suiting up at all. He sees nine minutes and is score-less; Webber scores 22 and grabs 11 rebounds in an 83–80 Wizards win, breaking the Hornets' streak. Webber, in fact, hits the game-winning bucket, a driving one-hander in the lane with under a minute to go. For Wizards fans, it's a comforting sight: Their big man taking it strong to the basket when it matters, not settling for an outside jumper with the game on the line.

Afterward, Strickland, who wanted the Wizards to sign Maxwell early in the year, is relieved he didn't have to put up with Max's ball-hawking defense for more than a few minutes. "Good D," he'd said to Maxwell in the first half, when Max cut off his path to the basket on a pick and roll.

"All our coach told us before the game was: 'Don't get Vernon mad,'" Webber says, smiling as he looks at a stat sheet. "'Don't get Vernon mad.' We didn't."

Four days later at Utah, Maxwell will come through on national TV. He gets fourteen minutes, hitting six of nine shots, including a couple of hanging-in-the-air prayers, for 14 points in a 111–85 blowout of the Jazz. When, on a three-on-one, he pulls up and drops a three, TNT broadcaster Hubie Brown shrieks: "Now *that's* confidence!"

Meantime, the premier issue of *ESPN Magazine* has come out and it includes a short sarcastic item, pegged to the news that the Supreme Court wouldn't hear his appeal, about Maxwell's legal travails—diagramming them as though they were a play on a chalkboard. By now, he is used to it, the way his misdeeds of years ago get resurrected, time and again. "That's the only thing still hanging over my head from my past," he says, standing at his locker. When he spots one of the Hornets ball boys, he digs into his pocket and excavates a twenty, holding it out to him. "This for you. Give it yo mama, hear?" he says, pulling the twenty back as the boy tries to snatch it.

"You gotta give this to yo mama, okay?" he says. When the youngster nods, Maxwell gives up the cash. "Yeah, that Houston shit, man. No matter what I do, no matter what kind of person I try to become, it's like no one will just let that old shit die. They won't let it die."

He doesn't know just how prophetic that is.

FOURTH QUARTER

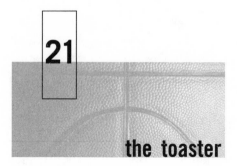

21

the toaster

two hours before game time, the television in the Detroit Pistons' locker room plays a tape of tonight's opponent: the Toronto Raptors. But no one is watching. In fact, only one player is in the room. Jerry Stackhouse sits at his locker, dressed in jeans and a gray PISTONS T-shirt, frowning while he intently peels an orange, pausing only occasionally to glance at the screen.

A couple of kids with locker room access passes draped around their necks come rushing through and abruptly halt when they notice Stack, their eyes popping. "Wow! It's Stackhouse!" one exclaims as though the player were out of earshot—or a museum piece.

"What's going on, men?" Stack calls without unfurling his knotted brow or looking up from his orange. The kids stand there for a second, awestruck, and then they're off, rushing out the door, whispering excitedly about their interaction with a real-live NBA star.

Stackhouse's mind seems miles away, however. His minutes and scoring average have picked up of late, but he's worried, nonetheless. For one, there is horrific flooding in his hometown of Kinston, North Carolina. He has called there repeatedly and been reassured that, as he puts it, his "people are okay."

Also, Shondra and Jay have been away for two weeks and his house has grown so quiet without them, he had to get out. That's why he's in the locker room so early. "I can't wait to see them," he says. They are due back tonight during the game and he'll have to bear down, if given the chance, to keep his mind in it, and off them, until then.

But the real source of his consternation is, as it's been for much of the season, the uncertainty of his career. "Houston," he says, looking up momentarily, as if he's testing the sound of it. "Yeah, Houston. That'd be a nice spot for me. Clyde's retiring, huh? What about Mario Elie, he gonna be back there?"

"I doubt it," I say. After the team tried to trade him, Maloney, and others in the deal that never was, Elie blasted Rocket management in the Houston papers. This is something to be expected of the league's stars—can you imagine how Barkley would have sounded off if treated this way?—but role players, even good ones like Elie, can't be so outspoken and still hope to be taken care of come contract time.

"I hear they got some room under the cap, too," Stackhouse says. "That may be the spot."

He is quiet, entertaining the fantasy: a long-term deal in Houston. But that still wouldn't be his first choice. Ever since his first trip to Pheonix his rookie year, he's wanted to play there. Great weather, a state-of-the-art arena, a coach in Ainge who players really like and who runs an up-tempo game, and, most importantly, a roster loaded with guys whose deals are winding down. In others words, the Suns have the potential for a lot of cap room.

The cap is a critical concern and makes any talk about

where he might play next season premature. Stackhouse, who still sees himself as a $10 million per year player, qualifies for the Larry Bird exception: The Pistons can go over their cap to sign him.

But who knows if the cap will be the same next season? Within the next two weeks, the owners will vote on reopening the collective bargaining agreement. That's the worst thing that could happen to Stackhouse now.

"You don't think they're going to reopen that thing, do you?" he asks. "I mean, that wouldn't be smart. If Michael retires, they can't afford to do that. It's too risky."

There are other worries, too. His deal with Fila is up next season and the endorsement market doesn't look promising. Sneaker sales are in an industry-wide slump, in large part because boots, designed by Caterpillar and Timberland, among others, have replaced sneakers as the hip fashion choice of urban youth. Consequently, public companies like Fila and Reebok and even Nike are expected to cut back on their multimillion-dollar deals with pro athletes; they've learned that, with the exception of Jordan, a celebrity endorsement costs more than it brings in.

Once the season ends, Fila is expected to reevaluate its deals with its stable of stars, including Stackhouse, Webber, and Maloney, while honoring Hill's seven-year, $80 million deal. Similarly, Reebok is expected to let Shaquille O'Neal's $3 million a year deal expire.

Stackhouse and Shondra don't even know where they're going to live during the off-season, though they think they've settled on moving to suburban Atlanta, right near where Vernon and Shel live. Now Stackhouse's teammates start filing in. He removes his Fila Stack IIIs from his locker and starts to get undressed. It's an hour before tip-off, and he still hasn't smiled once.

Tonight Stackhouse gets in first-half foul trouble and has to sit, although, while toiling on the bench, his face finally

widens into a toothy grin: He's spotted Shondra, carrying
Jay, finding her seat behind the Pistons' bench. The Pistons
will go on to down the hapless Raptors, 105–99, raising their
record to 31–36; but while there is still a slim chance that
Detroit can make the final playoff spot in the East, with
fifteen games remaining, they have no time to waste. A run
has to start tonight in order to catch up to Orlando, New
Jersey, and Washington.

Stackhouse scores 13 points in twenty-five minutes, one
of his poorer performances of late. In the eight games following his lunch with Lucas in Houston, he continued to
press and struggle, playing twenty-six minutes and scoring
just 11.6 points per game on anemic 35 percent shooting.
But then came a trip to Los Angeles.

There, Stackhouse met with Gentry and team president
Rick Sund and told them he didn't think there was anybody
else on the team, besides Hill, who could do what he could
do on the court: get his own shot. Everybody else, even wily
veteran Joe Dumars, needed others to get them free. Stack
argued that the team needed him and needed his scoring.

That night Stackhouse was, as usual, the first off the
Pistons' bench; Kobe Bryant was first off the Lakers'. Interestingly, Bryant had faded since all the hype about him at
the All-Star Game. He was down in every statistical category
and was increasingly playing as though he were feeling the
pressure to replicate what was coming so naturally early in
the season. His entry into games of late—not unlike Stackhouse's during the few weeks prior to their meeting—was
characterized by forced shots and sloppy mental errors.

When they both entered the game, Stackhouse immediately took Bryant to school, as though they were back in
that Philadelphia gym over two years ago and he had a
score to settle. He blocked Bryant's shot and scored on a
soaring jam. He hit his midrange jumpers. He made eight
of nine shots and scored 23 points, while Bryant seemed
lost, scoring just four points. The Pistons had no answer for

other points of the L.A. attack, however—Shaq had 32 points—and the Lakers won, but the game elevated Stackhouse in the estimation of Gentry.

That was six games ago and, since then, Stackhouse has averaged 17.6 points on 55 percent shooting while getting thirty minutes a game. Now, after beating the Raptors, the Atlanta Hawks come to town and Stackhouse again goes off, hitting eight of nine shots, scoring 23 points in thirty minutes, including a clutch jumper late in the game, leading the Pistons to a 105–98 win. It's been a strange season. Now, all of a sudden, things feel like they did when Stackhouse first arrived in Detroit under Collins. Gentry is running plays for him and he is again an integral part of the Pistons' attack. But has it come too late—for him and the team?

Grant Hill is starting to show signs of frustration. He's posted almost identical numbers to last season—roughly 21 points, 8 rebounds, 6 assists per game, but criticism of him has gone beyond his statistics. He disappears late in games, the argument goes, and his game is too nonaggressive or "soft"—a common lament aimed at jocks, like Hill and San Antonio's David Robinson, who practice a gentlemanly demeanor off the court.

Moreover, he's sick and tired to being held up as the Anti-Iverson. Two years ago, GQ put him on its cover and asked the question: CAN GRANT HILL SAVE SPORTS? Inside, Tom Junod's provocative story was a meditation on the meaning of Hill in contrast to the NBA's scourge of hoodlums. Hill was deeply wounded by the article. "I thought it was racist," he says. "It felt like a setup, like using me to reinforce stereotypes about black athletes being hoods."

The truth, Hill often argues, is more complex and more about age than race. "Guys like Allen Iverson just need a chance to grow," he says. "I'm not worried about the future of the league. If Michael retires, it's not just one guy who has to step up and fill his shoes. Right now there are a whole lot of us who have to be All-Stars on and off the court. When they were twenty-two, Hakeem and Charles and Michael didn't act like they did when they were thirty-two." Indeed, in Jordan's rookie year, it has since been forgotten, he showed up for the All-Star Game not in a Donna Karan suit and Kenneth Cole shoes but in baggy jeans, sneakers, and gaudy jewelry, much to the dismay of veterans like Isiah Thomas.

After a recent screaming match with a heckling fan at home, Hill unburdens himself further about not having to fill Jordan's Nikes, either. "When I first came in, I was consumed with wanting everyone to like me," he tells *The Detroit News*. "One of the problems was the marketing. People are so eager for a new Jordan, they tried to place it on me, or Kobe, or Penny. I say let him retire and someone will emerge. People can say I'm not like Isiah, I'm not like Jordan, but I've decided I'm just going to be me. People criticize Allen Iverson, but I respect him because he's being himself."

Hill's public bemoaning of how his icon-in-training status has hindered his play by ratcheting up the pressure on him should be fodder for bonding with Stackhouse, who has undergone a similar experience, if to a lesser degree. But the pace of the season is such that the two, while cordial, remain distant. Besides, while Stackhouse doesn't know precisely why his minutes have suddenly soared, he's not particularly interested in dwelling on it for fear of jinxing his good fortune.

Of course, it's possible that, just as his cut in minutes had more to do with Gentry's need to placate Hill, his resurrection reflects a realization on Gentry's part that the best way to go from being interim to permanent head coach is to make a playoff run. And the best way to do that is to play your most talented players.

So he's just going to ride the wave. Two nights later, he scores 22 points as the Pistons beat the Spurs, 103–94, for their fourth straight win, a streak that started with the win over Toronto. In the fourth quarter, Stackhouse energizes the entire Detroit team, getting a key block and steal against the Spurs' Vinny Del Negro. He finally seems to have gotten past the blow to his ego left by his removal from the starting lineup. Now he seems to actually enjoy coming off the bench. "I'm not the Microwave yet, but I'm a toaster," he tells *The Detroit News* after the Spurs game, a reference to longtime Pistons' sixth man Vinnie "the Microwave" Johnson, currently the team's radio analyst, who was renowned for coming off the bench and instantly heating things up.

For Stackhouse, the four-game winning streak is the longest he's known since college, a lifetime ago. More important, the Pistons are now just two and a half games out of the last playoff spot, with twelve to go.

But a one-point overtime loss at Cleveland deflates the team, though Stackhouse continues his improved play. Against the Cavs, he gets forty minutes—the first time he's hit forty minutes in a game since Collins played him forty-one on January 30 against the Wizards—and he posts 26 points and 6 assists.

But the Cleveland loss is followed by a blowout in Atlanta. Then comes a nationally televised game at Chicago in which Stackhouse scorches Jordan for 22 points, 7 assists, and 4 steals. His usual reserve is a thing of the past; he trades trash talk with Jordan all night and even gets a technical foul called on him. TNT broadcaster Doc Rivers talks ceaselessly about this new, energized, passionate Jerry Stackhouse. But the Bulls—because they are, after all, the Bulls—pull the game out, 106–101, for the Pistons' third straight loss, negating the previous winning streak.

After the game, Stackhouse concedes to himself what he's long suspected: We're not making the playoffs. I have to finish strong for myself now.

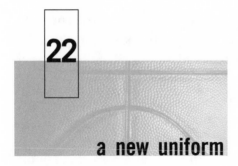

22

a new uniform

vernon Maxwell looks worried. He's trying to shrug off the reports that are coming out of Houston with his customary coolness under pressure, but there's something about his bug-eyed stare that belies his calm veneer.

"Ain't no way this can be some big deal," he is saying, dressing in front of his locker at Philadelphia's CoreStates Center, where the Hornets have just lost their third in a row, 109–101, with just six games left before the playoffs.

Maxwell played just seven minutes tonight, scoring 4 points, but four nights ago, he scored 14 points in twenty minutes against the Heat. More importantly, a cryptic conversation with Larry Brown tonight has him convinced that his first pro coach would want him on his team next season. And he'd love to play in Philadelphia again.

But Maxwell's mind can't stay focused on basketball. He's spent the day talking to Dwight Manley on his cell phone, who has been talking to Ron Wilson, the Democratic state representative in Houston and Maxwell's attorney there. The district attorney's office has been talking to the press, it seems, making noise about Maxwell coming back and serving his time, now that his appeals have all been exhausted in the four-year-old possession of a gram of marijuana case.

"I mean, they ain't going to extradite me for a damn misdemeanor, you know what I'm saying?" he says, grabbing his gear and heading for the team bus. Before boarding, he whispers: "This shit do got me scared, though."

A day later, Harris County officials in Texas issue an arrest warrant for Maxwell. They ask North Carolina police to place him under arrest and transport him to Houston.

After conferring with Wilson and Manley, it is agreed: Maxwell must turn himself in. He plays his final game for the Hornets, a 99–87 loss to the Hawks, and then he heads to suburban Atlanta, for one of the hardest face-to-face meetings he's ever put himself through. Before sitting Little V down at the kitchen table, he allows Shel to see him cry. "They treatin' me like a muthafuckin' mass murderer or something," he says. "I haven't hurt nobody."

It would no doubt surprise those who buy into the Mad Max persona to know that Maxwell can be a disciplinarian as a father, a hands-on parent who, for example, has severely curtailed his son's Internet privileges because "he's just like me—a little pervert—and I don't want him getting into all that stuff on-line when he should be studying."

Similarly, Maxwell uses a "Do as I say, not as I do" approach when he tells his son what's going to happen. "You know, yeah, they're screwing me, by treating me like a criminal," he tells Little V, whose mouth quivers around his tightly shut lips. "But I gotta go take responsibility for what I did. You hear me? I'm taking responsibility for my actions. It's something I gotta do, to get my past behind me."

Little V nods and hugs his father. The next day a crowd
of autograph-seekers surrounds Maxwell at Houston International Airport. He signs each and every autograph, before
Wilson escorts him to the Harris County Jail, where they
avoid the TV cameras that have been camping out all day.
The Associated Press account begins: "Charlotte Hornets
guard Vernon Maxwell traded his red-white-blue wind-
breaker for an orange prisoner's jumpsuit Monday . . ."

Wilson will continue filing appeals, to no avail, while his
client begins serving a ninety-day sentence.

One gram of marijuana wouldn't even make the sorriest
of joints. It's the equivalent of a "roach," the dregs of a joint
smoked so short you need to use a clip to keep from burning
your fingers. That's what Maxwell is serving time for.

Of course, there's more to the case. Wilson, a leading
civil rights voice in Houston, maintains that his client is
being treated more harshly than a noncelebrity would be,
because he's "a millionaire black man with an attitude." Indeed, the state of Texas had never before extradited someone
for a misdemeanor, as they were prepared to do in Maxwell's case. Moreover, there is the possibility that, by challenging his arrest all the way to the Supreme Court, Maxwell
fueled the zealotry of the Houston powers-that-be. District
Attorney John B. Holmes, Jr., has, after all, a reputation as a
tough, no-nonsense, modern-day gunslinger of a prosecutor.
Maxwell's legal challenges could not have sat well. "There's
no bond, no appeal," Holmes told the *Houston Chronicle*
when the warrant was issued. "He owes the state of Texas
ninety days. We're not running a hotel. It's not 'Come in
when it's convenient.' "

According to Assistant District Attorney Connie Spence,
Maxwell's priors could have contributed to the harsh sentence. In 1993 there was a resisting arrest charge; the next
year he faced a weapons offense, a Class A misdemeanor.

Still, Spence concedes, Maxwell probably would have been fined for the joint and given a suspended sentence—like other Class B misdemeanor offenders—had it not been for his defiant conduct while the case was winding it way through the legal process.

"He was an exceptional asshole," Spence would explain later, after Maxwell served his time. At one point, during a hearing on his motion for bond, for example, Maxwell tried to use a phone outside the courtroom. When a prosecutor asked who had given him permission to do so, he said it was none of her business and called her a "bitch." When the prosecutor raised the incident before the judge, according to the *Houston Chronicle*, Maxwell "showed her a profane hand gesture."

"He can't keep his mouth shut," said Spence. "We had our words, sort of a 'Fuck you' match outside the courtroom. It's not something I'm particularly proud of, but he doesn't like me and I don't like him. He relied on his celebrity status, and it was not going to help him here."

But should justice be meted out based on whether someone acts like an asshole or not? "That's how the world works," Spence said. "If you murder someone and are remorseful, a jury may take your remorse into consideration and give you less time. Or you can take the stand and say, 'Fuck you' to the court and the jury can slam you. Vernon thumbed his nose at the judicial system because he thinks he's above the law. I really think had he kept his mouth shut and showed respect, he wouldn't have gotten the time he got."

So Maxwell sits, incarcerated, doing time as much for his attitude as for smoking a joint. In effect, he's paying the price for his "keepin' it real" ethic. Had he just made a slight accommodation or two along the way, had he simply refrained from flipping off a prosecutor in court, had he checked his urge to glare at judges, maybe all this

could have been avoided. But that would have been un-
principled; that would have meant being a "phony
muthafucka."

The first five days he's in maximum security lockdown.
For a muthafuckin' joint, he keeps tell himself, shaking his
head in disbelief. The only natural sunlight he sees glimmers
through the slot that opens just long enough for a tray of
food to be slid into his cell. The only visitor he sees is a
blind priest. For those ten minutes a day, he is bereft of the
bitterness he is otherwise wallowing in. For those ten minutes, he is steered toward forgiving those who have put him
in this place, at this time.

It's not an epiphany. The priest will leave and soon Maxwell will again be full of rage. He is angry at a system that
has him right where it wants him. A young black man in
jail. He doesn't know the precise figures, but he senses them:
While blacks make up 13 percent of the national population
and 13 percent of monthly drug users, they account for 35
percent of drug possession arrests, 55 percent of convictions,
and 74 percent of prison sentences. His wealth, his fame, his
high-priced lawyer, they count for nothing.

So he paces, angry. But then he'll thumb through the
Bible left him by the priest—he wishes he knew his name,
so he could thank him properly when he gets out—and he'll
come across the verse in Psalms 51:17, the one that reads,
"A broken and a contrite heart, O God, thou wilt not de-
spise," and he'll read it over and over. He won't be asking
for forgiveness; he's got nothing to apologize for. But he'll
be asking God to forgive those who put him here—even if
he can't bring himself to do the same, yet—and he'll be
hoping God understands his anger, whether it's directed at
the judge who issued the warrant, the prosecutor who has
overzealously pursued him, or the father whose void he's
never been able to fill.

After five days, he gets transferred to the new Harris

County facility across the street, where he'll be in a bar-rackslike setting with other drug and DWI or DUI offenders. He'll be released at the end of May.

But the playoffs start in two weeks on April 21.

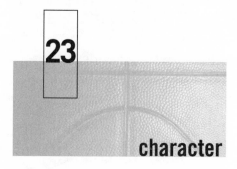

23

character

this is the worst yet. Each time Chris Webber has found himself at the heart of an image-soiling controversy, he's told himself that it's a test, that it's God's way of leading him to become a man. But this is the mother of all tests.

Over the last week, Chris Webber has been branded a sexual predator. On April 7, it was reported that Webber and Howard were being investigated for a sexual assault that allegedly took place at Howard's home the previous evening, where a party lasted until about 4 A.M. Both immediately labeled the charge "ludicrous," but the Montgomery County, Maryland, authorities have been speaking to witnesses and preparing to convene a grand jury.

Now things are only getting worse. Webber finds out about the fallout of the news back home, in Detroit, where his little sister Rachel—"my baby," he calls her—broke into tears at his aunt Charlene's house after camera crews showed up at her school, Detroit Country Day, seeking comment from her classmates about her brother, the school's most infamous alum.

As the investigation continues, strain has developed, if not between Howard and Webber themselves, then between their respective posses. "I'm finding out who my friends are," Webber says.

He has never been this down. Not during the timeout debacle, nor the Nelson flare-up, nor this season's arrest. When he ambles off the team bus parked outside Manhattan's Marriott East Side—the Wizards play the Knicks the next night with only the slimmest playoff hopes dangling before them—he keeps his headphones on and scans the lobby for pursuers, whether press or the law or jeering fans. His eyes dart everywhere. He is careful not to make eye contact with bystanders. If spoken to, he responds in a terse monotone. He can't wait to get to his room.

There, alone, Webber realizes he's hit rock bottom. In his words, he cannot see tomorrow. He calls Erwin. "I don't want this life anymore," he tells his agent and mentor. "Could I just go over to Europe and play? How do I get to Europe? If this is what it takes to be a star, I don't want it. I reached my dream and made it to the NBA and if I can't have this and be happy, I don't want it. I don't want this if it's going to be a curse."

Erwin knows it's not a serious request. He lets his client fulminate before counseling patience. "You know you're telling the truth," he says. "It may take time for the truth to come out." In the meantime, there are other things Erwin can do: He's suggesting that the authorities administer lie detector tests to both Webber and the woman, Melissa Reed, who has not been named publicly. If Webber passes and she does not, Erwin wants the matter dropped.

And Erwin shares with him a case in his own past, when he was subject to an unfounded lawsuit by a disgruntled client but settled nonetheless. "To this day, it's my biggest regret—and that was fifteen years ago." Erwin argues that, while understandable, the urge to quit and escape to Europe would similarly bear second thoughts.

Chris Webber will fight on, but the weight of these charges feel overwhelming because of their very nature. They go to the heart of who he is; indeed, they imply he isn't who he *says* he is. Throughout his time on the public stage, whether in the Nelson controversy or on the ESPN race roundtable, he has tried to argue for a simple principle: respect. Now comes a charge that he's disrespected a woman.

When it's all over and he's vindicated, he vows, he'll sue this woman. And he'll donate the money to Weight Watchers, because, he reasons, if anyone saw a photo of her—how ugly she is—they'd know these charges can't be true. "There you go," he says as if addressing his accuser. "You want to play like that, well, okay."

His anger lasts until he thinks again of Rachel, running from school to Charlene's house in tears. A wave of sadness rushes over him and he again starts fantasizing about Europe or anywhere, really, where he can be just a ballplayer and not a star. He has this image of his baby sister in his head, crying, and he thinks, Nothing is worth that.

Even before this latest distraction, Webber's team was having a rough time. After winning seven of the ten games following Webber's triumphant return against Barkley's Rockets, the Wizards have dropped nine of their last thirteen. One of the rare wins in that streak came at New Jersey in a game fraught with playoff implications. Webber had 25 points, 8 rebounds, and 4 assists in a 102–100 win, but the game was remembered for a Webber postgame move: At the final buzzer, he pantomined a throat-slitting that was played throughout the night on ESPN.

It gave the Webber naysayers fresh ammunition. "They [the Wizards] spend too much time showboating instead of playing hard-nosed, grindstone basketball," Barkley opined in *Sports Illustrated*. "It's okay to have one or two flashy plays a game, but it's the other one hundred plays that win a game. They concern themselves so much with making highlight plays that they forget the fundamentals."

Once again, Webber was seen as classless. Nets announcer Bill Raftery, whose commentary often takes sudden dramatic turns, was particularly offended by the throat-slitting gesture, arguing that Webber was a great player, but there was no place for this schoolyard junk—as though only Raftery has the right to get excited about what happens on the court.

Just days before, Webber had played with the two-year-old daughter of a friend on her Michael Jordan kiddie hoop, and he dunked on her while flexing his muscles and growling like a wild animal and she giggled and imitated him. Just as when he made the throat-slitting gesture, Webber was playing a cartoonish character. The two-year-old got it; Raftery and the playa-haters didn't.

Now, though no sexual assault charges have been filed against Webber or Howard, the pundits are having a field day questioning their judgment. Mike Lupica says, "Chris Webber has to ask himself if he just wants to be remembered as another rich punk." The *Post*'s Tony Kornheiser writes: "Why were Howard and Webber partying until 4:30 A.M., with the playoffs on the line? . . . Is that how they prepare, by partying until dawn? Is that how little they think of their responsibilities? . . . It's not 'all about the Benjamins, baby.' It's about being a professional ballplayer."

Of course, it could be argued that Webber and Howard met their responsibilities the next day: They didn't have a game, after all, and were both at the 11 A.M. practice ten minutes early. Moreover, gathering at a teammate's house for what Webber calls a "get-together" has been common practice for these Wizards, as General Manager Wes Unseld knows. "We always have these gatherings at our houses so

we don't have to go to clubs," Webber says. "We can drink
at home, play cards, eat. And then guys can stay over and
go home in the morning if they get too wasted."

Throughout the season, these "get-togethers" were fre-
quented by people known by the players. On April 6, however, Melissa Reed and three of her friends, all unknown to
Webber or Howard, showed up. In fact, in the days following Reed's accusation, the *Post* published a story detailing
Reed's history of arrests in violent domestic disputes with
her boyfriend and offering quotes from her Connecticut
neighbors in which they complained about the couple's wild
parties: "This is a quiet neighborhood, except their house,"
said one resident of Reed's community.

Even as public opinion swelled against Webber and
Howard, many players took this story as proof that it was
another trumped-up charge. False charges against prominent
athletes have become something of a trend of late; most recently, Dallas Cowboy Michael Irvin was falsely accused of
similar offenses by a woman seeking a payday.

Still, in the court of public opinion, fans (and nonfans)
tend to side against the high-profile jock, who many deem
deserving of a sweeping comeuppance. In part, the perception is the natural by-product of playa-hating; the masses
love to see the mighty fall. But it may just go deeper where
sex and millionaire ballplayers are involved. Promiscuity,
after all, runs rampant among athletes, often of an unsafe
nature. While it should come as no surprise that men so
conscious of their own bodies, so attuned to the physical,
would have highly charged libidos, there's an added ele-
ment: the wholesale lumping of women into a convenient
"other" category. "Cross-cultural research demonstrates that
whenever men build and give allegiance to a mystical, en-
during, all-male social group, the disparagement of women
is, invariably, an important ingredient of the mystical bond,
and sexual aggression the means by which the bond is renewed," writes Professor Peggy Reeves Sanday of the Uni-

versity of Pennsylvania in her book *Fraternity Gang Rape: Sex, Brotherhood, and Privilege on Campus.*

In the NBA, however, there is something even more so-phisticated going on, a Kabuki dance between the players and the women they know are out to "get" them—whether by freezing used condoms or filing paternity suits. It's a consensual game played out in after-hours clubs and hotel suites on the road. Increasingly, it's getting harder to discern just who is using whom. The existence of this subplot can't excuse the athlete's promiscuity, however, which is directly proportional to the amount of temptation literally thrown his way.

"Typically, sexual promiscuity among high-achieving, high-profile people is about things other than sex: It becomes a way to handle stress, pressure, and boredom," says Dr. Al Cooper, a Stanford professor of psychiatry who runs the San Jose Marital and Sexuality Centre, a clinic that treats several hundred "sex addicts" a year. "For instance, sometime after number ten thousand, I doubt it was about the sex for Wilt Chamberlain." As Cooper suggests, it should come as no surprise that athletes, whose professional failures are among our culture's most public moments, yearn for those climactic split seconds when they are at their most abandoned, when their minds are most clear, when they are most free of stress.

By all accounts, Webber isn't even promiscuous, not by NBA standards anyway. Besides, consensual sex is a far cry from violence toward women and, for Webber, being grouped with those who would exploit and victimize the opposite sex is the real wound. All the rest—the pronounce-ments about his lack of character, the hand-wringing about being at a party until dawn—he knows what that's all about. He thinks it's no coincidence that the outcry prompted by these charges came after his throat-slitting performance in New Jersey. "For people to judge me like they are, this is their chance, you know?" he says. "The people who had always resented that Chris talks a lot of junk on the court, he always speaks his mind. It's like they've been saying, 'He better not ever slip up.' "

Tonight Spike Lee has arranged a special screening for us of his new film, *He Got Game*, starring Denzel Washington and the NBA's Ray Allen, but Webber is too depressed to head out. When, a couple of weeks later, he finally sees the film, it resonates deeply. To Webber's way of thinking, Spike nailed it, from the way the main character, phenom Jesus Shuttlesworth, played by Allen, instinctively knows at age seventeen: "People don't care about me—they're just trying to get a piece of Jesus, that's all," to the way he shows the temptations thrown Jesus' way on his recruiting visits to major colleges. "Every recruiting visit you make, you think you've fallen in love and met your wife," Webber says. Yes, *He Got Game* documents the degree to which guys like Webber and Stackhouse have been seen as commodities since they were wide-eyed adolescents by relatives, coaches, agents, and girlfriends alike. But it also shows something else: The only characters not seeking to exploit or capitalize on Jesus' status are his own teammates. "That movie helped me realize how blessed I've been to play with the guys I've played with," Webber says. "No matter what happens, with this season, or in the future, I'll always have my family of teammates, the guys that I went to war with."

It's game day. The Wizards have four games left in the season, including tonight's against the Knicks, and they must win them all to still have a shot at the postseason. It's not going to be easy. They're without Strickland, who is out for the remainder of the year with a torn quadriceps.

Even with Strickland, it would be tough. The charges against Webber and Howard have deflated the team. On a personal level, the other Wizards have supported their two teammates unconditionally; on the court, though, they look like a group of players going through the motions.

And they can't escape the distractions. Before shootaround, the phone in my hotel room rings. It's Webber. "Did you see this morning's *New York Times?*" he wants to know.

It's a page-one story, headlined OZ ELUDES CAPITAL WIZ-ARDS and written by Mike Wise, the same author of the state-of-the-game lament published during All-Star weekend. This piece runs through all the controversies involving this seemingly dysfunctional team, from the Strickland and Murray fisticuffs to Webber's arrest to the sexual assault charges. "I'll just say this," Coach Bernie Bickerstaff is quoted as saying. "There's more to winning than talent."

At the close of the article, Wise interviews Jesse Jefferson, who runs a D.C.-area after-school program. "We tried to tell kids to look closer to home for their role models," Jefferson says, before noting that the players "do have an obligation to maintain a certain behavior. These guys get treated like prima donnas from elementary school on up. I don't think they're good role models."

Webber has no idea who Jesse Jefferson is. More importantly, he doesn't know who Mike Wise is. The article has a quote from Webber and one from Howard, but both were taken from other pieces. "How is that good journalism?" Webber wants to know. "That writer should write for the *Star* or the *National Enquirer.* I do all sorts of things for kids, man. Shouldn't he have asked me about that?"

Webber has set up the Chris Webber Foundation, a community-minded charitable organization that grants academic scholarships to underprivileged kids. Then there's his Rebounds for Kids program, in which he donates $30 per rebound—and local corporations match his contribution—to the Children's Cancer Foundation. "Shouldn't those things have been mentioned, instead of just talking to someone I've never heard of?" he asks.

He sighs. On his way to the team bus, he changes his alias at the front desk from "Bumpy Johnson" to "Barry Sanders" because too many people know of the Johnson moniker. After shootaround, he's going to sleep. The more he sleeps, the sooner he might awaken from this nightmare.

Somehow the Wizards pull it all together on the court. They get a lead on the Knicks, who come roaring back, making a seventeen-point run. But the Wizards hang tough. Webber scores 19 and hands out 6 assists and the Wizards win, 104–102. They are still alive—barely.

There are three games left, two at home—a distinct disadvantage, given the way the Wizards' fans have been raining down boos and catcalls on their team. Webber knows the odds are against his team. But after the game, surrounded by media, he patiently answers questions. It's been quite a season: He's been arrested, his best friend has been vilified as Public Enemy No. 1, and now sexual assault charges hang over his head. He is twenty-five years old, the de-facto leader of this room full of men, and he is doubting whether he wants this life anymore. Yet, when asked about the possibility of making the playoffs, he responds with noticeable conviction, and something in his voice leaves no doubt: He's talking about the adversity he's stared down all season, not just about basketball.

"It's not over," Webber says, looking his interlocutors in their collective eye defiantly. "You know, your real heart is shown when times are tough. That's when your true character comes out."

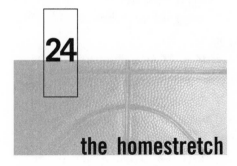

24

the homestretch

heading into the final weekend of the regular season, much is still to be determined. There are home-court playoff advantages that remain undecided, not to mention the individual scoring race, where Jordan and Shaquille O'Neal are neck and neck—it would be Jordan's tenth time leading the league.

O'Neal's Lakers have the glitterati excited again. Jack Nicholson, Dyan Cannon, and Magic Johnson have all returned to courtside, watching O'Neal pass out of the double team better than ever before to teammates such as Van Exel, Eddie Jones, and the still inconsistent Bryant. The Lakers are one of three teams in the West that could challenge the Bulls. The others, of course, are the Jazz and the SuperSonics. In the East, only the Bulls will join these three as a 60-win club; perhaps an astute general manager this off-season will notice the one thing three of these four elite teams have in common: veterans who have been together for many years. Utah, Seattle, and Chicago are proof of what wins in the NBA—long-term, stable rosters.

The latest cliché in sports is that "chemistry" wins, though hardly anyone ever defines the term. The Bulls, for instance, feature Rodman and Pippen, who have a history of ill will between them and who currently, at best, tolerate each other. But they've been dominant because of their *on-court* chemistry, because they know and trust each other on the floor. Familiarity breeds chemistry. The same is true in Utah, where the nucleus of Malone, Stockton, and Hornacek reign, and Seattle, where Payton, Sam Perkins, and Detlef Schrempf have had the benefit of playing together for years. Similarly, every year the pundits write off the Knicks as too old and too lacking in talent, but every year they win behind the longtime leadership of Ewing, Starks, and Charles Oakley; this season they'll be the playoffs' seventh seed, facing Riley's Heat in the first round, and Riley knows not to count his former team out. As Coach Phil Jackson of the Bulls explains in his book, *Sacred Hoops: Spiritual Lessons of a Hardwood Warrior,* winning is what happens when, over time, a coach can mold disparate egos and personalities into a cohesive unit that, as he puts it, puts "we before me."

In Philadelphia, Larry Brown's team is a good example of the alternative. With Coleman, Iverson, and Joe Smith, who was acquired at the treading deadline, the 76ers have three players who were the league's top overall draft pick in their respective years: Coleman in 1990, Smith in 1995, Iverson in 1996. Yet, as Brown has been known to lament, they haven't yet come close to playing as one. That's why, in the season's final week, Brown praised Coleman for coming to the aid of Iverson in an altercation, an act that resulted in Coleman's ejection from a close game. To Brown, it was a positive sign: Iverson got the message that Coleman was watching his back.

This is not to say that talent can't compensate for a lack

of chemistry, as the Lakers have proved. Del Harris's team, a combustible collection of young talent, recalls the 76ers squad in 1977 that featured Julius Erving, George McGinnis, Doug Collins, World B. Free, and Darryl Dawkins—a group of individuals playing as individuals but talented enough to pull it off, most nights.

The problem is fitting the right pieces together. Basketball aficionados are proficient at measuring who can run fast, shoot well, jump high. But, as Harold Katz, the owner of the 76ers when a seemingly endless string of complementary players were ushered in to play alongside Barkley, once said, "The toughest part of this business isn't judging talent. It's judging heart. It's answering the question: Who wants to win? And then putting as many of those guys together as you can."

Chemistry might be the issue in Charlotte. While Maxwell's lawyers file motion after motion to get their client released from jail in time to make the Hornets' playoff roster, Dave Cowens's team becomes wildly inconsistent. Their record in April will be 5–5 and there is acrimony behind the scenes between the outspoken Mason and his low-key coach.

Before leaving the team, Maxwell knew the Hornets were in trouble come playoff time. He and B. J. Armstrong—the only other Hornet to wear a championship ring—would talk late into the night about how they know what it takes to win it all in this league and how this team doesn't quite have it.

"It takes defense," Maxwell would say over and over. "That's one thing you learn, man. To work harder on defense than on offense."

Now, serving his time, Maxwell still has hope that his defensive acumen will rescue his team next week when the playoffs begin. He fantasizes about stepping out of a jail cell and into an NBA arena and lighting it up. But all his mo-

tions for bond are denied and the Hornets have no choice
but to leave him off their playoff roster.

His team may be out of the postseason race, but Jerry
Stackhouse is ending this topsy-turvy season on a high note.
Two nights ago, he posted his second superb performance
against Jordan—leading the Pistons to an 87–79 win with 20
points and 6 rebounds. Most importantly, he played with
the same passion as before, squaring up in Jordan's face,
refusing to back down.

Now, the night before the final game of his third season,
his Pistons can once again play the spoiler. They play the
Nets in New Jersey; if the Nets win, they're the East's last
playoff team. If the Pistons win, Webber's Wizards sneak in.

But Stackhouse couldn't care less about the playoff picture. He's just hoping someone was watching the last month,
when he squared off against Jordan twice and dogged him
both times. In his final five games of the season, he'll wind
up scoring 19.8 points per game on 49 percent shooting,
while handing out 4.8 assists per game. For the season, he
averages 15.8 points and a career best 43.5 percent from
the floor.

But he feels as though his biggest strides were made in
his own head over the last four weeks. He seems to have
taken Lucas's advice and has let go of much of the pressure
that so weighed on him after Collins's departure. Of his
April performances against Jordan, he says, "Hopefully,
someone saw what I did. If not, fuck it. What can I do?"

There are indications the Pistons want him back. During
the last month, their most effective unit consisted of Hill,
Stackhouse, and Dumars—who will be coming back for one
final season—on the floor all at the same time, with Stack
guarding the opposing point guard.

He no longer fantasizes about going to Houston or Phoenix; instead, he's content to be a sixth man in Detroit next
season and to then inherit from Dumars the starting shoot-

ing guard slot. Of course, he doesn't want to play for yet another coach, but his concerns in that area are dealt with when Hill and Dumars both publicly endorse Gentry for the full-time job. Detroit management will go through the motions of interviewing other candidates, but the public show of support by Hill has, for all intents and purposes, sealed the deal: Gentry will come back.

And so might Stackhouse. He even seems resigned to the fact that he won't become a $10 million a year man, realizing that he's probably more of a $3 to $5 million player and that the resultant discrepancy of $5 to $7 million matters only to his ego. "What's the difference?" he says. "I ain't ever going to spend it all anyway."

Most importantly, Jerry Stackhouse is starting to learn about the work ethic required to make it in the NBA. In past off-seasons, he's returned to Chapel Hill, to take college classes and play in pickup games. Now he's realized his error. "Playing pickup doesn't really help me, you know what I'm saying?" he says. "I gotta work on sharpening my game." To that end, after he and Shondra head out to suburban Atlanta for some house-hunting, he'll be returning to Detroit, where the assistant coaches will work with him through the summer, putting him through drills designed to improve his weaknesses—like three-point shooting and ballhandling—and take his strengths—like conditioning—to an even higher level, so come next season, whatever uniform he wears, he will have the wherewithal to do what he does best: get out and run in the open floor. With the exception of some Fila-related trips and visits to Durham, where he will open a hip-hop clothing store called BIL—Brothers Inspiring Loyalty—Stackhouse will spend his summer in the gym.

Once the Pistons' season concludes, *The Detroit News* is effusive in its praise of Stackhouse. Calling him a "preordained superstar," beat writer Chris McCoskey writes: "He is twenty years old, hungry to learn, and, most surprisingly, has shown a mean, competitive streak. He takes losing hard and backs down from nobody, not even Michael Jordan."

Stackhouse smiles when told of the season-ending glowing review. "After everything I've been through," he says. "I can't believe I'm saying this. But I feel positive."

Growing up a Barkley fan, Chris Webber found himself often rooting against his hometown Pistons. The night most vivid in his memory was that late-season game in 1990 at the Palace, when Barkley and Mahorn led their overachieving team over the Pistons to clinch the Atlantic Division title—and Barkley kicked Bill Laimbeer's ass. Webber couldn't sleep that night, he was so pumped by his idol's display of in-your-face aggressiveness.

Now it's eight years later and the fate of his own NBA season rests on the very same Pistons. After beating the Knicks, Webber led the Wizards to wins over Cleveland, Miami, and, yesterday, Boston; against the Celtics, he almost registered a triple double, scoring 27 points, grabbing 13 rebounds, and distributing 8 assists. But there's nothing more he can do. If the Wizards are to face the Bulls in the first round for the second straight year, Detroit must do his winning for him.

To Webber, the game is even bigger than its playoff ramification. He faces an off-season trial on the midseason arrest and a grand jury is still hearing evidence in the sexual assault case. But if his season can extend into the postseason, it just might quell the rampant speculation that management will deal either him or Juwan this off-season, not to mention putting to at least temporary rest the widespread doubts about whether he can ultimately win at this level.

But it's not to be. The Nets get 18 points, 11 assists, and 5 steals from Sherman Douglas, playing for the injured Cassell, and the Nets cruise to a thirteen-point win. Stackhouse scores 20, but it's not enough. The Wizards are done. A season that began with the highest of hopes—Jordan's year-old endorsement feels like decades ago—ends with Webber in front of his big-screen TV, watching two other teams determine his destiny.

Statistically, it is Webber's best season. He is ninth in the league in scoring at 22 points per game and eleventh in rebounding, over 9 a game. But his numbers are the farthest thing from his mind. After the Nets clinch the playoff berth, he sits a good, long while. He's going to have to start ruminating on the meaning of this turbulent season, on the lessons, but for now, he sits and stares into space.

A week before the season's final weekend, it looked like the Houston Rockets might overtake the Minnesota Timberwolves and grab the seventh seed in the west. The Rockets were playing at Sacramento and had built up a 64–55 lead with four minutes to play in the third quarter. Charles Barkley was at the scorer's table, waiting to check in at the next dead ball, and turned to the crowd. "One more basket and they'll quit," he announced to the Kings' fans, gesturing toward their team.

Just minutes later, however, it was the Kings' fans getting the last laugh. At the close of the quarter, Barkley heaved a full-court shot at the buzzer and then proceeded to double over in pain. He tried to play at the start of the fourth quarter, but left the floor after one trip down the court.

The Kings, playing without star shooting guard Mitch Richmond, made a run behind a couple of clutch fourth-quarter buckets by Lawrence Funderburke, but the Rockets held them off, thanks to Olajuwon. After the game, Barkley's teammates heard the worrisome news: The sports hernia that kept him out of action way back in November and had plagued him ever since had returned. He might have to undergo surgery right away, which would force him to miss the playoffs.

On the night before the last day of the regular season,

Barkley's golf buddy Jordan pumps in 44 against the Knicks to win the scoring title. The next day, without Barkley, the Rockets follow their 102–95 loss to Minnesota with a thirty-point loss to the Suns. They finish 41–41 and are the eighth seed, but more distressing is their lack of late-season momentum: They haven't beaten a winning team since Indiana on March 25 and they are 3–10 against teams with winning records since March 1. And injury, meet insult: They're going to have to face the Jazz in the first round.

THE PLAYOFFS

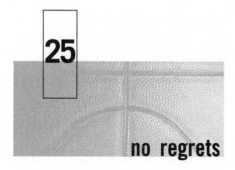

25

no regrets

before the first game of the Jazz–Rockets series, Karl Malone nods toward the visitors' locker room at the Delta Center in Salt Lake City and tells anyone who will listen: "Those guys are not number-eight seeds."

Malone is right to be concerned. The Rockets have struggled through a .500 season and Barkley's health is questionable—he'll suit up and try to play, although the hernia still has him in pain—but they are nonetheless a team with three all-time greats and an imposing cast of supporting actors, including Kevin Willis, Eddie Johnson, and Maloney.

Still, few expect them to steal the series from the team that edged out the Bulls for the league's best record—and none of those few, it seems, are in the Delta Center.

Salt Lake City is a Mormon town, but any semblance of reserved piety has been checked at the arena door. The fans are rowdy, obscene, and deafening, not to mention 19,911 strong. One particular heckler—a bald white guy with leather lungs known as "Jazzman"—starts riding Barkley during the pregame warmups. He's picked the wrong target. Without hesitating, Barkley storms into the enemy throng and goes shout for shout with the guy, a contest for which he'll later be fined $10,000. "If they curse me," he explains later, "I'm going to curse them back."

The argument is dangerous evidence of Barkley's take-no-prisoners mood. Close followers of his career have learned to sense when he's firing on all cylinders. Unlike most athletes, who wear dour and stoic game faces, Barkley engages his surroundings—talking to fans, yelling at referees, trash-talking his opponent, gesticulating to the crowd. At his best, he could rival Ali in the talking department and tonight he is in title fight shape. (Conversely, when Barkley is nonexpressive on the court, his game is similarly lacking in energy.)

From the moment he checks in, Barkley is on. Patting ref Dick Bavetta on the rump, he yells to Rockets' TV announcer Calvin Murphy, "Can you believe he was voted the best ref in the league?"

"Obviously, you didn't vote for me," Bavetta says.

"No, I voted for Mike Mathis," Barkley says and even Bavetta breaks up, laughing. Mathis is a longtime nemesis of Barkley's, going back to Barkley's days in Philadelphia, and one of four referees out of the league due to a tax-evasion investigation—which explains the inconsistency of a lot of calls this season.

Barkley's energy will indeed infuse the Rockets, who also get inspired play from Olajuwon. Together, they make the Utah crowd a nonfactor and open up a twenty-one-point third quarter lead. Maloney is playing Stockton, who has had an aching back of late, and he's giving no quarter. Using his muscle on him, Maloney harasses the usually sure-handed Stockton into three turnovers. Last year's playoff loss isn't far from his mind.

In that six-game loss to the Jazz, Stockton ran Maloney

ragged. This year Maloney's focusing on a more nuanced approach. Good defense, he has learned, doesn't have to result in a steal or deflected pass; it can also be virtually undetectable to the naked eye. Stockton is adept at getting the ball to Malone and his other shooters so that they're in perfect shooting position—"in rhythm," the players call it. If Maloney can bother Stockton just enough that he has to take one more dribble than he wants or has to deliver the ball six inches behind his teammate, thereby breaking the shooter's rhythm, he will have done his job. Tonight, in addition to Stockton's three miscues, the normally adept point guard is off-target time and again when trying to get the ball to teammates who are open for spot-up jumpers.

As expected, the Jazz make a late-game run behind their flawless execution of the pick and roll. At one point, Tomjanovich gives Maloney the green light to throw the Jazz a curveball; when they try and run the pick and roll, rather than chase Stockton around Malone's pick, he switches and finds himself guarding the NBA's premier power forward down low. Malone tries backing Maloney down, but Maloney won't budge while Stockton tries to find an angle to deliver the pass. The two continue to jostle in the lane, and it's a comical sight: the six-foot-three Maloney, forearm planted firmly in Malone's back, standing his ground. Suddenly Bavetta blows his whistle. Three-second violation on Malone. The Houston bench jumps up en masse, celebrating.

It's a turning point. Olajuwon finishes with 16 points, 13 rebounds, and, most importantly, 6 blocked shots; Barkley finishes with twenty-seven inspired minutes, scoring 12 points and grabbing 6 rebounds; and the Rockets finish off the Jazz, 103–90, stunning the basketball world. They'll get blown out in game two, but they head back to Houston for game three of the best of five. They've got the home-court advantage now and history is on their side: Their playoff record is 17–0 after winning the opening game. If they hold serve at home, they will wipe out the mighty Jazz.

*   *   *

"The NBA season is a marathon," Grant Hill observed earlier this season, "and the college basketball season is a sprint." He was explaining to me the difference between the two levels from a player's perspective, pointing out that, by late December, the NBA player has already played the equivalent of an entire collegiate schedule.

But Hill might just as easily have been explaining the stark contrast in game time atmosphere between college and the pros. The college game is all about emotion and enthusiasm, the fans as intense as the players. (Witness the Duke faithful who pass a prone Dick Vitale through the stands as a pregame drill.) But the NBA season is a test of endurance, for player and fan alike. On many regular season nights, the fans appreciate the artistry on the court but are lifeless when compared to the frenzied fanatics of the college game.

But not come playoff time. An hour before game three's tip-off, all the clichés uttered by the talking heads suddenly apply: There *is* electricity in the air, you *can* cut the intensity with a knife. For the intros, the lights dim, the fans scream en masse and the Rockets roar out playing their best defense of the season. Olajuwon leads the way and Barkley provides a spark off the bench and Maloney constantly bodies up the banged-up Stockton. By the third quarter, the Rockets hold a thirteen-point lead.

Then the Jazz make their run. After being fouled by Elie, Stockton hits two free throws with 44.3 seconds left and gives the Jazz their first lead of the game, 85–84. The fans don't get a chance to quiet down, however. Two Olajuwon free throws put the Rockets back up one with 37.6 seconds left.

Stockton sets up the tried-and-true pick and roll on the left side, with Malone. This is it, the moment Tomjanovich fantasized about last night, when he couldn't sleep at 1 A.M., the moment he opened shootaround with this morning:

"If it comes down to one possession at the end of the game, how are we going to defense the pick and roll?" he

asked his team just twelve hours ago. Maloney's switch during game one notwithstanding, the Rockets' defense is
among the more predictable in the league. So they decided
they would do something completely different.

Stockton dribbles patiently toward Malone, who picks Maloney and then spins to the basket, but suddenly Barkley jumps
out over the screen, as does Maloney, both of them frantically
waving their arms in Stockton's face. Coach Jerry Sloan of the
Jazz starts yelling, "Double team! Double team!"—only it's too
late. Malone rolls, but a stunned Stockton can't see where he
is. He picks up his dribble before awkwardly hurling a pass
to Bryon Russell in the corner for an out-of-rhythm three-
pointer. When it bounces off the rim, Drexler rebounds and is
fouled. His two free thows put the Rockets ahead 88–85.

When the Jazz call time, a giddy Maloney hugs Tomjanovich: "You know what we talked about at shootaround?
That was the play, right there," he says, hardly believing
that it was executed so flawlessly. The play even ended up
with Russell heaving a long-distance, off-balance three,
which is what Rudy had said he wanted: "You have to rattle
Stockton so it's like a broken play," he'd said.

Out of the timeout, Malone misses a jumper. Maloney
rebounds and is fouled with 7.6 seconds left, but none of the
16,285 fans know it, because their screaming drowns out
the PA system. Maloney calmly steps to the line and shoots;
the ball looks good, but it spins out. The crowd groans.

If he misses the second, the Jazz will have the chance
for a game-tying three at the buzzer. If he makes it, the
game is iced.

Just before he readies to shoot, Barkley approaches the
young point guard, stands in front of him. To the Compaq
Center's 16,285, it is a touching moment: the veteran offering
kind words of encouragement to the second-year player, who
simply impassively nods. But they don't hear the words.

"Make this or I'm gonna fuckin' kill you," Barkley says
to Maloney without the hint of a smile.

Maloney raises up, releases, follows through. Game over. The Rockets are a home win away from advancing.

Matt Maloney is starving. It is over an hour after the game and we can't find a place to eat. Houston's, across from the arena, is closed. So are a handful of other hangouts.

So Maloney, dressed in a white collared shirt, jeans, and loafers, makes a decision. We're off to Wendy's. Drive-thru.

He and Paul can't stop talking about the postseason prognosis as they scarf down a couple of chicken sandwiches, some fries, Cokes. Meantime, the fans are likewise riding high; already the sports talk show lines are lighting up with praise for the job Maloney's done on Stockton. His offense is struggling—he's averaging 7 points per game in the series—but that's because so much of his energy has been expended on defense. Paul tells Matt that San Antonio eliminated the Suns tonight.

"For me, it's probably better to play San Antonio," Matt says. "For the team, it would have been better to play the Suns. They can't contain Dream. For me, A.J. [Spurs point guard Avery Johnson] is a good player, but that's about it for their backcourt."

There is silence as the two chow down. Barkley's night is just getting started—he's out, clubbing—when they begin the trek home to Sugar Land.

At the Jazz's practice the next day, a member of the media suggests to Coach Sloan that Barkley would make a great Houston nightlife tour guide. Sloan will have none of it. "I wouldn't want to be around him," he says. "No way. That guy will kill you. He must be Superman. Anybody who can play with a hernia like he has has got to be Superman."

The first question put to the Caped Crusader when he arrives for Rocket practice is: "How did you sleep?"

He smiles slyly. "Who says I slept?" he says. Then he notices the chalkboard, where Tomjanovich's assistant has written today's practice itinerary. Barkley sneaks over and erases everything but WALK-THROUGH, giggling like a grade-schooler all the while.

Finally he gets serious. "If we can't win at home tomorrow night," he says, "we don't deserve to win the series."

It's going to happen. Before the end of the first quarter, it is clear: The number-eight seed is about to knock out the Jazz. The Rockets open the game still playing smothering defense. Seven minutes into the game, Utah has scored just 4 points; the Rockets lead by eleven after one quarter, holding the Jazz to 25 percent shooting.

When Tomjanovich calls on Barkley to enter the game, he jumps up and sprints to the scorer's table, ripping his sweatpants off with a dramatic flourish. This alone prompts a roar from the crowd.

On the floor, he's the Barkley of old—energized, active, asserting his will. He hits three of his first four shots and corrals 2 rebounds. With nine minutes till halftime and the Rockets up eleven, Barkley posts up Greg Foster. Foster goes for a fake and Barkley spins, going up for a left-handed layup under Foster's outstretched arms. The ball kisses off the glass and goes in, but Foster's elbow crashes down on Barkley's triceps; it's an impact he's no doubt weathered countless times throughout his career. But now he comes down cradling his arm, as though he's lost all feeling in it. A hush envelops the crowd as he leaves the floor.

He'll come back and give it a go for all of a minute, but he can't raise his arm and, without Barkley, the Rockets collapse in the second half. In a sixteen-minute stretch, they are outscored 40–16. In the final twenty-two minutes, they are beaten 55–22. The Rockets manage to score only four points in the first eight minutes of the fourth quarter. The final score is a humbling 93–71.

After the game, Barkley is soft-spoken. He says, "It would take a miracle to play Sunday." This is more than just a crucial playoff loss; what's lost may just be Charles

Barkley's last best chance for a title. Tomorrow he'll say, "In games like that, I just feel like I need to be the best player on the court. If I play like that, I know we're going to win. That's the way it was going to be in that game."

Before the team leaves for Utah and the deciding fifth game, I ask Barkley how he's feeling. In seasons past, whether his year has culminated in a heartbreaking game six loss to the Bulls in the NBA finals or a dreary regular season finale, he has found himself brooding over his future, publicly thinking aloud about retirement. Such is the case now.

"Hey, I got no regrets," he says. "It's been a great fourteen years."

He will repeat this line over the coming days, as if the more he says it, the more he'll believe it.

In game five, the Rockets fight gallantly, but they are undermanned, tired, and on the road. The Jazz move on, 84–70. Maloney is off to Vegas for two weeks of rest and relaxation before returning to Houston, where he'll work on his basketball game in the mornings with John Lucas and other pros who come to Houston in the summer, guys like Cassell and Van Exel. In the afternoons, he'll work on his music. In the evenings, he'll watch "The Simpsons."

Barkley will have surgery, first on the triceps, then on the hernia. He will be thirty-six next February, but the Rockets are nonetheless interested in his playing one more year, for $10 million. But he doesn't need the money. Over the years, thanks to the conservative investments made by his agent, Glen Guthrie (who provides Barkley with $10,000 in spending money per month), he's got some $32 million tucked away. Besides, he has other things to do: he wants to finish college, learn to play the piano, embark on his political career, and get really, really fat.

But those things won't bring game four back. They won't rid him of the feeling that he's been cheated in his pursuit of a title. By the time the second surgery is completed, he's not ruling out playing just one more season.

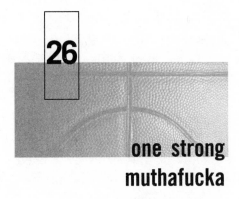

26

one strong
muthafucka

he can tolerate the everyday indignities of incarceration, of being told, in the harshest of terms, where to be and how to act, of having no control. What Vernon Maxwell can't put up with is thinking about what he's missing.

"This be my time of the year, man, the playoffs," he says, separated from me by a pane of Plexiglas, dressed in a bright orange uniform that boldly reads COUNTY JAIL across the back. His hair is growing out, dark and kinky, and a wispy mustache and beard surround his mouth. "They could have used me the other night. See, the Hornets be a jump-shooting team, and that shit don't fly in the playoffs. You gotta take the ball to the hole, make shit happen. Can't be afraid of taking hits."

The Hornets have their work cut out for them. They've eliminated the Atlanta Hawks and are now facing the Bulls. Maxwell would have gotten the chance to go against Jordan;

unlike many in the league, he wouldn't have run from the challenge. "I love battlin' that dude," he says.

As he speaks, other visitors and inmates can't help taking long glances at the facility's resident celebrity. "I seen you on TV!" calls out a leggy female visitor to an inmate who bumped fists with Maxwell upon his entrance to this room, where prisoners can meet with family or friends for up to ten minutes.

The days in here are the slowest Maxwell's ever lived. Though his sentence is ninety days, chances are that he'll have to serve only forty-five, since he begins each day pushing a broom through the hallways at 6 A.M., giving him a two-for-one credit on time served.

He reads the Bible, the one left by the minister during those first five horrific days. Those are the days that will stay with Maxwell; he will not soon forget being treated, in his words, like "I walked into a muthafuckin' post office and murdered some muthafuckas."

Now, at least, he's among others and can receive visitors. After the broom, he spends his days doing sit-ups, reading, and drinking Kool-Aid, though he believes it when other inmates tell him the authorities have put something in the Kool-Aid to "keep your dick from getting hard." The only NBA player he's heard from is Barkley, who called and inquired about coming to visit him. But Ron Wilson, Maxwell's lawyer, discouraged the idea, fearful of upstaging and further agitating the district attorney's office.

He's twenty-one days from release, from serving his forty-five. But one transgression while he's in here and he knows he'll have to do the full ninety. And he knows there are those who want to see him screw up, who want to see him do another forty-five. He knows it and tells himself every day not to snap in the face of provocation, yet he's come close. But he's keeping his eyes on the prize: twenty-one more days.

The problem for Maxwell is not among the prison population. Fellow inmates have welcomed him with affection and respect. He is, after all, someone who stood up to the Man, who took Johnny Law all the way to the Supreme Court, and who is constitutionally incapable of public acts of contrition in order to save his own skin.

The guards have been another matter. One, a hard-chinned, chiseled young black man, has hassled him since day one. "Why you wanna see that asshole?" he asked one recent visitor. Another time, he threw Maxwell up against a wall; Maxwell suppressed the urge to charge right back, but the two called each other every possible variation of "mu-thafucka" known to linguists.

After the confrontation, a gray-haired black guard took Maxwell aside. "Look, my young brother, some of these guys are jealous 'cause you a young brother with money," he said. "You gotta remember you don't got no NBA uni-form on in here. You got that orange shit on. You got to grin and bear it. Swallow that pride, get through this, and then get on back to the NBA."

Maxwell nodded and walked away. Still, every day, there are potential land mines. Yesterday, for instance, he was on the basketball court, which is outside, adjacent to the jail. It is fenced in on all sides, including top to bottom, and the hoop hovers just below the rooftop fence, thereby severely curtailing the arc of Maxwell's rainbow jumper. But he was horsing around nonetheless, minding his own busi-ness, when another inmate walked onto the court, smoking a joint.

"Yo, Max," he said. "Wanna hit this?"

Maxwell looked at the brother, then at the joint being extended to him. These bitches are trying to set me up, he thought to himself before grabbing his ball and heading back inside, where his Bible awaited.

He will get out in twenty-one days, and he will high-tail it out of Houston, where, beginning with the pistol-whipping a year ago, only bad things have happened to him of late. He will return to the refreshing solitude of his family and then head out to L.A., where he'll hang with Rodman and work out with a personal trainer. By that time, the Bulls will have faced the Jazz in the Finals; he will have seen Jordan once again accomplish the superhuman.

On the court, Maxwell knows, he's still got game and he knows he's showed it. Convincing general managers that these latest headlines are solely about his past and that he's tried over and over to do the right thing ever since the pistol-whipping might be a difficult task. But he's faced tougher spots.

I visit him one last time, after the Rockets have bowed out against the Jazz, and I am reminded of a sudden confession he made to me late that night at Stayin' Alive, the Charlotte club. "I know I'm bad, I know I'm a bad person," he'd said, apropos of nothing. "But I'm really trying, man. I'm really trying."

I said nothing. But his observation spoke of the power of media; even he, it seems, has bought into the soap opera–like hype about himself. Vernon, bad. Jordan, good. Now, as I'm about to leave, I try and say what I should have said that night, something to the effect that we're all more complex than the simplistic labels attached to us, that none of us want to be judged on our worst days. That effort and perseverance and the nurturing of one's gift, not a string of very common and human mistakes, are the true benchmarks of character. Yet he knows where I'm going before I get there. He puts his hand up from behind the Plexiglas divider and waves, quieting me. "You ain't gotta worry about me," he says, smiling. "I'm one strong muthafucka."

epilogue

the off-season that didn't want to end began as any other. Players took time off before returning to the gyms and hard courts while the league's powers-that-be saw fit to institute a lockout. The players were undeterred. In Detroit, Chris Webber ran the fastbreak at St. Cecilia's, bumping bodies with Derrick Coleman and Steve Smith. In Houston, Matt Maloney checked Sam Cassell and Nick Van Exel. Meantime, they all waited for word from their agents that the labor dispute had been settled.

That call didn't come until after the new year, however. Many players were in the same boat as Maloney, Maxwell, Stackhouse, and Barkley: free agents unable to strike a deal with a team while the lockout raged on.

For Webber, it was a different story. With two years left on his roughly $9 million-a-year contract, he was looking forward to putting his nightmare season behind him. Indeed, over the summer months, he (and Juwan Howard) would be cleared of the sexual assault charges (the grand jury failed to find credible evidence to indict) and, later, he would be acquitted of all misdemeanor charges (resisting arrest, marijuana possession, second degree assault, and driving under the influence) stemming from his January run-in with officer Raymond Kane. Nonetheless, just prior to the lockout, he was traded to the Sacramento Kings for veteran all-star Mitch Richmond.

Of course, the pundits loved the trade, despite the fact that the deal violates not one but two accepted dictums: Never trade youth for age and never trade big for small. In Richmond, the Wizards are getting a veteran shooting guard while giving up a 25-year-old big man who is often capable of dominating a game.

Still, the trade was widely lauded because Richmond is seen as someone who can provide much-needed maturity to the youthful Wizards. *Sports Illustrated,* for instance, praised Wizards' general manager Wes Unseld: "In trading away Webber, he has already shown he is serious about re-vamping the Wizards . . . Wizards fans are lucky to have [Unself] on their team, too."

In the aftermath of the trade, the only dissenting voice—tellingly—was Washington point guard Strickland, who lamented that "they traded the wrong guy," a pointed reference to Howard.

Much had been made of the fact that the Wizards had the league's sixth-highest payroll, but little attention was given to the team's lack of depth, not to mention the wisdom a few years back of handing leadership of the franchise over to two then-22-year-olds—Webber and Howard. In retrospect, a few years of growing pains should have seemed inevitable.

Just weeks before the trade, Webber sat for a two-hour interview with the *Post*'s Bucher, explaining that he wanted to come back to the Wizards, that he'd had "some revelations . . . I used to fight unwinnable battles and I don't plan to do that anymore . . . My whole attitude has changed."

"I felt like a jackass," Webber recalls when asked about the article that came out just before he'd been dealt. "I had been loyal to this team and this is how they did me. They put all this on me, when I had played when I'd had two surgeries on my shoulder, I played when guys like Gheorge weren't showing up. They knew, Wes knew, how hard I worked. That all I wanted was to win."

Being traded to the Kings frosts him in particular. Sacramento has become the league's Siberia, a place where players like the once-stellar Mahmoud Abdul Raouf go and are forgotten. On Draft Day 1998 Webber was convinced that Sacramento would trade him to the Knicks. Watching the draft, he saw the Rockets imperil the future of Matt Maloney in Houston by choosing Valparaiso's Bryce Drew in the first round, whose game resembles Maloney's. He saw the Kings surprise the cognoscenti and choose Jason Williams out of Florida, a vastly talented shooting guard—"that muthafucka will pull up on a dime and drop a three on you," reports Maxwell, who monitors his alma mater even if it wants nothing to do with him. (Following in Max's footsteps, Williams has run into off-court legal troubles.)

And he saw the Knicks go ahead and make a blockbuster deal for a power forward, but not for Webber. New York traded longtime leader Charles Oakley to Toronto for Marcus Camby.

At least Webber knew whose uniform he'd be wearing when the season rolled around again. Thanks to the lockout, Maloney, Maxwell, Stackhouse, and Barkley were all in limbo. Maloney had surgery to remove the chips in his elbow and worked out on his own with John Lucas in Houston, concentrating on becoming more of a prototypical point guard. Barkley underwent hernia and tricep surgeries and spent the summer traveling: to Philly, to Alabama, to Los

Angeles, where he was a guest on Pamela Anderson's syndi-
cated talk show and where he dined at Spago's. After his
release from jail, Maxwell split his time between Alpharetta,
Charlotte, and Los Angeles, shrugging off a couple of television reports that included him in the litany of players who
have fathered children out of wedlock. And Stackhouse
worked out in Detroit while making frequent trips to New
York to take part in the labor negotiations.

In New York, the man who is credited with saving the
league was overseeing its possible destruction. David Stern's
brinkmanship had brought the NBA perilously close to the
edge. In his capacity as hired hand for the owners, he'd
invented an economic crisis and was refusing to blink.

Still, Stern's reputation as the Jordan of sports league
commissioners remained unblemished. Even as his stub-
bornness was resulting in the first-ever canceled NBA
games, sports pages waxed lovingly about his job performance. Even the *New York Times Magazine* got into the act,
claiming that Stern "established a new paradigm for the
marketing of sports" and that he'd helped turn Jordan into
"one of the world's most recognizable people."

Once again, the chorus of agreement among the purvey-
ors of conventional wisdom drowned out the facts. Stern,
after all, hadn't become commissioner until 1984, a full four
years after Magic Johnson and Larry Bird had already begun
to save the league. When Jordan's star began to rise, it was
not thanks to Stern. Credit the foresight of Jordan, su-
peragent David Falk, and the folks at Nike for that.

In fact, it could be argued that thanks to Jordan and
Nike the NBA began in the late eighties to transcend its role
as just another sports league and stake out new territory
as a larger cultural happening. The first step was Nike's
groundbreaking set of commercials featuring Jordan and
Spike Lee, in his Mars Blackmon persona. Jordan became a
pop culture phenomenon and he was carrying the NBA on

his back. Suddenly, movie stars were filling courtside seats: Jack Nicholson and Dyan Cannon in L.A., Spike Lee and Woody Allen in New York. Madonna wanted to get busy with first Barkley, then Maxwell, then Rodman. The NBA, in short, became the hippest of sports leagues, each game an event that had little to do with Stern selling team T-Shirts.

But the league had been made by its assets, the players. Now, in the summer of 1998, David Stern seemed committed to take back what he perceived to be *his* game.

"In Las Vegas, the house always controls at least 51 percent of the odds," says Rick Burton, director of the Warsaw Sports Marketing Center at the University of Oregon. "What we're seeing now is David Stern's intention to redo the economics so the players never again control the house."

Make no mistake: When an agreement was finally reached in January, Stern had won. For the first time in history, a sports league's players agreed to a limit on their earnings; the days of six-year, $126 million contracts for the likes of Garnett would be a thing of the past. The maximum yearly salary would now be $14 million.

Stern and the owners got what they wanted. Under a system guided by free market principles, they couldn't contain the rate of growth of player salaries; the Timberwolves, after all, didn't fork over all that cash to Garnett at gunpoint. Stern's hard-line stance resulted in givebacks from the union that would protect the owners from themselves.

For their part, the owners justified their position by pointing out that they found themselves in a wholly irrational market, by virtue of their unique position vis-à-vis each other: They both compete against one another and are in business together. To which Jordan had a levelheaded response: That's your problem. The lockout is unjustified, Jordan argued, because "the owner paid these athletes what they felt they were worth." Owners who can't afford to pay their players, Jordan maintained, ought to make way for owners who can.

When it was all over, even the Larry Bird Exception had been eviscerated. Under the new deal, even though a team could still exceed the cap to re-sign its own player, the amount of that contract would be severely curtailed. Ironically, it was the owners who once insisted on the Bird Exception, and it worked as they'd hoped it would: Compared to other sports, like baseball, player movement has been kept to a minimum. The Pacers are and have always been Reggie Miller's team, ditto the Knicks and Ewing, Sonics and Payton, Rockets and Olajuwon. Indeed, Jordan would no doubt have jumped to the highest bidder had the Bulls not been allowed to exceed the salary cap to re-sign him.

What went largely unreported was whether the new economics ushered in when the league signed its new TV deal made any of this—the lockout, the givebacks—necessary. As Barkley pointed out the moment the deal was struck, the $2.64 billion windfall over four years—up from $1.1 over the same time span—represented an annual jump in national TV revenue for each team from some $9 million to $23 million. If a team couldn't afford to pay its players 57 percent of its basketball-related income before, it certainly can these four years, while the TV deal is in place.

In short, despite appearances, the impasse was not about economics. Not at a time when franchise values are skyrocketing, irrespective of annual profit/loss. After all, as more and more media conglomerates like Comcast, Cablevision, Disney, Fox and Time-Warner get into sports ownership, the less germane team profitability becomes. The new breed of sports team owners are buying loss leader programming for their media outlets. And that value is hard to put a figure on.

So, if the labor stride isn't about economics, what is it about?

Control.

Stern's penchant for stamping his imprimatur on what he deems as his game has been well-documented. It was on display when he publicly vowed to "take back the game" from the trash-talking, preening, and boorish Dream Team II. And it was most clearly displayed in the aftermath of 1997's Game Five between the New York Knicks and Miami Heat, when he suspected Patrick Ewing and others for the most technical of violations—wandering a foot or two away from the team bench during an altercation they were not involved in. Hiding behind a "rules are rules" mantra, Stern rejected all calls for clearheaded discretion (the same type of discretion his referees exhibit during games, when a foul can be called on literally every play), and prevented the season from being decided on the court. No doubt it was a great public relations move; it announced that David Stern was in control. But fans who invested their hearts and souls into an entire season sat through a watered-down Game Six and Seven that featured the best players in street clothes on the bench and were deprived of another gripping Bulls-Knicks playoff series.

Throughout the lockout Stern seemed once again preoccupied with appearances. How else to explain the invented crisis? The league's unwillingness to take the union up on its offer of third-party mediation? The owner's refusal to share revenue among themselves, as their counterparts in football do, before demanding givebacks?

But David Stern is nothing if not smart and he won the public relations battle. After all, it's hard for the public to sympathize with millionaire athletes like Kenny Anderson, who told the *New York Times* that, if the lockout continued, he just might have to sell one of his eight cars. Or Theo Ratliff, who says the dispute is "about feeding our families." Or Shaq, who, during the lockout, went on "The Howard Stern Show" and talked about how, instead of a maid, he owns a robot that cleans his house and makes his bed.

Clearly, the players are not as skilled as Stern in setting the parameters of the debate. But when the context is simple fairness, it's hard to find fault with Jordan's pro-capitalism argument. We're entitled to what the market will bear, he's said, and you guys have set the market.

And, alas, irony of ironies: Stern, the man who so many have lauded as the savior of the league, argued for and obtained an artificial restriction on salaries at a time when he makes a reported $9 million a year, far more than any other sports league commissioner in history, and more than all but ten players. And he doesn't even have to stay in shape.

Before the union's capitulation, as David Stern was going about devaluing the game, NBA fans were reminded of what makes it valuable. At a time when players were moaning about management and management was seeing eager to jeopardize an entire season, bookshelves across America carried a reminder: The game is fine. Even if the commissioner sucks.

The book is *Values of the Game* by Bill Bradley. In it, Bradley expounds upon how the game teaches life lessons, how it advocates and rewards discipline, effort, and selflessness. "I can learn more about people by playing a three-on-three game with them for twenty minutes than I can by talking with them for a week," he writes.

Indeed, it's as evident today as in Bradley's day. Rodman's selflessness, Barkley's will, the Bulls' spirit, and Maxwell's passion all echo the character traits once displayed by Reed, Russell, West and the Celtics. The game is fine.

This becomes clear one morning during the lockout at the Gold's Gym inside the Beltway Plaza Mall in Greenbelt, Maryland. It's not your run-of-the-mill workout facility. The first sign of its uniqueness is a poster adorning the wall: An image of a black hand and a white hand clasped together, above the message "True Friendship Is Enhanced By Embracing One Another's Difference."

The second is the gym's attached basketball court. Walled by floor-to-ceiling windows, shoppers wander by, stop, and take in the action. On this day, they get an eyeful. They see the health club's owner and his friends working out.

Here is majority owner Chris Webber going at it, hard. He is joined by his longtime friend, veteran Billy Owens, a free agent who toiled in Sacramento the last few years. Also playing is Chris' brother, David, a fleet-footed point guard who will be attending Central Michigan in the fall and who is currently draining threes over Owens's outstretched arms, dramatically blowing on his fingers as though he were cooling off a pistol each time the ball tickles the twine. Watching his little brother's display, Chris can't help but break into a crooked half-smile; he recognizes the joyous flair for on-court theatrics.

For those watching, the fun the guys are having can mask the hard work they're putting in. This isn't just a pick-up game. The workout began with extensive drills, followed by a round-robin one-on-one war, and, now, this scrimmage. But it's not a run-and-gun fest. For all the trash-talking—at one point, Owens backs Webber down, talking all the while: "Which way I'm gonna go? Left? Right? Which way, baby?" before nailing a tough turnaround fadeaway—there are real fundamentals at work. Screens, back-picks, defensive help, selfless passes to the weak (or non-ball) side of the court. All the things Bradley writes about. All the things the owners and the media and the bitter fans can't take away from them.

"Basketball," Bradley writes, "allowed us to feel the thrill of fresh creation . . . to transcend our circumstances however dire they appear, and to reply to the common wisdom that says we cannot soar by saying, 'Just watch!' "

I am reminded of Bradley's words as Webber and his brother run the pick and roll and when Owens foregoes an open jumper and instead zips a no-look pass to a teammate. Yes, many NBA players have fathered children out of wedlock. Some have even smoked pot. One has choked his coach. But like Barkley, Bradley would recognize that we err in anointing them our moral beacons. What they are is what they show themselves to be on this court, where the booming echo of the ball and the stop and start squeals of sneakers are drowned out only by the guttural grunts of the best athletes in the world banging their bodies into one another at the highest of speeds for no ostensible reason other than to experience the thrill of competition and the joy of soaring, both athletically and economically. They are at once artists and craftsmen, laborers and capitalists. They are, warts and all, the embodiment of the American Dream. And they are proof that the game is, indeed, fine.

acknowledgments

the author wishes to thank the following people for their assistance in putting this book together:

David Black (and his posse) for his invaluable prodding and encouragement.

Stephen S. Power, whose intelligent editing was always accompanied by refreshingly good humor, and the folks at Avon Books.

Bob Baber, Joey Joe Martell, Tex Cobb, Janet Ake, Eric Riley, and John Lucas for being constant sources of inspiration. Andrew Corsello for his comic relief. Linda and Mac of Houston's state-of-the-art Westside Tennis Center for their hospitality.

Bob Huber, Roxanne Patel, and Ben G. Wallace for their insights on early drafts. Ken Shropshire and Scott Raab for their clear-headed guidance. A host of magazine editors foolish enough to have actually paid me over the years: Eliot

Kaplan, Loren Feldman, Marty Beiser, David Granger, Michael Caruso, Duane Swierczinksi, and Tim Whitaker. PR mavens Jodi Silverman, Tim Frank, and Maureen Lewis and their staffs. Leah Popowich, editorial assistant, for her efficiency and professionalism. Elwood Boone for being one cool little brother.

Special thanks to Dad and P.J. for showing me at an early age that American men use the subject of sports as a proxy for discussions of values, ethics, and character.

Finally props to Charles Barkley, Chris Webber, Jerry Stackhouse, Matt Maloney, and Vernon Maxwell for putting up with the constant presence of a short, bald, white Jew who was always asking annoying questions. Their good-natured tolerance makes them true role models.

index

about the author

Larry Platt, thirty-five, is a senior writer at *Philadelphia Magazine* and has written for *GQ* and *Details* magazines as well as the *Philadelphia Inquirer*'s Commentary Page. His game consists of an uncanny two-handed set shot that he has yet to get off in a pickup game.